THE
FRIENDSHIP KEY

to

Lasting Peace,
United Communities,
Stronger Relationships,
Equality, and a Better Job!

DR. WINFRIED SEDHOFF

Copyright © 2019 by Winfried Sedhoff

All rights reserved. No part of this publication may be reproduced, stored in a retrieval system or transmitted in any form or by any means, electronic, mechanical, photocopying, recording or otherwise, without the prior written permission of the copyright holder.

Some of the examples in this book represent experiences of real people. Names have been changed and identifying details omitted to help protect their anonymity. The original work of this book and its suggestions are in no way affiliated with other courses and books regarding friendship. Any similarity or resemblance is purely coincidental.

Published by Senraan Publishing
Brisbane, Australia

Cover design by Laura Duffy
Book design by Karen Minster

978-0-9946091-6-8 (hardcover)
978-0-9946091-7-5 (paperback)
978-0-9946091-8-2 (ebook)

First Edition 2019

To a New and Promising
Era of Friendship

Contents

Preface xv
Introduction xix

PART ONE

The Friendship Crash and Rise of a Beast 1

1. Friendship Made Simple 3
2. Rise of the Beast Within 17
3. Slavery and Our Exploitation 31
4. The Destruction We Support: Empires 45

PART TWO

The Friendship Key— Empowering Positive Change 65

5. Friendship: Prosperity, Peace, Respect 67
6. Using the Ten Desires Day-to-Day 87
7. Deeper, Lasting, More Satisfying Relationships 118
8. Fixing our Relationship with Friendship 144
9. Friendship, Better Pay, Jobs, Businesses, and Global Stability 172

10. Bringing Back Community   203
11. Government by Us for Us   222
12. The Salvation in Us   249

FURTHER READING 253
NOTES 255
ABOUT THE AUTHOR 263
ACKNOWLEDGEMENTS 265
INDEX 267

Comprehensive Contents

Preface xv
Introduction xix

PART ONE
The Friendship Crash and Rise of a Beast 1

1. **Friendship Made Simple**   3
   Basic Human Desires: The Bird Brain in Us 5
   Balance of Self Model 6
       Desires of Personal Self 7
       Desires of Family Self 7
       Desires of Community Self 8
       Land 8
   Revealing the Ten Desires of Friendship 10

2. **Rise of the Beast Within**   17
   Farming: The Rise of Wealth, Power and Status 18
   Need for Status 21
   Need for Power 24
   Birth of a Beast 27

3. **Slavery and Our Exploitation**   31
   Importance of Wealth 34
   Beliefs 36
   Uncontrolled Desires 39

4. The Destruction We Support: Empires   45
    Wars and Massacres 53
    Terrorism and Extremism 55
    Mass Poverty and Starvation 58
    Environmental Destruction and Poisonings 60
    How We Unwittingly Support Empires 63

PART TWO
The Friendship Key— Empowering Positive Change   65

5. Friendship: Prosperity, Peace, Respect   67
    Countering Slavery 68
        Reducing Wealth and Debt's Power 68
        Reducing Hierarchies 71
        Countering the Beast 73
    Countering Empires and their Devastation 75
        Countering War and Massacres 75
        Countering Terrorism and Extremism 76
        Countering Poverty and Starvation 77
        Countering Environmental Destruction 77
    The Power of a Single Question 79
    When to Ask the Friendship Question 82
        Major Life Decisions 82
        Relationships 82
        Work 83
        Everyday Activities 83

6. Using the Ten Desires Day-to-Day   87
    Close vs Casual Friendship 87
    Ten Desires of Friendship 89
        Valued 91
        Noticed 93
        Appreciated 95

Heard 97
Sameness 99
Validated/Approved 102
Respected 105
Cared For 107
Supported 109
Protected 112

7. **Deeper, Lasting, More Satisfying Relationships** — 118

   Desires at Play in Relationships 121
   Basics of a Successful Relationship 122
   Successful Attraction 123
   Successful Compatibility 124
   Applying the Ten Desires in Relationships 125
      Gender Differences Matter 125
      How Gender Roles and Identity
        Became Confused 126
   How to Meet Gender-Sensitive Friendship Desires 131
      Valued 131
      Noticed 132
      Heard 134
      Sameness 135
      Validated/Approved 137
      Supported 139
      Protected 141

8. **Fixing Our Relationship with Friendship** — 144

   Friendship Desires Where
     Gender Matters Less 145
      Respected 145
      Appreciated 147
      Cared For 148
   Fixing Relationships with Friendship 151
   Three Steps to Fixing Relationships 151
      Step 1. Recognize it's Broken 151

Step 2. Stepping Up 154
Step 3. Fill the Holes 156
Avoiding the Cliff 161
Relationship Friendship Rules 162
    Keep up the Maintenance 162
    Keep Your Closeness Exclusive 163
    Keep the Trust and Secrets 165
Friendships Make Relationships Stronger 166

9. Friendship, Better Pay, Jobs, Businesses, and Global Stability 172

Business Structure 175
Co-operatives: Friendship-Friendly 178
Mittelstand:
  Friendship-Friendly = Global Success 180
Friendship-Friendly Business Characteristics 183
    Flat Hierarchies 183
    Worker Loyalty 183
    Customer Loyalty 183
    Shared Values and Goals 184
    Long-term Stability 184
    Family Focused 184
    Community Orientated and Environmentally Responsible 185
    Improving Work Environment 186
The Ten Desires for Managers 187
    Valued 187
    Noticed 188
    Appreciated 188
    Heard 188
    Sameness 189
    Validated/Approved 189
    Respected 189
    Cared For 190
    Supported 190
    Protected 190

The Ten Desires for Workers 191
  Valued 191
  Noticed 192
  Appreciated 192
  Heard 192
  Sameness 192
  Validated/Approved 193
  Respected 193
  Cared For 193
  Supported 194
  Protected 194
The Ten Desires for Customers 195
  Valued 195
  Noticed 195
  Appreciated 195
  Heard 196
  Sameness 196
  Validated/Approved 196
  Respected 197
  Cared For 197
  Supported 197
  Protected 198
Fortifying the Ten Desires in Your Business 199

10. Bringing Back Community 203

More Community, Please 206
Five Guiding Principles for United and Satisfying Communities 207
  Group Size Matters 207
  Face-to-Face Contact Matters 209
  Regular Contact is Good 210
  Shared Facilities 211
  Walking Can Promote Talking 212
Applying the Five Principles 213
  Housing and Community Halls 213
  Organized Community Sub-Groups and Social Bees 216

11. Government By Us for Us   222

  Six Principles of Friendship-Focused
    Government 223
    Flatter Hierarchies Work Best in Long Term 223
    Consensus is Fundamental 227
    Group Meeting Size Matters 227
    Individual Liberties Need Respect 228
    Rules and Laws are Critical 230
    Individual and Social Responsibility 232
  The Best Government for Us 234
    Types of Governments 234
  Women-Friendly Democracy 237
  How we can Improve our Governments 239
    Prioritize Friendship:
      Ask the Friendship Question 239
    Vote and Be Active 239
    Form Local Social Groups 239
    Meet at Community Halls 240
    Help the Marginalized and Disadvantaged 240
    Create and Support a Village 241
    Be Responsible 241
  A Thousand Years of Peace 242
  Governments Countering War from Within 243

12. The Salvation in Us   249

  FURTHER READING 253
  NOTES 255
  ABOUT THE AUTHOR 263
  ACKNOWLEDGEMENTS 265
  INDEX 267

Preface

I was raised a friendship skeptic. Work, study, and career came first; a notion instilled in me from a very young age. Friendship was no more than an accessory, nice if you had it, but other priorities were far more important. It took me decades to learn I had been taught a lie. Friendship had plans for me, to ensure I would see it very differently to how I had known, read, heard about, or witnessed. It forced me to see what I didn't want to see, then gave me compelling reasons to share.

It would be fair to say, friendship had not been kind for most of my life. Difficulty making friends in primary school then years of being ostracized in high school, weeks when I couldn't walk the school yard without being called names, was devastating at times and often left me feeling sad and alone, an alien among colleagues and peers. But being friendship's pariah meant extra hours in the library, and eventually saw me accepted into medicine. By the time I was in my second year of postgraduate training—to become a medical specialist—I was struck by a profound depression that had dogged me on and off for many years. The intense and prolonged low mood threatened my life. My solution was extreme, but I felt driven to try it, no matter the personal cost. It was also pivotal in beginning to see friendship as I had never imagined.

I had a promising medical career in front of me, but it meant nothing, not if I felt like this. So, I resigned, isolated myself in a one-bedroom rental in Sydney, and over many months strived to find a sense of all-knowing that I intuitively believed would liberate me. Facing my deepest fears and emotional pains, immersing myself in them, stepping past them, crying many times, within months I finally found what I was after. Part of what I discovered can vaguely be described as a way to understand myself and the world from within, through a connection with all things found inside us, through feelings. It offered a completely new way of seeing the world, free from how I wanted or needed it to be, and offered a set of practical tools for honest self-exploration. It was also a useful resource I would fall back on regularly.

Twelve months after resigning I finally returned to medicine as a Family Physician—General Practitioner, GP. Depression had left me; no longer was I dogged by profound sadness. Over time I felt more comfortable sharing some of what I had learnt. To my surprise the insights gained on my internal quest helped others overcome depression and anxiety too. They even correlated well with many already known approaches. After years of refining the ideas and methods—treating some counselors, no less—I decided to share some of them in a book: *A Balance of Self: A new approach to self understanding, lasting happiness, and self-truth*. Whilst writing this book friendship began to reveal its deeper, fundamental, self; its role in making us feel satisfied as social beings—we will explore how soon. The real breakthrough came with writing my next book, *The Fall and Rise of Women: How women can change the world*.

As I researched I learnt women were once great supporters of each other, especially when we lived in peace as nomadic tribal people, but now, too commonly, they were acting more as competitors than friends; trying to have it all but attempting it alone, trying to appear successful, better than other women, yet left with impossible burdens. I noticed this all too frequently in my practice; in women suffering stress, depression, anxiety, loneliness, and low self-esteem. I wondered why, what had changed? What could drive women once supportive of each other, like a sisterhood, to become so combative and isolated? Then it became clearer; it wasn't just women that had fallen—women were no longer treated with the respect they deserve, the premise behind the book—so had friendship.

Suddenly, as a GP, I could recognize it all around me. Evidence of friendship's decline: among the lives of lonely and depressed patients, of families divided, children being bullied and ostracized at school, adults intimidated and disrespected at work, in relationships struggling, in the mothers pushed to breaking point and beyond trying to balance work with being a mum, among men and women competing and feeling stressed, lonely, and unsatisfied. In my privileged work as a GP, being able to peer intimately into the lives of so many people of different backgrounds, daily I was seeing emotional pains, struggles, and illnesses that were clearly a direct result of friendship's decline; most avoidable or preventable. I could even begin to see evidence of the destructive effects of friendship's decline globally (we will focus on some of this in a moment). I couldn't believe it at first; could friendship be so critical?

Then came an even greater revelation that shocked me to my core, and still alarms me to this day.

Surprisingly, seeing friendship in this new way revealed evidence of a great malevolence that I had no idea existed. A creation inside us that could easily—since it has remained unrecognized, and unseen—completely overpower friendship, and by doing so wreak havoc around the world, as it has for millennia and now threatens the world today with war and global destruction. We will explore what this malevolence is, get just a glimpse of its immense destructive ability and how it negatively impacts all our lives, in the early chapters. When I realized the existence of such an insidious and malicious influence, and how we have been missing the obvious for so long, failing to recognize let alone work to contain it, I realized I needed to share, to offer it for consideration. Hence this book.

I should clarify. This is still primarily a self-help book. Its aim is to help us better understand friendship, to improve our relationships, families, and communities. It just so happens that by being better friends—satisfying basic friendship needs we will consider in a moment—we also do so much more socially, and globally.

Does this book claim to have all the solutions to life's problems, or those of the world?

No.

This book was written to share insights, opinions, and methods. It is just one approach to many of the problems we experience every day and seem powerless to fix. All the better if it stimulates some discussion and self-reflection about our choices; raises friendship and its potential into our consciousness to help clarify for us how we want to live and where we really want to be heading into the future. As a doctor I have had the honor of sharing and refining these methods and insights with others over many years; discussing and developing them into a practical form. Now, over 28 years since friendship began to reveal itself to me—during the months of my internal quest—I am privileged to be able to share them with you.

Looking back, I recognize that had I learnt but a fraction of what I am about to share with you, none of the traumatic social events of my childhood would likely have happened—I would have been far better equipped to both understand and make friends. I know I would not have suffered depression, let alone needed to isolate myself to discover a sense of genuine self. I can see that if friendship had been a priority in our society and around the world before I was born, not only could most of my traumas could have been avoided, but so too those of most of the people I've met and see around me. Perhaps in this book's sharing many others will not have to know so many unnecessary traumas either. I was reluctant to see it but now I have no doubts, seeing friendship in a new and practical way can offer us enormous potential for positive change. The question is: are we prepared to properly consider it, and take up its challenge?

Introduction

His weathered face much older than his 40-something years, Steve seemed rightly frustrated. 'I just don't get it!' he said, hands in the air in exasperation. He was recalling being in hospital a few years ago for a medical condition. Only his father sat by his bed, for hours at a time, his wife stayed only a few minutes a day, his mates—those he thought were his mates—later told him they didn't know he was even in hospital. 'I was away from work for weeks and no one asked, *I wonder where Steve is?* I helped these people. I thought they were my friends.' Steve felt abandoned. This year, he had the added trauma of a tough separation and divorce.

It had been over nine months since he realized—for the first time—that his wife of 20 plus years didn't treat him well; with kindness, affection, and much-needed emotional support. Intimacy had been extinct for well over a decade and a half. He now felt used and neglected. I once asked him if he was ever close friends with his wife, since they met in their late teens. His eyes stared into the distance for many long seconds, then he coldly replied, 'No, we weren't.' But they seemed to get on ok for a few years or so, or it would have ended at the start. What troubled Steve the most now was why he didn't see it, why he didn't leave much earlier, in spite of his obvious unhappiness in the relationship after it turned in those early years. Finally, one day he told me, as if born from an epiphany.

'I was so lonely, I needed someone to come home to,' he said, tears welling in congested eyes. Steve shared how he felt let down by others all his life. When friends or colleagues needed help he'd be the one they called on, even in school. But when people didn't want anything from him no one showed up, no one seemed to care, like the time he was in hospital, only this went back decades before. So painful was the possibility of being alone Steve felt it better to come home to someone who at least hung around, who at least seemed to accept him, for whatever reasons, than to return each day to the stark solitude of an empty house. He was so lonely during his relationship, he said, 'I didn't want to see how bad it [the relationship] was.' He remained in his emotionally distant liaison to avoid an even greater emotional pain and realization: loneliness.

Steve was a broken man in repair.

He was also a father, fearful for the future of his now young-adult children.

'The world has gone crazy!' he said, leaning back as if resigned to the fact. 'I love my children, don't get me wrong,' he added. 'But when I look around I wonder if it had been better they'd never been born.' He was talking about the troubles of the world he wanted to ignore but said he couldn't; the wars, the terrorism, the broken communities and families, the greed, the gross inequality, and governments in the pockets of the rich. We had discussed these topics now and then, as he tried to make sense of his life and the world. 'Maybe we should blow the whole place up and start again,' he recently commented, struggling to find hope, to see the realistic prospect of a better future for his children and generations to come. His personal sense of powerlessness filled the room.

In Steve, we can find a part of ourselves. How many of us have stayed in relationships we weren't satisfied in because we were afraid of being alone? How many have been let down by so-called friends, people we tried to actively help but were never there when we needed them most, even our partner? How many of us have looked at the world, or our lives, with sad despair, tried to ignore how bad it really is, and felt powerless to make a real difference? With so many troubles it can make us question if it is even real. Are we just being negative? Perhaps we are we just blowing these problems all out of proportion, letting our imagination run away with us?

Perhaps not. Consider the following.

Statistics tell us over half of all US families are remarried or re-coupled,[1] with the average relationship only lasting seven years. According to infidelity stats, 74% of men and 68% of women said they would have an affair if they knew they wouldn't get caught.[2] If our modern relationships are so great why are over two-thirds of us in relationships so quick to look for satisfaction in the arms of someone else, and so quick to leave? How great have relationships been for you?

By 2030 an estimated 38% of US jobs, and 30% of UK jobs, will be wiped out by automation, in areas from retail, to transport and storage, to manufacturing.[3] To make matters worse, businesses are being lumbered with too much debt to survive leaving workers on the unemployment scrap heap. This is especially true with the rise of purely profit-driven private equity firms who load up newly purchased businesses with massive debts, setting most of them up to fail.[4] The collapse of Toys R Us in September 2017 is a classic example. In 2005 equity firms Bain Capital and KKR & Co, and Vornado Realty Trust used a leveraged buyout leaving Toys R Us with huge unserviceable debt. The result: over 31,000 unemployed.[5] Private equity firm numbers are on the rise; in 1980 only 20 private equity firms existed, in 2015 there were over 6500.[6] Stable, well-paid, satisfying, jobs are under threat. Do you feel jobs are as stable, plentiful, satisfying, and well paid as they should be?

Inequality is entrenched and just won't quit. Since 2009 salaries have skyrocketed by over 54% for the top CEOs of US firms while regular wages haven't increased—in real terms—for most of us, even though costs of living have gone up.[7] The last year has seen the biggest increase in the number of billionaires in history—there are now over 2043 [dollar] billionaires worldwide. At the same time 82% of all growth in global wealth went to the top 1% while the bottom 50% saw no increase at all. The richest 1% continue to own more wealth than the rest of us combined.[8] How often have you wondered how unfair it is, that a few should have so much at the expense of the rest us?

Big money has hijacked our governments. In the last eight years, over three billion dollars has been spent annually by companies to lobby the US government.[9] You read right, three BILLION dollars, enough to run a small country, just so special interest groups can have their way instead of us. Governments have united with corporations—the rich—to form government/corporate hybrid empires that compete around the world inciting terrorism, leaving war, misery, poverty, and destruction in their wake. (We will explore how shortly.) In 2018, at least 40 wars are raging globally, such as those in Syria, Yemen, Iraq, and Afghanistan, to name a few.[10] Now we have the prospect of the worst wars ever on the near horizon. Tensions are rising in East Asia, and even more so in the Middle East—there is talk of nuclear conflict. The death and destruction from such wars would be beyond imagining. Our best and bravest—and innocent children, no less—continue to be killed in wars that show no sign of stopping. Aren't you sick of war, the death, the misery, and corruption? I know I am.

And amid the global turmoil, our communities are being torn apart.

Community spirit seems to have died or gone on life support; we have become communities divided. It is estimated the average American moves residence 11 times in their lifetime.[11] How can we maintain lasting close communities if we don't hang around long enough to build them? To make the problem worse, many of us live busy lives and barely have the time to get to know and help each other—how many of us even know our neighbors, do you? We look to money for help—our savings, credit cards, and insurance policies—not people. Dividing us even more is modern technology—it is making us lonelier and splitting us into intolerant, conflicting, groups. Dividing us further still is rising hate.

Hate crimes increased in New York City during the year ending 2016 by 12.4% compared to a national increase of 4.6%, the levels stubbornly staying there in 2017.[12] In Britain in 2016 a national crime survey suggested 225,000 hate crimes took place.[13] We can readily see it in the media, innocent people are being targeted, and all too frequently killed, simply because of their color, race, sexual orientation, or belief. People are scared to be pulled over by police. We have become too terrified to be close.

Look around and we see rising levels of depression and anxiety, ongoing problems of drug and alcohol abuse, domestic violence, sexual discrimination, and bullying at school and work. Incarceration rates are way too high, and people of color or indigenous descent take up a much higher proportion than whites.[14] Our natural world is being destroyed faster than it can recover. Adding icing to the cake, loneliness has become a major problem. The UK government even created a whole department and appointed a Minister for Loneliness to help counter the epidemic.[15]

No, this isn't a product of our imaginings; the problems are real, and causing genuine misery and devastation.

So, what do we do about it? To be more specific, what can you and I, as individuals, do to make a real difference to all these issues? After all, we are only one person; we are, like Steve, struggling just to sort out our own life problems let alone try to help solve so many others that seem beyond our control.

Perhaps we can do far more than we are often led to believe, in a very basic way.

What if there was a simple way to not only make relationships easier and more satisfying, improve our jobs and pay and make them more stable, reduce loneliness, unite communities, and return governments to the people, help the environment, and finally see the real prospect of creating lasting peace?

The notion sounds absurd, doesn't it? How could that possibly be?

Perhaps sometimes the best cures are those under our noses, waiting for us to finally recognize them, to see them in a different light. Maybe we have been missing the obvious for far too long. Like our discovery of the existence of vitamins.

Amazing as it might seem, it wasn't until the late 1800s we had any idea vitamins—such as Vitamins A, B, C, or D—even existed.[16] Even though Captain Cook in the late 1700s prevented scurvy, an often-fatal bleeding disease of long distance sailors, by insisting his crew eat fresh fruit and vegetables, it wasn't until 1920 that Vitamin C was recognized as the cure. As we all know, Vitamin C is present in fresh fruits and vegies. Now we know many vitamin deficiency illnesses exist—such as beriberi, pellagra, scurvy and rickets—they've existed for thousands of years, but it wasn't until we considered the idea of nutrient deficiency, that vitamins were essential for our health and wellbeing, that we saw what was under our noses all along and found lasting cures.

There can be no doubt we live in troubled times. Many profound and troubling problems scream out for a cure, and have plagued humanity—us—for far too long. But what if a large part of the cure—or the key to a cure—is simply to recognize and correct a single yet profound and destructive deficiency we have yet to fully appreciate, one that has been just waiting to be recognized and appreciated?

What if the illness that has caused many of the greatest troubles that plague us now, and have for millennia, is simply a deficiency of friendship, pushed so low it became pathological and began to damage—and continues to damage—our families, communities, relationships, governments, and the natural world under our feet?

Put simply, what if the problem resides inside us, created out of a fluke of nature, and has unleashed untold devastation and misery, but is part of a deficiency we can all easily begin to correct?

Sadly many of us have grown to feel powerless to improve our life situation. We feel too weak and inconsequential to improve the troubles we so commonly experience around us. We are often taught we are small, insignificant, we have no real power; what can we possibly do to change any of these huge problems in our lives and around the world?

It would seem we are far from powerless.

As we are about to see, friendship, seen and used in a new way, even without much effort, can positively empower us as individuals and help us fix more problems in our lives and the world than we might have imagined.

What is this new way of seeing friendship, and how can it help?

It is an approach that focuses on, and recognizes, our deepest desires.

Think of friendship and most of us might imagine being around people we trust and like, of having a laugh, sharing stories, hanging out with people similar to us. We might think of people we know in social media—such as Facebook—who we call friends and never meet, people we get along with at work, or catch up with when we drop our children to school. Some friendships could be casual, and we barely meet, others we catch up with regularly. Some friends can be so close it feels like talking to a soulmate, even if it has been ages since we last caught up. There are many ways to consider friendship. But behind them all we can see friendship in terms of the basic human desires that define them, desires we can know in our hearts. Desires, once recognized and understood, that uncover a largely untapped hidden potential of insight and positive change.

What are basic human desires?

Basic human desires can be considered the desires nature wrote inside us that ensure our needs are met as human beings. So we do what we need to do to survive as a species. In other words, they ensure our basic human needs are met, needs such as those for water, food, and shelter, to find a partner and have a family. The feelings you have when you get flustered meeting someone really attractive are a reflection of just a few of these desires. So too the cosy feeling of sitting in front of a warm fire on a bone-chilling night. Among these many desires that make us human we can recognize those that drive us to be with others like us, to be social and form closely bonded groups. We can call them our Desires of Friendship.

Human beings were made to be social, we thrive best when we unite and work together.

Friendship is the glue that brings us together and binds us as well-bonded and co-ordinated groups.

We can distinguish Ten Desires of Friendship. We will describe them in a moment. This new way of looking at friendship offers us many advantages.

To begin with it can help us unite. To know we have something in common to all of us independent of race, culture, sexual orientation, or belief, offers us something we can use as a common bond. It offers us a way to help bridge our differences. How it can do this will become obvious soon.

Seeing friendship in terms of desires also offers us a framework, a powerful tool to help us improve our lives, and make a difference in the world. Most of the following chapters will focus on how we can use these desires to do this.

And lastly, and most importantly, understanding our basic human desires and the Ten Desires of Friendship helps us identify the emergence of three new desires, prominent in almost all of us, that have gone virtually unrecognized until now and done nothing short of wreak havoc upon the earth for thousands of years.

A malevolence has lurked under our very noses for millennia, grown through a fluke of nature to become so powerful it would

ensure the fall of friendship and bring us ongoing war, misery, famine, global destruction, and a growing inequity that would tear our societies apart.

Nature invented inside each of us a beast responsible for unmentionable acts and it still dominates us today.

Where do we find evidence of such a beast?

We can see it in workplace bullying, where three-quarters of workers have claimed to have witnessed it happen to co-workers.[17] We find it among the over one in five CEOs in the US considered sociopaths,[18] quick to step on others to get to the top, not caring what happens to those below. And we recognize it globally in the form of authoritarian rule still existing in almost one-third of the world's countries, where leaders such as Kim Jong-un of North Korea live in luxury while they oppress the masses beneath them and threaten to bring major devastation upon the world. The beast even imposes itself on our daily lives, in our relationships, work, and in our governments; how and where will become apparent very soon. Understanding the Desires of Friendship helps us uncover this darker part of ourselves, bring it into the light, and reveal how to counter it.

Put simply, friendship, when viewed in terms of the basic human desires that define it, can be a key that unlocks new, and practical, hope.

Part 1 of this book will be devoted to revealing friendship's importance, how it fell into decline, and some of the terrible consequences. In Chapter 1 we will start by learning the fundamentals of what makes us feel lastingly satisfied and fulfilled as human beings; we will introduce our basic human desires. As we shall see nature made it very simple: do, or expect to do, what it needs of us and we can feel great, don't do it, or expect we won't, and our lives can be horrible. Are you finding life isn't feeling as great as you know it should or could be? In this chapter we begin to learn fundamental reasons why—what we need that is often missing. We will introduce and give a brief outline of the Ten Desires of Friendship, a critical group of these desires/needs, such as those for respect, feeling valued, and appreciated. Who doesn't want to feel valued, respected, and appreciated? We will use the insights and practical recommendations garnered here throughout the rest of the text.

It might seem incredible considering the current state of affairs of our world but there was a time in human history where, for the most part, we lived very peaceful and fulfilling lives. Friendship was a priority; we enjoyed the company of many close friends and cherished them—later we will introduce examples of tribal societies where this was true, such as those of Australia and North America before the arrival of Europeans. Then we took a troubling path.

In Chapter 2 we will see how the simple invention of farming guaranteed friendship's decline by ensuring the rise of a new desire we all take for granted today, but completely underestimate in power and destructive potential: a desire for wealth. We don't think much of owning our own homes, cars, gadgets, savings accounts, or shares these days, but for most of human existence wealth, and a desire to have it, never really existed. However, once it arose this one desire also ensured the associated creation of strong desires for status and power. These three desires have had devastating consequences; the rise of civilization has created brutal competition, and extremes of inequality that remain today. In this chapter we glimpse their destructive potential; largely due to their inherent insatiable nature. Ever wondered why many of us feel we can never have enough and are prepared to do whatever it takes to get it, even at someone else's expense, even if it means millions starve and we destroy our planet in the process? Here it will begin to make practical sense.

Then we will explore two examples of our uncontrolled desires for wealth, status, and power at their worst, two compelling reasons to prioritize friendship: exploitation and slavery, and empires.

Slavery and exploitation are rife. Many of us all too readily experience the exploitation at work; being offered minimal pay, poor conditions, treated with disrespect, struggling just to find a well-paid, stable job. Slavery, an extreme form of exploitation, has become so widespread today there are more slaves now—by numbers—than at any other time in history. In 2016 alone there were an estimated 40 million slaves, one in four of them children.[19] And slavery is closer to home than many of us may think. Shamere McKenzie, for example, a student on an athletic scholarship to St John's University, became an unwitting sex slave, brutalized, and bashed, as she simply tried to get by on restricted money available—we will consider her case in more detail later. As will become apparent in Chapter 3, the same basic fundamentals that allowed Shamere and many others over thousands of years to become slaves also ensure we continue to be exploited now. We will examine three fundamentals that easily lead to the creation of slavery and exploitation, and barbaric abuse: the importance of wealth, our beliefs, and our uncontrolled desires. As we shall see, the abuse and exploitation won't stop, and the scars that fuel racial hatred and division won't heal, while these fundamentals remain unchallenged. This chapter will help us discover how we can finally turn this tragic state of affairs around once and for all.

Many of you may remember the stark images: a young boy in red t-shirt and blue shorts lying face down, drowned, on a beach; a refugee who died to escape war. Or the distressed survivors of the Twin Towers collapse running desperately, covered in thick, grey, toxic, dust. We are regularly bombarded by pictures in the media of ongoing wars, terrorism, mass starvation, the rise of extremism, and pollution; a small reflection of the true levels of misery and devastation gripping our lives and the world. Behind it all is arguably the most destructive force the world has ever known: the empire. In Chapter 4 we will see how we create empires and the rise of the most destructive empire of all, the corporate/government hybrid empire, one that has garnered our support today, without us even being aware of it!

We continue to support wars, massacres, terrorism and extremism, and contribute to the destruction of the natural world through our often-unwitting support of empires.

Empires by their nature foster misery and devastation, and always will. The classic empires we are more familiar with are less obvious today, morphed, though into a no less destructive form. We will learn of the role of our desires for wealth, power, and status in the rise of empires and how they took their current state. This will help us later see how friendship has the potential to make empires extinct; ending wars, saving the planet, and helping bring about a lasting peace.

Once we have seen how seriously destructive our new desires are, in Part 2 we will then learn how we can use friendship to counter them and improve our lives.

In Chapter 5 we will learn how friendship empowers us to naturally counter each of the destructive results of the desires of our inner beast, from the three fundamentals of exploitation and slavery, to each of the destructive consequences of empires, including wars, massacres, terrorism and extremism, poverty and starvation, and environmental destruction. For example, friendship helps reduce the destructive power of wealth and debt through sharing and working collectively; reducing our individual burdens and need to exploit others. It dissolves empires at their source by eliminating—or countering—the desires within us that are needed to foster and grow them. It also prevents wars by reminding us of our commonality rather than our differences—we are less likely to want to go to war with people we relate to who seem similar to us.

Friendship makes each of us the potential instigators of massive positive social and global change.

However, all too easily we can unknowingly be the source of our problems rather than the solution. It can happen when we simply decide to work the extra hours to pay for the new kitchen, the new house in a better suburb, the new car, TV, mobile phone, computer, or designer clothes. It can be when we try to impress others, step over, or push others out of our way at work, at home, or on our streets. Unfortunately, most of the time we can be driven by the desires of our inner beast without being aware of it. As we shall soon see, one of the features that makes our inner beast so powerful is its ability to remain hidden, ignored; followed out of habit. Thankfully, we can readily counter that.

In Chapter 5 we will also learn how friendship can counter the fundamentals behind slavery, exploitation, and empires. We will begin to cage our inner beast through the act of asking a simple question: am I putting friendship first? As we are about to learn, just this one question can be a critical first step to creating the change we want and can be an invaluable tool. It alone has the potential to be life and world transforming.

Then we will get down to making friendship a practical and important part of our lives. We will learn how to apply the Ten Desires in general and then in specific areas of day-to-day life such as in our relationships, at work, and in our communities and governments. As we shall see, applying the Ten Desires isn't difficult, but to get the most out of them requires more than a one-size-fits-all approach if we are to avoid potential pitfalls and gain maximum benefit.

Chapter 6 will be devoted to learning the friendship basics. We will start by looking at close versus casual friendships and why it is important to distinguish between the two. For starters, being close friends with everyone is unrealistic and impossible; there are way too many people to be close friends with. But we can aim to at least be casual friends, create an environment of friendliness around us. Next, we will look at each of the Ten Desires, one at a time, and see how we can apply them to our daily lives in general terms. The key, as we will see, is to satisfy them in others first. We will go through simple steps as to how we can do this. The more we apply these steps the more people will want to be around us and like us; the more we will be seen as friendly and worth wanting to be around. Then we will look to tweaking how to meet the Ten Desires in more specific important parts of living.

Want to improve the closeness and satisfaction of your relationship? Want to be able to find a 'keeper' more easily and know how to make sure they hang around?

In Chapters 7 and 8 we look at how to apply the Ten Desires to relationships. Yes, we may all want the same Ten Desires satisfied by everyone, but how we meet them in relationships can either bring us closer or tear our relationships apart. More than just the Ten Desires are at play. We will look at some of the other desires and how to meet them, so we can have the great, lasting, and stable, relationship we desire. For example, desires of attraction—what drives us to want to physically be with each other as men and women—play a critical role. So too desires that ensure we maintain a strong sense of self and don't lose the genuineness of who we are. Lose a sense of self and we become unattractive, often needy, and no matter how we try to satisfy the Ten Desires for each other we can still find ourselves drifting apart. We will also look to what we can do to fix broken relationships, learn basic rules to prevent us sabotaging the close friendships within relationships we have built, and how we can use friendship to make relationships easier at every stage, even before we meet.

Wouldn't it have been wonderful, for instance, if we'd already learned how to be close friends from a young age, learned to prioritize friendship so we had more like-minded people around us to choose from, and more time and opportunities to meet?

As we shall see, finding 'the one' doesn't have to be so difficult. Friendship can make it easier in many practical ways.

Then we will look to our work.

Most of us work; it forms an important and meaningful part of our lives. Whether we are an employee, owner, manager, or simply buy from businesses the Ten Desires can have enormous personal, social, economic, and environmental benefits. For example, if we own or run a business the Ten Desires can help increase innovation and adaptability, help us become and remain internationally competitive, be a global success. Among workers they help us create a happier place to work so we want to be there, such as by eliminating bullying and increasing a sense of mutual respect and appreciation. As customers the Ten Desires make us powerful advocates for workers' conditions and the environment by helping us recognize which businesses are worthy of our support. Buy from a friendship-friendly company, for instance, and we can take solace knowing we are promoting friendship in the workplace, friendship between businesses, reducing exploitation, slavery, and poisoning of the natural world. Applying the Ten Desires to work isn't just transformative of businesses, it helps transform communities and lives around the world.

In Chapter 9 we will apply the Ten Desires to business in two main areas: business structure and improving our work environment. We will consider the example of two business structures where the Ten Desires are already being successfully applied both globally and locally: the co-operative, and Mittelstand companies. From them we will distil specific friendship-friendly business characteristics to look for worthy of our support such as flat hierarchies, worker and customer loyalty, shared values and goals, family focus, and being community and environmentally responsible.

Successful business doesn't have to mean brutally prioritizing profit ahead of people, it can mean supporting families, communities, and improving work–life balance while creating more stable, fulfilling, and meaningful jobs.

Having considered how to apply the Ten Desires to business structure we will then apply them to the work environment—on the floor—in three main areas: among managers, staff, and customers. As we shall soon learn, applying the Ten Desires to all three areas not only makes for a better, happier, more effective and efficient work environment it also increases sales. Applying the Ten Desires to business means more happy customers. Thus we can look forward to a stable and growing business.

As we shall see, friendship isn't the enemy of business, it is its greatest asset.

Finally, we will look to how we can use the Ten Desires to improve our communities and governments.

Restoring community spirit, being able to trust our children will be safe with our neighbors, a place where we help and support each other, is long overdue. The Ten Desires can help us not only restore a unifying community spirit but raise it to new heights. In Chapter 10 we will learn five guiding principles to help build fulfilling, united, communities founded on satisfying the Ten Desires. As we shall see, group size matters, so does face-to-face contact, shared facilities are enormously beneficial, and so are places where we can walk and talk. We will learn how we can personally apply these principles in our neighborhoods and suburbs to bring back and enhance community spirit and unity, to transcend fear, division, and hate. Recreating a village-style environment, for instance, can be a great help. New Urbanism is an example of such an approach already being successfully used. How we organize our housing or use our streets can also be beneficial. For example, building houses around common areas such as honeycomb housing provides a central area for families to meet, or using footpaths to grow food for everyone to share, promotes social contact. The five guiding principles can be used to help restore community in many practical ways. Then we will learn how to take back our governments and make them better than ever before.

In Chapter 11 we will learn how to fix a broken system, without tearing it apart or by revolution, but from the grass roots, from remaking the foundations. We will use six guiding principles, distilled from the Ten Desires, to help us determine what type of governments we should be trying to support or create. As we shall see, many types of government have been tried but only a few satisfy the principles, democracy being one of them. Unfortunately, we are all too vulnerable to being dictated to when we are afraid or under threat. We will learn how and why that makes democracies fragile, and what makes this especially relevant today.

If we want representative governments we need to constantly work to ensure them.

Rules and laws are essential if we are to get our governments to work or we can be cursed by acts of revenge and infighting. Personal social responsibility is also paramount. You and I can take many practical steps to make better governments real; to improve our governments here and now—to take them back.

Applying the Ten Desires to governments and our lives offers us enormous hope and promise. As ambitious as it sounds, they provide us the potential to lay down the foundations for a thousand years of peace. When we recognize states and governments behave like people we can counter the malevolent desires in them just like we can in us, preventing unnecessary conflict. In Chapter 11 we will learn what some of these malevolent desires are—hint, there are more than just the desires of our inner beast—and offer simple approaches that can counter them. As will become clear, we can't underestimate how vital our personal role is in making lasting peace, perhaps to last a thousand years, a realistic possibility. Understand the fundamentals that prevent peace within and between us and we can, perhaps, finally make war an endangered species.

Chapter 12 concludes by helping us to recognize the wondrous opportunity nature has given each of us to create a positive future for us all.

When so much division, fear, intolerance, hate, conflict, and inequality exists in the world, it is easy to lose hope, throw our hands up in the air like Steve, wish our children had not been born into such a worldly mess, and come to believe we can personally do nothing to change things.

The challenge isn't for you and I to create a utopia, but to make each day better, so we manifest a more fulfilling life and a better place for us and the generations to follow.

Understanding our basic human desires, and especially the desires related to friendship, can be the tool we need to help personally guide us to make that change. Even if we don't want to change the world, if we simply become better friends with those around us and make friendship a greater part of our life by learning to use the Ten Desires, we will notice remarkable improvements.

Tomorrow grows from the seeds we plant today.

PART ONE

The Friendship Crash and Rise of a Beast

He was jailed for the term of his natural life and was accommodated in a damp cell so small that, if he laid down its length, he could feel his head against one wall and his feet against the other. It was cold and bleak, and in winter rarely above 40 degrees Fahrenheit (4 degrees Celsius). His blanket was so worn it was almost see-through. He had to complain heavily just to get a pair of trousers to replace their prisoner shorts—they slept fully dressed, it was too cold not to. Even then he wouldn't accept them unless all the other prisoners had them too. He went into prison at age 44. He suffered terribly in these confines for over 27 years. He had every reason to hate the penal system, and the men who ran it. But Nelson Mandela, a black South African fighter for freedom, justice, democracy, and non-racialism in a white dominated—racist—country, had another way.

On 11 May 1994, the day after his inauguration as the first black president of South Africa, Mandela met Afrikaner John Reinders, the chief of presidential protocol during the reign of the last white president, FW de Klerk, and the president before him, PW Botha. Reinders had been part of the correctional services that had treated Mandela so badly and was a member of a political organization he vehemently opposed. But instead of showing hostility, resentment, or disdain—he certainly had every reason to—Nelson Mandela greeted him warmly. Reinders said, 'Mandela treated him with the same respect as he showed the president of the United States, the Pope or Britain's Queen.'[20] He recalled that he treated all his staff, no matter how humble their position, the same way. Reinders and Mandela developed a close and emotional bond; he came to love Mandela like a father.[21] During the five years serving by his side, he said he was treated with nothing but courtesy and kindness.

Mandela, certainly in his later years, was an example of friendship personified, an exemplar for us all. No matter your station in life, what reason he might have to dislike or disagree with you, it seems he always practiced one of the most important of the Ten Desires: respect.

Perhaps we can learn to develop a personal code of friendship, a standard by which we ensure respect for each other, like the inspirational Nelson Mandela. A sound foundation towards spreading friendship everywhere.

CHAPTER 1

Friendship Made Simple

STRANGERS ARE JUST GOOD FRIENDS THAT YOU HAVEN'T MET YET.

—*Margaret Lee Runbeck*

At a casual glance Toby looked like he might rip your head off! He didn't mean to, but not making eye contact, fists clenched, body piercings, and obvious agitation made it appear he just wanted to get into a fight. He came along at his wife's suggestion; he was getting angry easily and seemed a bit down. We sat down over a few visits to see if, together, we could work things out. Getting to know him, he was very different to how he appeared.

Toby was a shy, slim, mostly gentle guy in his mid-20s. It soon became obvious he was having trouble with depression and anxiety—his mood was constantly low and he was often very anxious. Much of this started after his first daughter was born several months ago. Toby found it hard to find a long-term job, and he was desperate to be a good father to his new baby girl. He didn't have many friends and often wouldn't go out. It wasn't that he didn't want to be out with his mates as much as all the pubs and clubs they wanted to go to wouldn't let him in. He hated being out these days; it made him even more anxious, and self-conscious. He said he felt frustrated. He soon broke down, his hands to his face, sobbing.

Like many of us Toby didn't know how to communicate in a way that worked. Having had a tough childhood, he suffered more than his fair share of verbal and physical abuse; there wasn't anyone there to teach him how to get on with others in a way that let them feel calm and want to be around him. Instead he was always on guard, and on the defence. It was like he was just waiting for the next person to attack him, and some did. After a while we started talking about friendship needs and desires—what people want from us to feel comfortable and satisfied in our company. The next I'd see him was several months later. I almost didn't recognize him.

Gone was the shy guy hunched forward trying not to look you in the face, now he stood tall, seemed calm, and almost had a smile on his face. I couldn't wait to ask what happened. He said it was simple.

All he did was treat people like friends, and they just treated him differently.

During our sessions we had spoken about how others quickly try to judge us when we first meet them to see if we will be a friend or foe—can we be friends, or should I be on guard? He simply applied some of what we discussed when he went out. All the clubs and pubs that had previously refused him suddenly let him in!

How did he do it?

He said he just went up to the bouncers—security—at the door and asked them about their night, started talking about football, and any other topic he thought they might be interested in. He had a quick laugh with them, and that was it.

In short, he found his way to meet the Ten Desires of Friendship we had talked about. These skills were also helping him get on better with his wife and mates. He even had a part time job—his newfound confidence helped him there too. When I asked him about his depression and anxiety he told me 'Oh, I don't think about that; it doesn't bother me anymore.' Today he was here for his daughter; she had a cold. It was great to see how just learning a few basic principles and techniques had begun to change his life.

We might not think much about it but simply learning to understand the basic human desires that drive us, that make us do and feel what we do every day, can be enormously useful and powerful, like they were for Toby.

What are these basic human desires, and how do we know they even exist inside us?

We can gain a much deeper appreciation of what basic human desires represent by considering the Australian brush-turkey.

BASIC HUMAN DESIRES: THE BIRD BRAIN IN US

Ever met, or seen, an Australian brush-turkey? They are a scrawny black turkey-sized bird with a bald red head, and a yellow dangly bit coming from around their neck; the older the bird, the longer the dangly bit. They live up and down the east coast of Australia, and just about every avid gardener in this region hates them! Why? They scratch around among leaves and mulch, dig holes—like they did in my small garden, and make a right old mess. Not good if you like a reasonably tidy garden, like me. Why do they do it? Not to annoy slightly anal gardeners, though that might be fun. It isn't just to find food; they find the insects and grubs under the litter and in the soil. It is also how they make a humungous nest.

The brush-turkey lays around 20 eggs in a meter-high pile of mulch or leaves. The male makes the nest so that as the mulch breaks up it gives off heat around the eggs to keep them warm. It then hangs around after the eggs are laid, and the female has taken off, to keep the temperature of the mound just right by pulling it apart and adding to it as needed. The most amazing thing about these creatures is they are almost totally solitary.

Why is this amazing?

From the moment they hatch they run off, alone, into the bushland. Without learning from their parents—who are elsewhere by now—they know what to eat and where to find it. They know to climb branches at night to find a safe place to sleep. They know how to avoid dangers they have never been shown or taught to be scared of. Then, at just the right time, the males know how to build a nest and attract a female. Then they know how to mate and keep the mound just the right temperature. They know how to do all of this without learning one piece of it from each other. How do they know all this? Nature wrote inside them what it is to be a brush-turkey and gave them the desires and drives to ensure, at just the right time and right place, they do what a brush-turkey is supposed to do to survive.

How is this relevant to us?

This helps us recognize that nature wrote something common inside us all; the thing that makes us human.

Look past all our complex language, our detailed explanations for how the world and our brain are supposed to work. Look past our dreams, beliefs, expectations, culture, and all the technology we interact with every day, and we find a basic creature, a human being, driven, as a brush-turkey is, by the drives nature wrote inside it. Only in our case we find the drives to be human, not to be a brush-turkey.

Search into our feelings and we find basic desires—the fundamental drives and motivations—of every human being.

Where is the evidence that the basic human desires exist in all of us? We find it by sharing what we know in our hearts. We see it in the basic understanding that we are biological beings with our own part to play—our place, different to other living things—in the natural world; we find it in the commonality of our humanity. Yes, we are all human and can recognize this in the common desires to eat, drink, and avoid temperature extremes, to share the love of our children, and desires to feel safe and secure.

What are these basic desires instilled in all of us independent of race, beliefs, or culture?

I find them easiest to make sense of using a simple Balance of Self Model.

BALANCE OF SELF MODEL

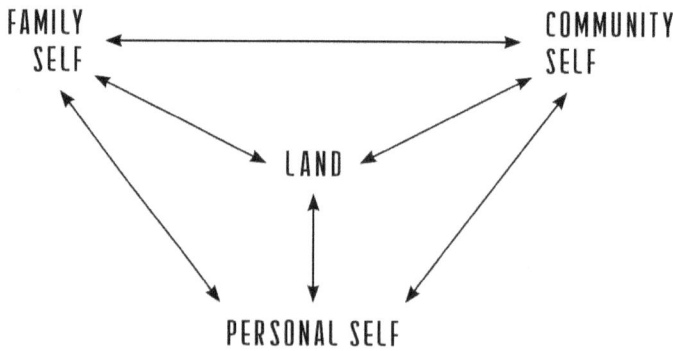

Figure 1.1 Balance of Self Model

The Balance of Self Model represents all the desires—or drives and motivations—we know nature must have written inside us and breaks them into three main functional groups.

Desires of Personal Self

Our Personal Self desires represent the desires that keep us alive as individuals in our own right. They include such desires as hunger, thirst, and need for shelter. If we find ourselves alone these desires ensure we are still alive and kicking. They also define our individuality; to have a strong sense of Personal Self is to have a strong sense of knowing who you are in your own right; what you think and feel when you are not worried what others think, or when you aren't out to impress. We might all have the same overall desires and basic human needs but at any point in time the profile of these will be different; we won't always want or need the same things at the same time to make us satisfied. For instance, I'm not necessarily going to be hungry or thirsty when you are, need to be with a friend, or need a relationship when you might. Personal Self helps us see we can only live a satisfying life if we are genuine and true to our own desires; true to ourselves. The Desires of Family Self relate to our needs to be part of families, and have families of our own.

Desires of Family Self

We all know human beings survive better in families, especially if you throw us out into the natural world. So, we can expect to have desires to be part of supportive families, and to find a partner and have a family of our own. The desires to have sex, to find a long-term and suitable partner, and to be men and women as opposed to childish boys and girls, can be found here. Amid all this we have strong desires to form groups, or communities, beyond our families.

Desires of Community Self

Nature didn't make us to be like brush-turkeys, to be solitary creatures; we lack the feathers for a start. Instead it made us find safety and security among others of our kind. Like a wolf, a social animal that also hunts and survives better in groups, we thrive if we work together as a unified and co-ordinated group, or community. If the bear or tiger attacks then together we can quickly send it on its way, or kill it. We can even bring down more, and larger, game; we can hunt better in a group. A classic example would be the Cro-Magnon of early Europe, working together they could bring down large mammoth, something they could never hope to do alone. Nature determined we are to be social and so it gave us what we can recognize as Community Self desires, which drive us to come together and work as an integrated collective, a team that can act as one. We are made to find safety and security in numbers. We can recognize our Community Self desires as our desires, or needs, of friendship; we will be focusing on these throughout the book. We will list them in a moment.

Then we have Land.

Land

Land in the diagram represents everything that isn't human. It includes the plants, animals, sky, etc. It is there to remind us how the land affects the expression of our desires. For instance, the type of land or environment we grow up in can determine our family size—how we satisfy our Desires of Family Self. The more food available, for example, the bigger the family we might have. It also affects if we come together to form communities. If we can farm the land, for instance, we can create much larger communities such as towns, villages, and city-states, than if we are simply nomadic. Land can also be used as a tool to help us increase our sense of Personal Self. If you wish to learn how, I recommend you read, *A Balance of Self: A new approach to self understanding, lasting happiness, and self-truth* (Vivid, 2011). Like tribes of old I have personally found the land can be a profound and honest teacher about ourselves and our place among all things, if we are prepared to listen.

What about the arrows in the diagram that connect the groups of desires?

They remind us that all our desires are connected.

For example, trying to satisfy our Family Self desires will determine how much of an individual we become and how much we respect or value ourselves; our level of Personal Self. If our family is abusive, neglectful, or our parents never cared for themselves, for instance, then our Personal Self will be low because they will have taught us we aren't worthwhile or worthy of respect; we will have learnt by their example not to care for ourselves. Similarly, if our community doesn't value or respect us as an individual we will have a low Personal Self too—how others treat us affects what we think about, and how we treat, ourselves. Yet if we have a low sense of self—Personal Self—then both our relationships and friendships will suffer and we will never truly be satisfied by them because we will not be true to ourselves or genuine. When Personal Self is low our Family Self and Community Self desires will not be as satisfied as they could be.

The diagram itself is insightful. It clearly reminds us we aren't just part of a family, or a community, and we aren't just individuals. A whole gamut of constantly changing desires inside us affect, compete, and interact with each other differently depending on the time and circumstance. Friendship desires are simply just one part of this dynamic, and when you affect one part you affect the balance of everything.

This is important to remember. In a book about friendship it is easy to forget that friendship and being social is just part of who we are. It is easy to fail to recognize we aren't just part of a community we are also part of a family, we are individuals in our own right, and part of a bigger world. Changing the nature of our friendships changes our communities, ourselves, and the world. As the diagram reminds us, they are all interconnected.

So, what are the Ten Desires of Friendship, where did they come from, and why ten, why not say 15 or 20?

REVEALING THE TEN DESIRES OF FRIENDSHIP

The Ten Desires almost arose by accident. They came from simply imagining a tribe of 30–60 or so people long ago, way before civilization, and imagining them as a close and independent group that suddenly had very little to eat or were under threat from a neighboring tribe; the threats of starvation and attack. I wondered what personal qualities might rally others in our group to us to ensure we had a better chance of surviving compared to the rest. When we are a close tribal community we don't want anyone to die, but what qualities might enhance our survival over others?

For instance, if we have a particularly vital skill, like being a very good hunter, would that mean others would make sure we survived compared to those who didn't have such a vital skill? There is a clear example of this recorded among the Lakota Plains Indians of the central United States in the late 1800s in a book—*The Land of the Spotted Eagle*—written by one of their former chiefs, Luther Standing Bear.

The Olga Lakota were a nomadic tribal people who lived off the bounty that was the great herds of buffalo: bison. They also lived off deer and other smaller animals when the buffalo weren't around. Having grown up until 11 years of age in the traditional ways Luther Standing Bear recalled a time when people were starving and how a woman sacrificed what little food she had to give to a warrior—a good hunter—so he would be strong enough to go out and bring back more food for everyone. She might go without herself, and suffer because of it, but her self-sacrifice would ensure everyone else's survival in the process. To have a valuable skill helped ensure the warrior would survive above others; to have food when others did not. To be a good hunter and warrior is a great skill and asset to have when a tribe is under threat.

In other words, by feeling valued—that we have something important to offer to the group—we can feel assured we have the support of others, and enhance our chance of surviving, especially if times are desperate. A modern example would be if we were the only breadwinner in a family doing it rough. The skills and ability to work makes us especially valuable to our family.

What other qualities might help us when times are tough, so we can be assured our group will be there for us no matter how hard things get, when it is literally life or death?

Suppose nobody noticed us, we have been so inconspicuous few people noticed we were even there. When times were dire could we really count on everyone to give to us what they could instead give to someone they knew and saw more regularly? Would you give your precious food to someone you barely saw or even knew existed compared to someone who regularly kept you company and was popular among the group? Being noticed in a tribe can help keep us alive.

What about if we treated others with disrespect?

Suppose you have not respected others, abused them, perhaps stolen from them, or constantly annoyed or angered them in some way. When times were dire could we really count on the people we disrespected to give us preference over those who were kinder and more respectful to them? If we didn't also have an important skill, it's doubtful.

Would we be more or less likely to want to protect and feed those who never listen to us, never validate our struggles, or our way of doing things? These are qualities that help unite us and act as if of one mind, enhancing our strength and safety. The person who regularly disagrees, invalidates us, and never listens will be more likely to act independently, behave like an outsider and weaken the integrity of our group. Are we really going to give preference of food and protection to them over someone who is more integrated and makes us work better together? It enhances our survival in a tribe to feel heard, validated, and approved.

And it is the enemy who is different to us that attacks us, not those like us; those who are the same or similar.

To be too different is like painting a sign in big letters on our back that reads: 'I'M NOT ONE OF YOU!' Can we really be expected to ensure the safety and nourishment of someone who is so different they also weaken the strength of our group's integrity? It's unlikely. Mind you, a little bit different is ok, it adds variety, new skills, and adaptability, but too different just sends a signal: we are a loner and can't be trusted to be there for everyone else when they most need us.

Of course we are going to want to keep alive those who most care for, support, and protect us. When we are injured we need to know someone will care for us and help make us well, tend our wounds and feed us when we can't feed ourselves. When we need to accomplish difficult tasks we need to know others will support us so we succeed and endure. And when we are attacked we need to know others will protect and defend us. Anyone fulfilling such roles will probably have preference over someone who doesn't, especially in times of threat or deprivation. By helping them we help ourselves.

If we summarize these qualities that enhance our ability to survive as an individual in an integrated group we arrive at the Ten Desires of Community Self. Only later, as I began to help people like Toby use them, did it become apparent that these were also the Desires of Friendship. It then became obvious, what kept tribes strongly bound to each other was to be among close and trusted friends. We become bound together as people by the Ten Desires of Friendship, listed below.

TEN DESIRES OF FRIENDSHIP

1. Valued
2. Noticed
3. Appreciated
4. Heard
5. Sameness (similarity)
6. Validated/Approved
7. Respected
8. Cared for
9. Supported
10. Protected

We will explain what each of these desires represents, and how best to use them, in later chapters.

So why just ten? We could have added empathy, compassion, and love, for instance, and several others. Why keep it to ten?

Basically, to keep it simple and to a minimum, and because often other desires can be explained by using these ten.

For example, empathy, being able to put ourselves in other's shoes, can be encompassed under the desire to be heard. For someone to really listen and make us feel truly heard requires some empathy—trying to understand what we are going through. To be compassionate is a combination of all of the Ten Desires, especially that of wanting to care; it is next to impossible to be compassionate if we don't care for others. And love—to feel loved by those around us—also encompasses caring, supporting, protecting, validating, respecting, appreciating, noticing, valuing—essentially being a close friend. We often feel most loved around close friends.

By now many of you may have noticed the desires are all closely linked; to satisfy one is often to satisfy many others. For instance, to be respected requires we are noticed and not ignored, appreciated and not disregarded, heard and not kept silent, cared for and protected, and never abused. Similarly, to notice someone, like seeing them in the room and letting them know by a kind and casual greeting, for example, is also a way to indicate they are valued and respected. And to let someone feel heard we need to respect, notice, value, care, and validate them—it is hard to feel heard if the other person doesn't seem to care or show an interest in what we are saying. To satisfy one need of friendship often satisfies many; they form a greater whole.

So how did Toby's approach, we described earlier, work? Why did people who usually excluded him suddenly let him in?

He began by looking the doormen—security—in the eye, approached them as potential friends and said hello: he noticed them. He respected them by behaving well. He offered to listen to them—to feel heard—by asking about their night. This also would show he valued their input and opinion, and suggest he cared. Then he made them feel the same—similar to him—with small talk, by talking about things they had in common, such as football. This was in contrast to not making eye contact, not talking, perhaps swearing if they didn't let him in, and not showing he cared about them by never wanting to interact with them. In short, he went from being a potential threat to coming across as a friend simply by meeting several of their friendship needs. The security let him in—even ahead of others in the line, so he told me—largely because he showed them he was their friend, as opposed to their enemy. A friendly guy, I suspect the security imagined, was also going to be less trouble.

This raises one further important basic principle about friendship we should point out before we move on.

It isn't for us to make others meet these needs in us, it is for us to satisfy the Ten Desires in them.

Consider it a moment, can you force someone to meet these ten needs in you? Could I make you meet these needs in me, for instance?

Well, I might try, but is that showing I respect you?

No.

If I respected you I wouldn't try to make, or force, you to do anything. Instead I would simply ask and let you decide for yourself—offer you the choice.

Having our friendship needs met doesn't happen by trying to make others meet them for us. It doesn't happen by us punishing them if they ignore us or don't listen, by abusing them if they don't seem to care, by threatening them if they don't protect or support us. Yet that is what we often do isn't it, punish others for not noticing, caring for, or appreciating us, especially in relationships? Just you wait, I'll give you the silent treatment, ignore you, shout at or slam you with abuse. I'll teach you! Of course, this actually makes matters worse as it destroys what friendship we have left; one more nail in the coffin of our relationship.

Put simply, our friendship needs get met best by us focusing on just meeting them in others.

How does this work?

Largely thanks to our desire for sameness (to be similar to everyone else). When we do it others are likely to do it too.

You will recall nature made us so we can act well together as a group. We can't do that if we are too different in our behaviors, beliefs, ideas, and actions. The more alike we are the easier it is to work together as one. It is one of the reasons soldiers dress alike and follow the same rules and march in unison. By being similar to each other they can act better as a single unit and be much stronger than individuals doing their own thing.

When we become an example others are likely to follow.

It may take time but once you show value, respect, care, appreciation, approval and support, then the people you show this to will be more likely to give the same back. Like Toby found when he went out and tried it with complete strangers; when he was friendly and met their friendship needs they did likewise in return, and he had a great night.

Want your friendship needs met by others, so you don't feel lonely, so you can feel someone really cares?

Then we need to learn to meet their friendship needs first.

We will work on specific ways and circumstances in later chapters.

Behind all the apparent complexities of ideas, beliefs, thoughts, and technology, deep down inside we are very basic; we are all driven by basic desires to be human beings. Common to all human beings are the desires for friendship; nature made us to seek out and find deep satisfaction among friends. Unfortunately, it also played a cruel joke on us that would lead to friendship's fall. It allowed us to start farming. (More on this later.)

Now that we can recognize the desires at play we can see how friendship fell into decline, its destructive impact on our history, and the devastating impact it has on us still.

KEY POINTS

- We can recognize basic human desires common to all, no matter our beliefs, ideas, thoughts, race, sex, culture, and technologies.
- If we satisfy these desires, or see how we can, we will feel good, satisfied, and fulfilled.
- We can break all human desires into three main functional groups: Personal Self, Family Self, and Community Self.
- Community Self desires drive us to unify as integrative, co-ordinated groups, to find safety and security around others like us; to be social.

- Community Self desires can also be recognized as our desires for friendship.

TEN DESIRES OF FRIENDSHIP

1. Valued
2. Noticed
3. Appreciated
4. Heard
5. Sameness (similarity)
6. Validated/Approved
7. Respected
8. Cared for
9. Supported
10. Protected

CHAPTER 2

Rise of the Beast Within

AM I NOT DESTROYING MY ENEMIES
WHEN I MAKE FRIENDS OF THEM?

—*Abraham Lincoln*

It was a beautiful sight. Young Aboriginal Australian children playing together in a remote community, the elder children caring for the young, the young playing with all ages, no bullying, no one excluded, and no fighting to be better than the rest. I recall it in a documentary I watched several years ago. The ten or so children varied in ages from teens to toddlers but shared smiles and grins all around; the children had learnt to be there for each other and the older children took care of the rest. Eventually I discovered Aboriginal carers actively encouraging independent play is a well-recognized part of traditional Aboriginal Culture and Law. It helps children learn important life skills, like responsibilities, such as to care for one another.[22] Looking back now I can see many contrasts to the public schooling I remember.

The schools of my youth in country Australia were riddled with competition, and a drive for kids to be better than everyone else. Status, and wanting to achieve it, was rife. In the playground, for instance, the kids who were in academically better classes would hang out together and avoid those from below. You were also something according to your ambition; the more prestigious the job you wanted—doctor, lawyer, architect, pilot, or even the Prime Minister!—the more you were accepted, Everyone was judged and treated according to their status, or the level of status they might have some day.

In the school of my childhood it wasn't uncommon for students to be bullied for being different, as I had been; the other children certainly didn't come around to protect those under attack and make them feel cared for and wanted. A broad friendship, like the type the Aboriginal children shared, wasn't there, or encouraged, among the children of the schools I remember, or among many of the children of the schools I see, or hear of from parents and students, today. I am told by teachers, parents, and students alike that pupils still form into smaller—exclusive—social groups and are all too quick to exclude others rather than be broadly welcoming.

From our schools we see a reminder of the contrast in the value of friendship from different eras. The broad, welcoming, inclusiveness, and protection from when we were tribal, and a less protective, caring, and more competitive spirit of modern times.

So, what changed to turn this around, to make friendship so much less important compared to when we lived in close and nomadic tribes?

We changed. We changed in response to the transformations of the natural world around us in a predictable, though disturbing, way.

FARMING: THE RISE OF WEALTH, POWER AND STATUS

Don't you just love farming? It is an astonishing achievement. For starters, it has filled our pantries and refrigerators, so we don't have to go out and hunt and scrounge for our food anymore. But it has also helped feed the world and given us civilization itself. For without farming there would be no cities, modern technology, and medicine. Farming has given us the resources to research the causes of illnesses and successfully fight off all manner of diseases—such as small pox and polio—that once killed millions. The antibiotics you get from your doctor to save your life are thanks to farming. Our modern life was built on farming. But it came at a price we are yet to fully comprehend.

Just over 10,000 years ago, in six places around the world, for the very first time in history nature gave us the right crops to cultivate (such as wheat, barley, corn, and squash), and the right animals to domesticate (such as goats, pigs, cattle, sheep, and llamas) to allow us to settle and farm. From the Fertile Crescent in the Middle East between the Tigris and Euphrates rivers in Iraq, to Egypt, China, India, Mesoamerica (Southern Mexico), and Peru it allowed farming to supply enough food to create the world's first primary civilizations; civilizations, or nation states, that developed away from the influence of any other. In all these places, as if by accident, it fashioned inside us a new desire we hadn't really noticed much before: a new yearning for wealth.

We take wealth for granted these days; our lives revolve around it. We think it is normal to 'own' stuff, such as a house, car, computer, TV, or mobile phone. And we give no second thought to pay for it with money, or some form of credit. But evidence suggests that for nigh on over five, perhaps seven million years, wealth—as we know it—never existed. Yes, we might have exchanged things, like a stone knife for a few spears or an axe or bartered for trinkets such as pretty shells we liked, but that wasn't about wealth. Wealth didn't happen until we started to farm.

What do we mean by wealth?

Put simply, wealth basically means having excess; far more than we need to survive. When we roamed and lived off the land we had no need for excess. In fact, it would actually be a burden.

For example, Aboriginal Australians for over 50,000 years, before Europeans invaded, had no need for wealth. They carried less than 20 items with them everywhere they went, such as some spears, and simple tools. There was no need to have lots of clothes or excess food, most of what they needed they could find—or make—as they went. To own too much would have slowed them down. That didn't mean they didn't cultivate some of their land, there is good evidence they did,[23] but when the seasons changed they could reliably find a more abundant place to live. What foolish nomad would hoard and carry around two dozen pairs of extra shoes, or clothes, or carcasses of meat? Nomadic hunter-gathers in ancient times had no concept of a need for what we now recognize as wealth, but to a farmer, reliant on the bounty of a small, local, piece of land all year around, wealth becomes a necessity.

Wealth is a farmer's life insurance; it can mean life or death.

Farmers have no way to accurately predict the seasons and know how good, or bad, they will be. But it only takes one bad season and we can be in strife. If we don't have excess—some extra grain in storage, for instance—our family dies. End of story. It's not like we have another resource to count on and can just wander off to find it, like our nomadic cousins could. And in early days big towns or cities rarely existed to go to for relief. If we didn't store enough, and our neighbors didn't do the same, we'd all perish. Excess—wealth—isn't a burden to a farmer; it's vital!

Farming created a strong desire for wealth.

But once you create wealth other powerful, and potentially destructive, desires need to protect it.

Imagine for a moment you are an early farmer among several others in your area. Suddenly a few bad seasons befall you and other's farmers' children are starting to die; they don't have enough stores to see it through, but you do, you have plenty. But if you share your extra with them your family could also die—you never know how long the bad times will last. At least if you can keep what you have your family has a chance.

Now suppose you are a parent watching your children starve to death, slowly. You plead for help—for food to feed your family—but none is forthcoming. What would you do? Would you fight, perhaps join with others, to take what you need from those who seem to have plenty?

Herein lies a major problem with creating wealth; when we create it, others are going to be driven—at some point—to want to take it.

The unfortunate reality is there will always be inequality in farming; someone, or some group, is bound to have less. Create farming and we don't only generate wealth, we invent a need to protect it. Like we have a desire today to protect the assets we have worked hard for, such as our home, our car, and funds for that rainy day or retirement.

How do we protect our hard-earned wealth as an early farmer?

We certainly won't be able to fend everyone off ourselves; there are bound to be too many. So, we need a new strategy: influence.

If we can influence others not to take what we have worked for then our excess will be safe.

How do we create such influence?

With status and power.

Create wealth and we also inevitably create the need—the strong desires—for status and power so we can keep it.

And this is where insatiable desires rise to great power, and the fall of friendship truly begins, with terrible consequences.

NEED FOR STATUS

Have you ever enjoyed feeling important, even just a little bit? Having other people look up to you, show appreciation, and let you know they want you around can feel great. Deep down we all like to feel important; the desires to feel valued, appreciated, and respected, as we noted earlier, are some of our Ten Desires of Friendship. When we are important in our society we can be said to have status. Status is especially helpful when we have wealth because it means others won't mind if we have more than them; they will allow us to keep it and won't try to take it.

Why?

They will want us to be secure.

What forms of status might help ensure our wealth?

That can depend on the society, and its situation.

For example, in a community at war or in conflict with another community, the fighters—warriors—will have great status as they protect all of us. If one particular fighter is especially skilled at fighting and strategy, then that person will almost certainly have the highest status. Like Alexander the Great, a king of Ancient Greece around 340 BC. Among a land of warring people he was a great leader going into battles from the front and held enormous status among his people. In contrast, if a society is riddled by infighting, but not necessarily war, the wise peacemaker—the resolver of disputes—can be important to the survival of the community and have great status. Those who heal, who make important tools, who can farm well, or build the best boats to catch the fish, will all have high status if they have the skills or qualities our community needs the most and can't afford to lose.

Another important skill needs special mention here, as it can easily be used as a powerful tool to feed our insatiable desires and help unleash untold misery. It is the claimed ability to converse with the supernatural.

Why would claiming to be able to converse with gods or spirits create high status in a farm-based community, let alone be a source of misery?

It has to do with our need for hope.

Farmers need rain, predictable seasons; fair weather that won't wash away their crops or animals so that they can grow, flourish, and offer great bounty. They need volcanoes overshadowing their farms to remain silent, so they don't get burnt by hot ash clouds, and the seas to be kind and calm rather than rough and stormy so they don't drown as they are fishing or travel out to sea. By changing the spirits we once believed in as nomads—such as those of the trees, forests, mountains, and sky—and transforming them into gods we can manipulate, coerce, and gain favor or somehow control, we make the world less heart breaking, and scary. We offer our communities hope.

Hope is powerful. To be able to claim direct connection to the divine gives us control of a major source of hope and can assure us of a very high status indeed and permit us great wealth. We can find evidence of people using a claimed spiritual connection to increase status, and allow them to maintain great wealth, going back as far as the world's first primary civilizations, and even find it readily today.

For example, in Ancient Egypt wealthy pharaohs had the support of influential priests or priestesses who claimed a connection to their specific gods. Either that or they made themselves gods. One pharaoh—Akhenaten—increased his divine connection and status by making himself the sole prophet of a single god—Aten, the sun god. You may know him as the husband of Nefertiti, or father of the famed Tutankhamen—the young boy-king and owner of the beautiful gold death mask often seen in photographs. To be a pharaoh was to have a divine connection or status associated with the supernatural. People might question the words of a man but who would dare question the wishes of a god? The pharaohs were enormously rich compared to their subjects. Powerful status through religious connection helped them keep it—it helped prevent the masses from overthrowing them and taking it from them.

The ancient civilization of Samaria, arising in the Middle East over 5000 years ago, also had many gods. Their elite rulers were considered priest kings, giving them a direct divine connection, and with it very high status that also assured their wealth. So too the Olmec of Mesoamerica, who lived in what is now lower central Mexico from as early as 1500 BC. Their elite ensured and legitimized their status by claiming a spiritual connection to the spirit of the powerful Jaguar, and glyphs (pictures carved in stone) suggest they held a connection with the divine spirits that controlled the weather as well.

Religion and spiritual belief has been a powerful way of increasing status to legitimize wealth for thousands of years.

We can even see a clear example of it today with the Catholic Church.

Many of you may not be aware but the Catholic Church has its own bank—the Vatican Bank—that manages over $7.3 billion on behalf of 17,400 customers. It also manages around €700 million of its own equity. It keeps $20 million in gold with the Federal Reserve and makes over $850 million per week—that's right, per week—through donations in North America alone. In 2011 the CIA estimated Vatican City to have revenue of $308 million for its 800 head population, equating to $365,796 per person per year, making it the richest state by this measure in the world.[24] The Catholic Church has considerable wealth thanks to enough people agreeing they have a sufficient divine connection to offer them status to keep it. Hence, despite great world poverty, they are not taxed and made, by the people, to share it.

We may even legitimize our wealth using the divine ourselves. How many of us claim that the wealth we have is a 'God-given right' or 'God's will', legitimizing for us why we don't need to share it? Using a divine power or connection to legitimize status, and hence our wealth, has been around for millennia. How this can lead to misery will become apparent shortly, when we briefly consider belief's role in slavery in the next chapter.

Of course, we can gain status to ensure our wealth in many other ways.

For example, we can have status by having jobs that are recognized as being important or having some prestige. For instance, being a judge, lawyer, doctor, dentist, high-ranking politician, or CEO of a large company. We also give status to people who touch our heart with their creativity and help us escape into fantasies such as writers, actors, movie directors, and producers (being able to escape is very important to us in our society and creates enormous status). Actors, for instance, are often treated, or considered by many, to be a form of royalty and given very high status. We even give enormous status to people in our society just because they look good! For example, Kim Kardashian West, the selfie queen, made over $45 million in 2017,[25] her sister, Kendal Jenner, made over $22 million as a model the same year.[26]

The bottom line is status means others will allow us to be wealthy—others won't mind so much if we have more than them; we permit it. Mind you, having wealth by itself can also give us status too, and we will discuss this more in a moment. But what about if we don't have any status, what can we do to be allowed to keep our excess then?

The next option is power.

NEED FOR POWER

By using force, threat of force, or the use of payment or bribery, we can influence others to follow our wishes; we can convince them to help protect our excess or deter them from taking it. We know this level of coercion as the use of power.

Exerting power is often a form of thuggery and corruption. Through bribery (such as gifts or inducements), threats, violence, or threat of violence, we get our own way; or at least try to. We basically become a brute who uses intimidation, fear, and coercion to get what we want, much like Al Capone did during Prohibition, or the Mexican drug cartels do today. If you don't agree to work for a drug cartel in Mexico these days they kill you, or a member of your family. To prevent the law bringing the cartel leaders in they use threats, intimidation, and pay bribes to officials so they don't get raided. A classic example is the Los Zeta cartel that terrorizes great swathes of land in north east Mexico, bordering on Texas.

In courtroom proceedings in 2017 in Texas, witnesses described the level of Zeta control '…extended to city police chiefs, state and federal prosecutors, state prisons, sectors of the federal police and Mexican army, and state politicians'. Zeta was said to have 'paid bribes and integrated police officers in their hierarchy to ensure the cartel would be able to continue their illicit operations without resistance'. Sadly, in spite of Mexico's militarized crackdown against the drug cartels in the last decade over 200,000 people lost their lives, and over 30,000 went missing.[27]

Power as a form of maintaining, and acquiring, wealth is well documented throughout history. For example, during the Roman Empire, power determined who ruled and became the influential elite. In fact, if you had insufficient military support—military power—you couldn't be their head of state. Julius Caesar—who eventually became emperor of Rome—only achieved this thanks to support of the majority of the military. He did this by paying soldiers from the bounty of his conquests and offering promises of increased status and power (inducements) on their return. By wielding the power of the military he controlled Rome, and could maintain great personal wealth. Great wealth in Rome required great power. Power was similarly used to gain great wealth and leadership in China.

The Chinese dynasties, such as those of the great Mongol emperor Genghis Khan, and the many that came before and after him, arose out of fighting each other. As they exerted their power they collected taxes and bounty from those they conquered and forced into submission. They used their power to ensure they could accumulate—and keep—considerable great wealth. The elite of the Chinese dynasties amassed enormous wealth—even by today's standards—thanks to the use of power.

Today the use of power to create or keep wealth isn't just exerted by drug lords; we can see evidence in all walks of life. People threatening and intimidating others to get their way be it at home, at work, on the street in gangs—and in local councils. Recently, a wealthy property developer coerced local council members to vote for him just so the developer could remain deputy mayor and pass property development approvals. This would allow the deputy mayor's development company to make millions of dollars. It isn't just individuals doing this, many companies use power to increase wealth every day.

For instance, in the USA we see millions of dollars 'donated' by companies, and wealthy individuals, to fund huge media driven campaigns to ensure the political candidate that agrees to their agenda will get elected. We also see it in lobbying, as mentioned earlier, where billions of dollars are currently spent. By buying political influence—a modern form of legal bribery, or inducement—they then help ensure the majority of the people don't decide to take their wealth from them through taxation or regulation, so the wealth might instead be used to build schools, pay for social supports, or medicines. They use their power to maintain their wealth and their wealth to maintain their power, a strategy that has, again, been used for thousands of years, and remains common today.

As you can probably see by now a close link exists between wealth, power and status. They are so closely linked they can be considered virtually inseparable; have one and you almost invariably have the others. Wealth can buy power, power can give us wealth, and both can give us status—if we are wealthy and powerful we will often be an important influence in our society. And by having status we can further legitimize our wealth—if we are important enough people will be less inclined to want to take it from us; they will say we deserve it or won't mind if we have it. How many people have you met, or seen in the media, with considerable wealth who don't have status or at least some significant power, who don't have considerable influence? They usually have all three. Some run huge media companies. Some CEOs oversee multibillion dollar businesses. Some even run for president!

The powerful desires for wealth, power, and status were an inevitable consequence of becoming farmers and no longer being nomadic. They are still powerful influences now.

Why are they such a problem when it comes to friendship?

By their nature they are unquenchable, making them immensely destructive, and divisive. Farming didn't just create civilization, it unleashed a monster that still rules over us today.

BIRTH OF A BEAST

If I were to describe a being so powerful that it could spread fear and hate globally, drive one man to kill another and step over him without a second glance, let children starve, and let millions die in wars, and that this being would lay waste to the world and threaten our very existence, what would you call it? Calling it a beast would be an understatement. Yet that is what was created inside us without us even being aware it.

Have you ever, as a child, lived through really hard times? Times of great poverty where you went hungry some or most nights? If we suffer through severe deprivation our desire for wealth increases greatly; we never want to go through something so terrible ever again. Live in a society that has known deprivation and our increased desire for wealth will see us climbing over each other to get as much as we can from the same pot of limited wealth. Our strong desire for wealth creates brutal competition. This establishes a hierarchy, with a small number of elite owning almost everything, and the majority with almost nothing in comparison; extremes of wealth and poverty, like we see now. The problem is, no matter how much anyone accumulates they will never feel safe and secure.

In farming-based societies—like ours—we try to find safety and security by having so much wealth no matter what happens we will always have enough and our family will never go without. But we can never accumulate enough to protect us from every crisis. And we can never have so much that the majority won't take it from us. A good example of this was in the Russian Revolution of 1917.

In Tsarist Russia towards the end of World War 1, the masses of poor and starving people overthrew the autocracy. Tsar Nicholas II and his family were executed. One of the most powerful and wealthy families of the world lost everything within a matter of months. Not long after a whole new elite driven by a need for wealth, power, and status replaced them under the guise of communism. Even the wealthiest and most powerful were not safe and secure when the people decided their time was up.

When we are using wealth to try to feel secure and safe we make our desires for wealth, power, and status, insatiable.

We can never have enough to outlast any great disaster. Or that others won't be able to take it. But that won't stop us trying. The insatiable quality of these desires will, by their nature, send us beyond our borders in our endless quest for more, resulting in wars, death, destruction, and misery. They will even see us destroy our own planet—the natural world that sustains us—just to try to satisfy their unquenchable lust. Accumulating more wealth becomes so powerful and endless we will let nothing get in the way of accommodating our endless desire for more, to fill the bottomless pit. Now just three desires threaten our very existence, and the world. We wouldn't have nuclear weapons that could wipe us all off the planet tomorrow, and have poisoned so much of the planet, if it wasn't for these desires' all-consuming power and influence.

I think these desires deserve the title of 'beast', don't you?

What role does friendship play in all this?

Nature made us to quell our desires to feel safe and secure with friendship. We found security having enough to eat; with each other we could hunt more effectively and gather more food as a group. We found safety among others of our kind—our friends—who could be counted on to protect us from the savage beast or another tribe. Nature made us nomadic tribespeople, not farmers.

That is why we never feel deeply satisfied no matter how much status, wealth, or power we have; we were made to feel safe and secure among friends.

Unfortunately, when we live in a farm-based society that isn't what we see. Our desires for wealth, power, and status, overwhelm our desires for friendship; our fears of never having enough consume us.

While we continue to let our desires for wealth, power, and status go unchecked we will always be left with a hollow emptiness inside, and a world in turmoil and under threat.

It is said, if we don't learn from the past we are doomed to make the same mistakes. One of the ways to prevent history repeating itself is to better understand why things happened as they did. In this case we are trying to stop a destructive ongoing cycle. Two areas that help us better understand the destructive nature of our inner beast and how it creates such havoc are its role in slavery and exploitation, and the creation of empires. Recognize its extreme destructive nature and we better appreciate just how critical friendship is to stopping much of the misery and damage inflicted around the world. If we want friendship to rule our lives and improve them far into the future we must learn more about its greatest enemy, and how you and I can contain it.

KEY POINTS

- Farming created a new desire inside us that never really existed when we were tribal: a desire for wealth.
- With the desire for wealth came associated desires for status and power.
- Our desires for wealth, power, and status never make us feel truly safe and secure.
- The insatiable nature of these desires leads to conquest, wars, death, destruction, misery, and global destruction. They create an insatiable beast inside us that wreaks havoc on the world.
- Friendship can counter the destructive nature of the beast by satisfying the wants that drive it, by quenching our

desires for safety and security. Nature made us feel safe and secure among friends.

- While we continue to let our desires for wealth, power, and status go unchecked we will always be left with an emptiness inside, and a world in turmoil and under threat.

- If we want friendship to rule our lives and improve them we must also learn more about its greatest enemy, and how we can contain it.

CHAPTER 3

Slavery and Our Exploitation

… TO THEM THOSE WHITE PERSONS WHO ARGUE
IN FAVOUR OF MAKING OTHER PEOPLE SLAVES.
I AM IN FAVOUR OF GIVING AN OPPORTUNITY TO
SUCH WHITE MEN TO TRY IT FOR THEMSELVES …

—*Abraham Lincoln*

'The trigger was pulled but I was alive. For a few moments, I thought I was experiencing death with the ability to still see life, until I felt the blows to my head by the gun. This was when I realized there was no hope. I had to continue this life of being obedient to him so my family wouldn't get hurt, as he reminded me each day. I was alive, but not living. I was a slave.'[28]

Shamere McKenzie was on a student athlete scholarship at St John's University, New York, when an injury forced her to look to other means to pay her way. A charismatic man lured her into a relationship and offered her dancing work at a New Jersey strip club to pay the bills, and to move in with him to save on rent. Excited with the money she made dancing on one occasion she followed the man to a house in Brooklyn, New York, where she was expecting to dance privately for men. Taken aback when one of the men asked for oral sex, she refused, was then taken aside, choked, bashed, and threats were made to her family's lives if she ever left or told the police. 'From the very first beating when I was choked to the point of unconsciousness until the day he pulled the trigger on the miraculously unloaded gun in my mouth, I knew obedience meant survival.' Without shackles or a deed of ownership Shamere had become a slave. Eventually the man was arrested by the FBI. Shamere was also arrested for prostitution and spent three weeks in prison before being sent to a program for victims of sex trafficking where she received counseling and housing. She was now a registered sex offender! Once her legal matters were concluded she began life anew. Today she works as a Protected Innocence Initiative policy assistant for Shared Hope International, an international non-profit organization seeking to prevent the conditions that lead to sex trafficking, help restore victims of sex slavery, and bring justice to the women and children.[29]

We often like to think slavery is a thing of the past, after all we don't see slaves traded openly as chattel as they once were. Slavery was outlawed, in the US in 1865, Cuba in 1886, and Brazil in 1888. The United Nations General Assembly adopted the Universal Declaration of Human Rights stating, 'No one shall be held in slavery or servitude; slavery and the slave trade shall be prohibited in all their forms,' so it shouldn't exist. Yet there are more slaves today than any other time in history. According to the International Labour Organization (ILO) in May 2016 almost 25 million people were victims of forced labor, such as threats of physical harm and debt bondage. Some 4.8 million of them victims of forced sexual exploitation, usually women and children—being sold and forced into having sex.[30] Current estimates suggest there are just under 60,000 in America,[31] not including those we might consider slaves in detention around the country—an often-unrecognized source of modern slaves.[32] Slavery never died, not even in the United States.

Why is this relevant?

Firstly, the scars of slavery are yet to heal. If they don't we may never have peace in stable, friendly, united communities and neighborhoods, see an end to fear, oppression, hate, and intolerance; the end to racial prejudices founded centuries ago based almost entirely on the color of our skin. We may never see an end to the killing and profiling of innocent African Americans on suburban and city streets. We will remain divided and afraid and enduring friendship won't have a chance.

Secondly, to understand slavery is to recognize the reasons our bosses, and those wealthier than us, continue to treat us poorly and exploit us; such as preventing us having a decent wage.

So long as the fundamentals that led to slavery remain we will have to continue to fight being underpaid, abused, and treated like machines or livestock; a resource to be exploited rather than caring, feeling, human beings.

Unless we deal with these fundamentals the same problems of slavery and exploitation can be guaranteed to resurface again and again, making it next to impossible for the majority of us to have well-paid, respected, stable jobs.

And thirdly, this is relevant to every one of us because sadly, as we shall soon see, you and I have been supporting and fuelling these fundamentals; we have been keeping them alive and strong.

We have been supporting slavery, and our own exploitation and abuse!

If we don't recognize our part then we will remain complicit, we will be the reasons people become slaves like Shamere, not just in our country, but around the world. We will be the reason ordinary people, like you and me, and our sons and daughters, continue to be exploited in their jobs, or become someone else's slave.

The desires of our inner beast have manifest in an extremely horrid form.

What are these fundamentals that led to us justifying the creation of slavery, and the exploitation of other human beings we have been, mostly unwittingly, supporting?

Let us consider three of them:
- importance of wealth;
- beliefs;
- uncontrolled desires.

Later we will see how we can use friendship to counter them, and stop them ruling our lives.

IMPORTANCE OF WEALTH

How important is wealth to you? Would you be prepared to give up everything you own, the latest mobile phones, computers, TVs, clothes, shoes, cars or gadgets, right now, on the spot? What about the house you own and worked—or are working—to pay off? Suddenly it would be like all your efforts were for nothing; what a waste! And it is because wealth has become so valuable to us—we are all very reluctant to give any of it up—that we were bound to create slavery.

How did that happen?

It began by allowing us to create something else we didn't pay much attention to as nomadic tribespeople: debt.

Living in a tribe we didn't have much need for debt; owing someone something. If we wanted it we'd just exchange it, not promise to make it or swap it over later. Promises are nothing but trouble; if they aren't met they create tensions and can divide our group. Besides, what we exchange most of the time isn't going to be that important; so what if they forget to make the spear tips, pipe, or knife they said they would, or collect the special shells they promised, I can still live without them. Debt—in the greater scheme of things—isn't very important to a nomadic tribesperson, but it becomes much more critical to a farmer.

As we already noted, wealth is vitally important to a farmer and their survival. So, they aren't just going to give it away frivolously.

But suppose someone needs food now but can't pay us—has nothing to exchange that we need—what do we do?

We wouldn't just give it to them for free; how could we dare give away something so precious for nothing? We could be cutting our own family's throats. But there is something they can give us, that can help us replace what we have lost: their labor. We can get them to pay off what they owe us by helping us get more of what we need most, excess food—wealth. They can work for us. In that simple act, we have just created the foundation for slavery.

This was how the Aztec, an ancient farming-based civilization of South America before the Spanish invasion, created their slaves. In their culture, a person could place himself or herself into slavery to pay a debt they owed to someone else: they would become a slave to that person, a debt slave. They could also become a slave as a punishment for a murder. If the family of the lost loved one agreed, the murderer could become a slave, rather than be killed for the murder. This way they could pay off a debt for lost income the loved one could have provided. They called them Tlacotin.[33] They were regarded as a respected people in Aztec culture, but slaves none the less. Slavery developed in the Americas without them being aware of its existence on other continents.

The bottom line:

When wealth becomes paramount debt becomes important.

Soon we can start trading our debts with others—you owe me a chicken, the neighbor owes you a chicken, why don't I just get the chicken from the neighbor? We swap debts. This exchange of debts led to the origin of money. Money was originally a promissory note; we owed someone. Instead of running around with long notes of what people owed each other it was agreed to that a standardized note that represented a certain level of debt be created. Now we just know it as dollar bills, coins, and numbers in accounts. Today we pay people for their efforts—work—in exchange for promises we can give to others—money—so they give us what we want, such as food, gadgets, cars and houses. Behind all our money we created the basis by which we can own people, we created debt. We also created the desire to increase our wealth at minimal cost to us, and that is where slavery is ideal.

When wealth is important we are not going to want to pay people much. Consider the modern-day example of the minimum wage.

The first minimum wage law was enacted in New Zealand in 1894 to counter the exploitation of women and children in the sweatshop trade. The current federally set minimum wage in the United States since 2009, has been $7.25 an hour. A pittance compared to the average hourly wage in the United States in 2017 of $22 an hour.[34] It is so low about a quarter of all minimum wage earners, those working in restaurants and other food-service industries, have been made reliant on tips just to get by. Yet many businesses don't want a minimum wage at all, let alone an increase. They would rather send their jobs overseas.

In 2015, some 44% of companies in the US said they would increase the outsourcing of jobs outside the country if the minimum wage was ever raised to just $10 an hour.[35] Yes, they would rather leave the locals unemployed, without any job, hurt the people of their communities, leave them penniless than lose even some of their wealth. They offer a clear example of how far people who value wealth highly are prepared to go to keep it; preferring to pay people nothing at all. Our desire for wealth creates a desire for wanting—at some level—the perfect low-cost and low maintenance slave.

Farming didn't just give us stable food sources and civilization, it led to the creation of the fundamentals that allow one person to make another person a slave. Primary among them, a powerful desire for wealth, and its associated obligation, debt.

You will recall, our desire for wealth is primary among the desires of our inner beast. In effect, our inner beast enslaved us with debt.

But how can we possibly justify treating people—other human beings—so unfairly? We are all brothers and sisters, after all. That is where beliefs come in.

BELIEFS

I remember just a year or so ago a member of staff at a local teaching hospital told me of an incident where a nurse refused to assist a particular doctor in an operation because in India, where they both came from, the surgeon was born to a lower caste, or social class. That's right, even though the surgeon had higher status in Australia by being a surgeon it meant nothing to the nurse whose beliefs told her she could not mix with, let alone work under, a member of someone her religious inferior.

Beliefs are important, not only do they help us come together—such as at church on weekends—they also help determine how we treat each other; how we get along socially.

So, what situation could possibly lead to us creating beliefs that could allow—even justify—the creation of slaves, and actually condone exploitation? More than that, what beliefs help keep slavery afloat and exploitation and oppression rife in our societies?

Ancient Egypt provides some insights.

The beliefs of Ancient Egyptians reflected a culture developed from early farming. They developed an elite and aristocracy; a hierarchy with a few people of immense wealth, power, and status up top and the masses of poor below. Their beliefs reflected this. They believed in many powerful gods that also had a hierarchy, with the leader or head of the gods, Ra, the sun god who brought life to the world, and the other gods around him—the god-equivalent of an aristocracy. The gods toyed with the people and used them. This gave justification for their representatives—such as the priests, priestesses, and pharaohs—to do the same, to use them rather than treat them as equals. It gave them divine support to enslave people. Ancient Egypt, as we all know, was built on the back of slaves; slaves built many of their great monuments.

Create a society with a hierarchy and elite and expect to build a belief system with a similar structure to empower and justify it.

What would be the point of having an elite and aristocracy with a belief in gods that were all equals, democratic, or the same as us? It would contradict the order of things; it would motivate the people to overthrow their kings and leaders and treat everyone the same. It wouldn't allow anyone to oppress or exploit their neighbors.

But, you might be saying, they are just an ancient people's beliefs; we would never follow or still hold onto beliefs that support slavery today.

Are you sure?

Some of these beliefs have crept in from the ancient past and still affect billions of people—perhaps even us. Consider the following tale, one that many of you may be familiar with.

In 1597 BC the Babylonians, under the rule of King Nebuchadnezzar, invaded the lands of Judah, then under the rule of the Davidic king, Josiah. The invaders destroyed the sacred temples and burnt down the cities and towns. Tens of thousands of people were forced to live in a foreign land, but not as slaves. These people were given land to own, and many

Judeans prospered in Babylon. They did so well they could own their own slaves; slavery was common among the nations of this region at the time. The people, of course, were the Hebrews, and they engaged in slavery as much as the kingdoms and people around them, and before them. Seven Judean texts describing the lives of the Hebrews in Babylon make it clear they traded in slaves of two types: debt slaves, and chattel slaves. The first were like the debt slaves of the Aztecs: people placing themselves into slavery to pay a debt. The second were slaves who were captured by conquest—chattel slaves—who could be sold off like livestock. Slavery was a standard way of life for the Hebrews. It isn't surprising then that rules and laws pertaining to the treatment of slaves—that had the support of their God, a higher being as divine king or ruler—would appear in their religious texts, in this case the writings making up the Old Testament of the Bible.

That's right, beliefs supporting slavery, even how we should treat our slaves, survive today. They too create a hierarchy, only in this case instead of many gods there is one God, like a great king or leader ruling over all mankind, much like the kings of old that ruled over the Middle East and Ancient Egypt. They too create priests who have power over the people, who maintain this hierarchy, rather than promoting equality.

Take another modern example alluded to earlier, the beliefs that form the foundation of the caste system in India.

India can be regarded as the modern capital of slaves. It has over 14 million of them,[36] more than the populations of New York and Los Angeles combined! The core of their Hindu beliefs dictate the social order of their society. On top are the Brahmins, the priestly people; regarded as superior. At the bottom, the Shudras, or laboring class; regarded as the lowest of the low. In their religion they believe in a hierarchy of gods. This belief continues to contribute to creating more slaves than in any other country in the world. After all, if they believed all of us were equal how could they justify such horrid treatment of so many human beings?

Beliefs matter; they determine the rules and expectations of how we treat each other.

Creating a belief system with a hierarchy—with gods, or a god as king or supreme leader—is the perfect way of ensuring exploitation remains, it entrenches a justification for slavery.

We have a way of justifying that others are our inferiors.

In essence, our inner beast fostered the rise of its great compatriot in our beliefs and their messengers: the priests, priestesses, and prophets; representatives of the gods—superior beings—who ensure we continue to place enormous importance on wealth, status, and power. Beliefs that remain firmly entrenched in our societies, guaranteeing the beast's reign isn't threatened, and slavery, and exploitation, remain. How many of us still believe in a superior being or beings? How many believe we are somehow better than someone else, and can then justify treating them so poorly?

Add unchecked desires of our inner beast and suddenly slavery and human exploitation becomes next to impossible to stop.

UNCONTROLLED DESIRES

Imagine you grew up in a time of great poverty and desperation, like the great depression of the 1920s, or in a ghetto where poverty is rife. Now imagine seeing others around you doing much better, wealthier, not struggling, not getting beaten for scraps, not having to use crumpled up newspapers in their jackets just to keep warm. Do you think this might stir a desire in you to have what they have, to somehow make it, to never be poor and destitute, regarded as inferior, ever again?

Take the luxury goods mogul, François Pinault, worth over $14 billion. He had to quit school because he was teased so badly just for being poor.

Starbucks's Howard Schultz, now worth almost $3 billion, grew up in a housing complex for the poor knowing people on the other side of the tracks had more resources, more money, and happier families.

And Chelsea Football Club owner, Roman Abramovich, was born into poverty in southern Russia, orphaned at age two, and raised by an uncle and family in the subarctic regions of northern Russia. He is now estimated to be worth over $8 billion.

Many of us may look at them and be inspired, even make them our pinups, our idols. But what they reflect is something more sinister.

Painful memories of deprivation and suffering energize our desires of wealth, power, and status to great heights. We are prepared to do whatever it takes to get to the top.

We will clearly not be motivated to share, which would threaten our success. These highly charged desires ensure slavery.

It makes sense. As we noted at the beginning, human nature dictates that in a farming-based society, when food and safety are lacking, our desires for wealth, power, and status go up. In wealth we try to feel secure and safe. Threaten us in modern society and it is no different. Keep us poor, and afraid, make us feel inferior and vulnerable, under constant threat from those around us, tell us that others will fight us to get what we have, and we can expect our desires for wealth, power, and status to be elevated, for brutal competition to be raised to new heights. A perfect environment for wanting slaves so we can become the wealthiest and most powerful of all. China offers us a modern example of how this can happen.

China has the second most slaves of any country in the world, over three million.[37] Before it adopted a free market system most of its population lived in abject poverty. As the masses suffered, millions starving, they saw their overlords, leaders of the Communist Party, living in relative luxury. But only being a party member, and having the right connections, could in any way guarantee a means out of their desperate misery; only status and power could save them. Then, when China freed up its markets and damped down Communist Party controls—let the market decide the value of items, and how much should be grown or made instead of the state—suddenly desperate people had a new way to find liberation: wealth. How amazing must it have been for people to realize they could free themselves of poverty through toil and labor? But they had known the struggle. The desires for wealth, power, and status, had time to grow strong; they had seen examples of privilege and suffered under it. Some cite the rapid modernization of China as the reason for so many slaves, after all jobs were hard to come by and there was no shortage of unskilled labor; they could choose to pay them next to nothing. But just because they could exploit the people didn't mean they had to. If the desires for wealth, status, and power weren't so strong among the Chinese people to begin with they almost certainly would have shared their wealth and never let a slave or serf class still exist. In spite of the gains of creating a large middle class in recent years their country still fosters huge social inequality, a growing divide of wealth, with ever-more extremely wealthy billionaires and still a massive number of slaves and underclass.

More troubling still is how these energized desires can lead to indescribable levels of inhuman brutality.

How brutal?

Consider the example of early Spain, Christopher Columbus, and the conquistadors of the Americas sent as conquerors, but who became something far worse.

In 1492 King Ferdinand of Aragon sent Christopher Columbus in search of treasure—to find a new path to lands of Asia and valuable spice. When instead he arrived on the island he called Hispaniola—Haiti and the Dominican Republic today—he quickly, and savagely, enslaved many of its natives. Although the numbers of natives (*Taíno*) were estimated to range from several hundred thousand to over a million when he arrived, by 1514 there were only 32,000 on Hispaniola.[38] It is suspected many natives fell to diseases they had no immunity to such as small pox, but the brutal enforcement of making the men work as slaves in mines also prevented them planting their crops, meaning a lot simply died of starvation. Many others died from the enforced labor. So many slaves died within the nine years of Columbus's arrival—and they could no longer be resupplied from the natives—so in 1501 they sent for slaves from Africa. The brutality and enslavement continued—on a much larger scale—with the arrival of the conquistadors such as Hernán Cortés and Francisco Pizarro in South America.

Why would Spain do this?

Spain was trying to defend and expand its power in Europe—the desire for power and wealth were clearly strong and running rampant.

Unfortunately, things weren't going so well; they were near bankruptcy. Gold could be their saving grace. They would brutalize and enslave a people to get it.

How barbaric did it get?

On 22 May 1520 the Spanish conquistador, Hernán Cortés, had left the Aztec capital of Tenochtitlan to fight other Spaniards on the South American coast and left his deputy, Pedro de Alvarado, in charge. Moctezuma, the Aztec king, had asked permission of Alvarado to celebrate a festival in the Great Temple in honor of one of their gods. Spanish accounts suggest there were at least 600 people there, perhaps 1000[39] in the temple courtyard that day, including women and children. Everyone was apparently singing, dancing, and having a great time. Suddenly the Spanish arrived, fully dressed for battle. They blocked off all exits. Then they started slaughtering people.

The Aztec accounts were horrific; people having both arms cut off, others decapitated, and more still sliced open; their entrails spilling onto the earth. None were allowed to escape. Once they killed as many as they could they then searched house to house for more to slaughter. It is worth noting, none of these people had any weapons; this was supposed to be a joyous, peaceful festival. The motivation for such an atrocity is still debated today but what we can conclude is extremely powerful personal desires for wealth, status, and power back in Europe played a major role. Not only were these desires energized because of Spain's expansionist wars, they would have also been high among the soldiers, who would have seen and experienced poverty and witnessed those living with great wealth and power back home. A trip to the Americas was their chance to make their fortune, improve their—and their family's—social standing. Heaven help anyone who would get in their way, such as inferior natives, ripe for abuse, enslavement, and slaughter.

When the desires for wealth, power, and status go unrecognized, unchallenged, and unchecked, then our natural tendency to step over other people to satisfy these desires rises exponentially. It is easy to lose sight of the humanity in each other; other people become like

objects, or animals to use as a means to an end. **When greed clouds our hearts we become capable of atrocities.**

Put simply, let wealth and debt dominate our lives and we can expect exploitation and slavery. Maintain beliefs in superior beings, such as gods or one God, and we establish the notion of inferiors open to abuse and exploitation. Live in deprivation and see privilege around us—create visible gross inequality—and we raise our desires for wealth, power, and status to new heights ensuring even greater brutal competition, and a stronger and even more extreme hierarchy. We raise inside us desires of an inner beast that can drive us to all manner of inhuman brutality—we stop seeing each other as caring, feeling, and loving human beings.

How many of us live in societies powerfully driven by wealth? How many believe in superior beings, or one being, and look to them for salvation, to help us get to the top so we feel safer and more secure? How many try to achieve, and support, the attainment of extremes of wealth, power, and status? Yet all the time, by doing so, we ensure brutality, slavery, exploitation, and the inhumane treatment of other humans, including our children. We become complicit. The underlying cause.

Slavery once saw a people of different skin color be forcefully taken from their homes and seeded around the world. It enforced a notion that somehow, because of skin color alone, these people were inferior. Can we really expect the scars of the past to heal, for people of all colors to always be treated with equal respect, when the fundamentals that created them persist, fuelling the very notions we are trying to eliminate?

The same applies to exploitation.

While we let the fundamentals exist we can expect bosses to be driven to exploit their workers, for private equity firms to treat people as collateral damage in their fight for profit, for corporations to see us as a resource to exploit rather than a people to respect and cherish.

While we let slavery exist, in any form, we threaten our own job quality and security and those of our children and generations to come. We make it harder for them and us to find that better paid, stable, respected, job. It is in our interest to understand and overcome the fundamentals of slavery and exploitation inside each of us.

Our inner beast has created a horrible expression of our humanity in the form of slavery and exploitation, and we are still reeling from its effects, but it was nothing compared to the destructive manifestation it unleashed on us and the world in the form of empire. It even found a way for us to unwittingly support ongoing wars, terrorism, mass poverty, gross inequality, and destruction of our natural habitat, right now, today!

KEY POINTS

- We have been supporting slavery and our own exploitation and abuse by allowing the fundamentals that led to slavery to remain.
- **Three fundamentals lead to the justification and creation of slavery, and the exploitation of other human beings**:
  - The importance of wealth makes debt critical, leading to us wanting a low-cost slave.
  - When we believe in a god or gods we validate that others can be treated as inferior and support a hierarchy with an elite that can exploit us and treat us as slaves.
  - Painful memories of deprivation and suffering energize our desires for wealth, power, and status. We are prepared to do whatever it takes to get to the top, including treating each other with extremes of brutality.
- While we let the fundamentals remain we ensure slavery and exploitation continue and threaten our own job quality and security.

CHAPTER 4

The Destruction We Support: Empires

AN INVISIBLE EMPIRE HAS BEEN SET UP
ABOVE THE FORMS OF DEMOCRACY.
—*Woodrow Wilson*

Unable to swim, and after two days at sea in an overcrowded old fishing boat, Doaa, a 19 year old aspiring student, anxiously told her love, Bassem, 'We will never reach the shore. We will sink.' Two days later a rustier boat arrived. When Doaa, Bassem, and the others refused to get on, the people smugglers sunk the ship, with 300 souls trapped below deck. 'The sea went black,' Doaa recalled. 'I heard people screaming, and water crashing. I felt like I was going to drown.' Approximately 100 survivors soon came together in groups, praying for rescue. Saved by a water ring discovered by Bassem, Doaa witnessed men lose hope and take off their life vests. She watched her fiancé drown before her eyes, exhausted after two days of treading water. A man approached and left her his 9-month-old granddaughter, Malek. A woman approached, and left her 18-month-old girl, Masa. 'Save her,' she said, 'I will not survive.' After four long days in the water she was eventually saved by a merchant ship. Malek died in the boat's clinic. Masa made it.

Doaa was just one of over 130,000 refugees and migrants who have attempted to cross the Mediterranean; tens of thousands died for their efforts. Her family had been forced by four years of war in Syria to seek refuge in Egypt, but the Egyptians who had once welcomed them had become weary. It had become a scary and difficult place to survive. One day Doaa was almost kidnapped by a motorcycle gang. But Bassem, also a refugee, promised to marry her and take her safely to Europe. It was August 2014 when, feeling she had no choice, knowing more than 2000 refugees had died crossing the Mediterranean that year, she stepped onto the overcrowded fishing boat.[40]

Of the 19.5 million refugees in the world Syria remains the largest source with over 4.3 million refugees and another 6.6 million internally displaced.[41] A clash of empires has struck the world once more, and Syria just happens to be one of their current staging grounds.

We live in the extraordinary time of the rise of some of the greatest empires the world has ever known, new entities that make all others before them pale into insignificance in terms of misery and potential destruction. I'm not talking about the empires of old, such as those of France, Spain, the Ottoman and Dutch, which killed millions and subjugated or brutalized many more. But the new empires, a hybrid type of structure, now threaten to kill billions and destroy our world. As we are about to see, the malevolence of our inner beast has taken on a truly troubling form that threatens not only peace, but our very survival. The devastation and human suffering in Syria is but a small sample of its destructive potential.

Why decide to look at empires in a book about friendship?

For two main reasons. Firstly, because you and I, mostly unwittingly, are supporting them; just as we are unwittingly propping up slavery and exploitation. As we will soon see, we have become personally complicit in wars, terrorism, global poverty, mass starvation, and the poisoning of the natural world.

We are personally contributing to our own mass misery and devastation, and the possible extinction of all life on our world without even being aware of it.

Secondly, we need to look at empires because we, as individuals, can make a real difference. Friendship can have a huge impact on dissolving empires in a way that can ensure they never return. The more we understand the beast the easier it is to recognize how we can be the cure of most of the world's, and our personal, ills.

Ok, so what and where are these new, powerful and destructive, hybrid empires? How did they come about? How are we supporting them without even knowing it? And are they really that bad?

Let's start at the basics, by defining 'empire'. According to the *Oxford Dictionary* an 'empire' can be defined as:

> an extensive group of states or countries ruled over by a single monarch, an oligarchy, or sovereign state;
>
> a large commercial organization owned or controlled by one person or group.

The first part of the definition includes empires we are all familiar with, such as those of Ancient Egypt, Babylonia, the Aztec, or the empires of Europe, some mentioned a moment ago. The second part includes large business, or multinational companies. Combine a sovereign state ruling over other states or countries—directly or indirectly—with commercial organizations as empires in their own right, and we have what we can define as the corporate/government hybrid empire; the empires of today. Governments and corporations in bed with and feeding off each other to an extraordinary degree.

How did these hybrid empires come about?

They began as other empires. We have already seen the desires that create them.

You will recall that brutal competition driven by the insatiable desires of our inner beast leads to an elite bent on conquest. Eventually they conquer so many communities and city states they form an empire under their one rule. It can be the same in business, one company taking over others until we have corporate empires such as JPMorgan Chase, and Exxon Mobil.

How did they take their current hybrid form? After all, for thousands of years they were mostly just giant states or countries; the empires we are most familiar with from history.

It began with empires simply taking over and superseding others. The Babylonians and Ancient Egyptian empires, for example, overtaken by the Ancient Greek and Roman empires, then the empires of Europe always fighting and conquering each other.

The empire that perhaps set the tone—created the template—for today's hybrid empire was once the biggest of them all: the Great British Empire.

Want to learn how corporations hijacked our governments, and still do, how they pillage countries and keep millions of people poor, how they combined to become the most powerful and destructive form of empire ever? It all began with the signing of a single document by one of the most powerful women in the world.

On 31 December 1600, Queen Elizabeth signed a charter that granted 218 merchants a monopoly of trade past the Cape of Good Hope—the southern tip of Africa. The corporation these merchants founded would become known as the East India Company. The aim of the company was to trade in commodities such as cotton, silk, textiles, salt, indigo dye, tea, and saltpeter—a basic ingredient of gunpowder. Later they would also trade in opium—yes, they became government supported drug traffickers, several centuries before the CIA was implicated in drug running on behalf of the US government in Nicaragua. One of the many features that made the company particularly unusual was it also created its own army to expand its business through military conquest.

It would seem absurd today. Could you imagine giant companies, like Apple or Google, increasing their corporate power and influence by creating an army and invading other countries?

But this is exactly what the East India Company did!

For over a century and a half the East India Company (EIC) had only a few hundred soldiers and guards, mostly used to protect its goods. By 1778 it had 67,000. Eventually, by 1857, it had over 280,000 troops, more than many nations in the world at the time. These were mostly Indian soldiers trained by the company along European lines but led by company trained British officers. This formidable force could deter traders from other countries such as Portugal and Spain, but also take over their outposts. After the death of Aurangzeb, the Mughal emperor of much of India who allowed the EIC to establish a foothold, local rulers began to resist the continued expansion of the company. The EIC then used its own private army to take over each Indian state, starting with Bengal, and soon almost all of India came under the rule of the EIC.

That's right, this was a company, not a government or sovereign state, invading a nation!

Since the Civil War of 1651 the power of the monarch had been circumvented by parliament, so the EIC had to look beyond the monarch to support it. As their monopoly was up for renewal every 20 years the EIC needed strong backing in parliament for it to continue its monopoly, so it created a powerful lobby group. Edmund Burke—an Irish statesman, political theorist, and orator—commented at the time that the East India lobby was one of the most united and formidable forces in British politics. The lobby would get on the good side of the elite by showering them in gifts. Be they ministers, mistresses, or priests, all were 'kept in good humor by presents of shawls and silks, birds' nests and attar of roses, bulses of diamonds and bags of guineas'.[42] It even made timely gifts to the treasury when the state faced bankruptcy. Hence the birth of the model that vast and powerful lobbying corporations follow today.

Yes, for a time a private company helped keep a government financially afloat!

So not only did the EIC have great military power, for some time it held great political power as well, so it could ensure its shareholders—elite—great wealth. Many of its shareholders were members of parliament. This was a company like no other before; an empire with armies, its own navy, judiciary, laws, and currency, having the full support of legitimate government. The demarcation between corporation and government rule had blurred.

The good times didn't last forever, however. Eventually the EIC began to be pulled into line by the government, like reeling in a ravenous shark. In 1786 the British Government passed laws that made the EIC a subsidiary of the Crown. In other words, the company now needed to listen to and work for the government, much like a soldier or an employee. At this time, under government supervision, the company further expanded its territories through threats and coercive actions until it took over not only most of India but also Malaya, Burma, Singapore, and Hong Kong. For the latter, it had the help of British Navy as part of the Opium Wars that ensured the EIC could keep supplying a million plus Chinese opium addicts—illegally.

Eventually, after an uprising in India in 1857, the British government dissolved the company and took control of all of its assets, administrative powers, and armed forces. The biggest company the world had ever known was absorbed into government and what the company had captured and administered was now in the possession of the British government, now a great empire.

Thanks primarily to a company, driven solely to increase the profit of private individuals, Britain built an empire so vast that at its peak it controlled over a quarter of the landmass of the planet, and ruled over one-fifth of the world's population. Most of the world now speaks the English language due to how far its influence spread. The governments and elite of countries didn't need their own army to conquer new territories as much anymore, they had profit-driven companies to do it for them.

The British Empire would last for over 100 years.

The East India Company is a classic example of a corporation as empire.

It had its own hierarchy and elite, and its own military to invade and capture new territory, just like empires and states of the past once did. Yet it also became a servant of the government. For a time, it was the government's instrument for conquest and empire building. It didn't require government funding to expand its wealth and power, at least not initially, just its support. With the use of corporations to expand influence and power a new form of empire had been born that blended the interests of corporations and governments. The new empire was a corporation/government hybrid, the type of empires we can recognize today.

Where are these hybrid empires?

The new corporate/government hybrid empire can now be commonly found in the US, UK, China, Russia, and Brazil. Some are made of powerful private corporations that back governments, such as by helping the parties and politicians who are supportive of the corporate ambitions to get elected. The governments in turn support the corporations, such as by passing corporate friendly legislation, and using government military and intelligence so they can increase influence and power in other countries (more about that in a moment). Some corporate empires are owned directly by the state, such as those of China, Russia, and Brazil. Over 60% of large companies in China and 40% of the large companies in Russia, for instance, are state owned—the governments and corporations working together to increase wealth, power, and influence of the company and government globally—working as a hand of the government if you like. Why physically try to take over a country with soldiers unnecessarily when you have companies, driven by an elite seeking wealth and power, to do it for you? Send the large companies in with full government backing to gain as much wealth, power, and influence as possible and the more they control the more influence the government that supports them will have, and the wealthier their elite will become.

Author John Perkins in his book, *Confessions of an Economic Hit Man: The shocking inside story of how America really took over the world* (Random House, 2005) offers a classic, though disturbing, description of how governments use companies in this way.

Perkins was trained in the 1960s by a major corporation of the US (Chas. T. Main, Inc) to go into countries where resources could be exploited by US companies and convince the governments to take out massive loans with the World Bank with the promise of building infrastructure, such as roads, rail, electrical power plants, and improved sanitation. The companies would then come in, paid by the loan money, exploit the natural resources—such as minerals or oil—and export it at a great profit, giving very little money back to the country they were exploiting. As a result of the high interest rates with the World Bank, and little income received for resources from the overseas companies, the exploited countries would soon default on their loans. Since the World Bank was primarily funded by the US a deal would be struck whereby the companies from the US would get special concessions and their local government would come under greater US influence. Leaders of these countries were paid huge sums of money to go along with this scheme. If they didn't comply the government, according to Perkins, would send in 'Jackals' to eliminate them and replace them with someone more compliant. The US apparently used this technique in many countries of the Middle East and Middle America, including Iran and Panama.

In effect US and other hybrid empires learnt from the British Empire model. They found a way to conquer or have major influence in other lands without sending in their own troops.

The elite overseas, driven by the desires of their inner beast, would get very wealthy and powerful by sending their company in to exploit a country's resources and cheap labor and in the process leave almost nothing for the poor of the country they exploited. By using companies supported by their government the US could expand its corporate/government empire. But their approach wasn't foolproof.

In the process of expansion wars broke out, and thousands of troops and civilians died. Many resulted from the clash of the US and Soviet empires for power and influence. They occurred under the banner of what became known as the Cold War.

This clash of empires hasn't stopped. Not only is the US hybrid empire still at odds with remnants of the Soviet Union, modern day Russia, it also has a new great hybrid empire able to compete on its terms: China.

China has set up its own Asian Infrastructure Investment Bank (AIIB), much like the US uses the World Bank for infrastructure loans in countries it seeks to dominate. In 2015, China promised over $60 billion[43] in loans for investment in infrastructure—via the AIIB—across Africa alone, and is providing loans of billions of dollars across the Asia-Pacific region, such as in Papua New Guinea. If they follow the US model, and it appears they are, the money will go primarily to Chinese companies who will build the projects—or most of them—then leave the countries with unserviceable debt, giving China enormous political influence. The

Chinese have begun to perfect geo-economics—a use of soft power, not sending in troops—to manipulate governments to ensure their control and support. In turn allowing them to use and exploit the country's natural resources and send profits back to their homeland into the pockets of the elite, driven by desires of our inner beast. China, like the US, is using government resources—including military and intelligence—to shore up their gains, trying to expand, and prevent losses to the opposing side. It is creating an inevitable clash of empires as they both struggle for ever-more wealth, status, and power for their elite with the very real and likely outcome of wars, a scenario oft repeated throughout history.[44]

Why worry about empires?

Because by their very nature, as you have probably realized, they are extremely destructive.

How destructive?

Let us get just a glimpse of the devastating force we are up against in this manifestation of our inner beast, and can expect to continue, if we allow them to remain and keep supporting them.

WARS AND MASSACRES

Empires, wars, and massacres are as common together as a bushfire and smoke. Every empire in the past could only have become an empire by going to war—they all needed to fight at some point to increase or maintain their territory. Even the British Empire which fought in Asia, Africa, Australia, and North America fought to expand, or keep, its vast lands. In the process many conquered people were massacred.[45] Perhaps two of the greatest examples of empire building leading to war, massive loss of life, and massacres, happened just in the last century.

World War 1, often described as the war to end all wars, began on 28 July 1914. On one side you had the Austro-Hungarian Empire aligned to Germany and allied with the Ottoman Empire, and on the other you had the British Empire backed by the French and Russians. Estimated casualties from this war—including civilians—were over 37 million. That is the current population of California! An estimated 1–1.5 million

Armenians were killed, many massacred by Ottoman troops, in one of the world's worst genocides from 1915 to the early 1920s. Empires brought about this war and almost a whole people were wiped from the face of the planet. Worse was yet to come within 30 years.

In an effort to restore German pride (after its loss in World War 1 and subsequent crippling reparations), and inspired by past empires, Adolf Hitler began to build a 1000-year empire (Reich) of his own and started World War 2. To that end he sent German troops to invade Poland in September of 1939. An estimated 50–85 million people died, both military personnel and civilians, as a result of this conflict (more than ten times the populations of present day New York or London). Can you imagine ten New York cities being wiped out within six years?

During this global conflict Adolf Hitler began one of the worst massacres of history; now known as the Holocaust. Using systematic extermination camps his regime killed over 11 million unarmed people, many of them Jews and Gypsies.

The hybrid empires aren't bucking the trend here; they have fuelled wars and massacres too, and still are.

During the Cold War—a war between the hybrid empires of the USA and USSR we touched on a moment ago—several conflicts were fought, including the Korean War, the Vietnam War, the invasion of Afghanistan by the Soviet Union, and several conflicts in Middle America and the African states. Since the collapse of the Soviet Union we have had several more major conflicts including the two Iraq wars, a new Afghanistan war, and now the conflicts in the Crimea, in Syria, and Yemen. In Afghanistan alone, since war began in 1978, at least two million people have died. The vying for power and influence, including economic power, is still in play. Now we are even seeing China expand military bases into the South China Sea, and the US is building its own bases to try to contain them, threatening even more conflict. Empires of all types, even hybrid empires, lend themselves to creating war and conflict.

But empires aren't that bad; it's better than it once was, some of you may be saying. There are fewer people killed by wars as a percentage of population than at any time in history, especially in comparison to when we were tribal. This makes the rise of the hybrid empire seem a pretty good deal, perhaps it keeps order and makes us all safer and happier?

This is misleading.

For starters, it makes tribes seem like they were all at war. This wasn't the case. Many tribes lived in peace with each other and didn't constantly fight. The Aboriginal Australians, for example, didn't have pictures of war painted all over the rock walls of the country, and the Europeans who first encountered them didn't find a constantly warring race; evidence suggests they were a mostly peaceful people. A group of six local tribes of North West America, before European settlement, were united—so the legend goes—by the Great Peacemaker, to form the Iroquois Nation. They lived peacefully with each other for over a century. They held regular council meetings and learnt to resolve differences peacefully (we will discuss them more later). To claim all tribes were constantly at war and killing each other is inaccurate, and an oversimplification.

And besides, if it hadn't been for the deterrence of atomic weapons we might still have great armies of empires doing battle and wiping many more people off the planet to this day.

This apparent age of peace under the rule of empires is deceptive. The many basic desires driving these conflicts remain uncontrolled within.

Give us the opportunity and they come out, as continued fighting around the world, and the clash of hybrid empires, reminds us. The volcano may not have erupted in a while but that doesn't mean it isn't just simmering, on the verge of explosion.

While empires exist, we can expect a tendency to wars and massacres.

TERRORISM AND EXTREMISM

Who can forget the Twin Towers collapse, the result of a blatant terrorist attack by Al-Qaeda extremists on 11 September 2001? The people running away covered in light grey dust, the death of brave firefighters; it still haunts our memories. Now we are also seeing horrific scenes of decapitations and massacres by terrorists such as ISIS. Extremists are killing people in modern cities, such as Paris, London, and Sydney. The fear of extremism is hitting close to home with our youth being radicalized and wanting to go overseas to join malicious cults, and others seeking to spread their terror among us on our own soil. People turn to terrorism and extremism for many reasons, but it is important to recognize the role of empire.

By its nature empire creates extremists because it prevents people having basic human needs met; creating growing, or persistent, dissatisfaction.

Think about it a moment, are we really going to see radicalism and extremism in a nomadic tribe where everyone knows and supports each other—where we are all close friends, having our basic human needs met? Can we really imagine someone standing up in a tribe of their friends and claiming they are going to wage a holy war on everyone?

It just wouldn't happen.

Why?

To start with such religious ideas would never be created in a nomadic tribe—they tend to believe in spirits not gods, as we mentioned earlier. Secondly, the motivations that would have led to such an extreme reaction, even if it they did begin to arise, would have been calmed long before they could become an extreme conviction simply thanks to caring people regularly talking to each other—as friends do. If we get along, and most of our basic human needs are met, why would we want to rise up and fight against our own people, let alone others who aren't threatening us? People need a reason to fight and possibly die, take this reason away and they can live in peace.

Empire, by its nature, does not allow many of its people to meet basic human needs.

The empire does not, for example, let the majority of its people feel heard, valued, appreciated, or even respected; needs we can now recognize as basic social needs, or needs of friendship. Empires aren't really interested in listening to their people; they are more focused on ruling, dictating terms, and increasing power and wealth. Besides, there are way too many people to listen to. It saves time if someone, or a group of people, just leads and tells others what to do. Empires are also more likely to oppress people, not want them to be individuals, because individuals breed dissent and disagreement and can weaken the empire from the inside, leaving it vulnerable to its enemies or competition. They will also not make you feel valued unless you are one of the elite. This is also true of the hybrid empire.

As the hybrid empire spreads its influence around the world its aim is to make profit for its supporting elite. It is not there to share it with the people and make their life the best it can be. It is not there to listen with genuine care to the people of the country they are exploiting and let them be themselves; to behave like a good friend. Don't behave like a friend, however, and you become the enemy.

When a corporation does nothing to lessen inequality and help people meet their basic human needs, in fact it prevents it or makes it worse through exploitation, then the corporation isn't behaving like a friend but a foe, much like an invader such as the Spanish in the Americas. This creates growing resentment and hatred towards the companies and governments involved—a mounting dissent that can easily manifest through radicalism, extremism, and its associated use of terror, especially out of frustration and anger. Soon it isn't just the corporations that become the enemy it is the government and the people of the country of origin too, after all they are responsible. The religious beliefs and ideals that permit hybrid empires to exist can also become the enemy; these beliefs validate and foster the exploitative behaviors in the first place, and they are a shared quality of our oppressive 'enemy'. In time we not only have a battle between empires we can have religious wars, conflicts between the beliefs that foster the empires and help drive them, like those between Christianity, Islam, and Judaism, for instance. How many battles today have a religious component—one religious group fighting another—especially in the Middle East? Would they really still be fighting if empires weren't playing a pivotal role, trying to increase their power and wealth?

Empires by their nature spread the power of hierarchies around the world. They widen inequality and promote conflict and dissent; fertile ground for extremism and violence.

While empires exist we can expect radicalism, extremism, wars, and terror to continue.

MASS POVERTY AND STARVATION

Thankfully most of us have not had to watch our children cry because they need something to fill their empty stomachs. Nor have we held a starving baby—not more than a bag of bones—as they die in our arms of malnutrition. We haven't known real hunger, the type that lasts for days or weeks, and tears at your insides. It is usually the opposite, we eat too much. World-wide obesity has nearly tripled since 1975, and in 2016 over half of us were either overweight or obese.[46] Yet, in spite of there being more than enough food for us all the Food and Agriculture Organization of the United Nations (FAO) estimated over 815 million people went hungry in 2016, up from 777 million in 2015[47]—more than twice the population of the United States recorded in 2017.[48] Although starvation can be due to many reasons such as lack of resources and conflict, much of it is simply due to poverty. Empires have played—and continue to play—a crucial role.

Much of the poverty leading to hunger in many of the poorest countries can be traced back to effects of empires and the severe debts they imposed.

In 1996 the International Monetary Fund (IMF) and World Bank, following extensive lobbying by non-government organizations and other bodies, created the Heavily Indebted Poor Countries (HIPC) Initiative. The aim was to provide debt relief and low interest loans to cancel or reduce external debt repayments to more sustainable levels. As of March 2018, the HIPC Initiative identified 39 countries, 30 of which were in Sub-Saharan Africa, as potentially eligible for debt relief.[49] These were countries proven to have many poor people, and where the debt of their government was at least two-and-a-half times more than government earnings. You will recall—as John Perkins highlighted—severe debt was created with organizations like the World Bank and IMF by outside corporations and governments so they could strip the resources from countries, increase political control, and make great profits. There are still over 200 million people in Sub-Saharan Africa suffering from hunger as a result of this corporate/government approach—as the result of hybrid empires. Empires also play a role in the poverty and starvation of hundreds of millions of poor and starving people in countries that haven't been burdened by crippling debts.

As the International Food Policy Research Institute report (2014–2015) points out, half of the hungry people in the world—360 million—live in middle-income countries such as India, China, Brazil, Indonesia, and Mexico.[50] These are not totally impoverished nations who can't afford to feed their people.

The report cites rising inequalities in wealth as one of the main contributing factors to the hunger and malnutrition of so many people.

Empires have played a major role.

In India, for instance, we know the East India Company (EIC) contributed to entrenching a small and wealthy elite and a poor majority. Like the corporations of today the EIC went to countries to exploit them, not share their wealth. In the process they left the hierarchy common in the British Empire; the elite and aristocracy on top and a mass of poor underneath. This hierarchy remains today with a mass of very poor people indeed.

Take another example, Brazil.

In Brazil, established as part of the colonial empire of Portugal, the Portuguese also set up a hierarchy and elite, and ensured continued inequality that remains today in a large population of very poor people. The same can be said of Mexico thanks to the Spanish, and Indonesia thanks to the Dutch. Empires have sown the seeds of inequality wherever they spread, and masses of poor and starving people still exist because of them; the legacy of empire ensures mass poverty and starvation remains.

The most telling fact of all: in spite of the world recognizing the seriousness of this poverty, inequality, and hunger, corporations have usually not been the ones coming to the most desperate countries' aid.

Companies, and the elite that run them, own more than enough to make all this poverty and hunger go away within a few years, yet there has been less than a 7% improvement in the rates of hunger and poverty in over 20 years; even with the added help of the United Nations. If it hadn't been for the pressure of many not-for-profit organizations on the World Bank and IMF—not corporations or the wealthy—what little benefit the poorest countries received simply in debt relief wouldn't have happened. What does this say about the strength of the insatiable desires within the elite and the empires they are running?

Empires, thanks to the desires of our inner beast motivating the elite that create and support them, readily contribute to mass poverty and starvation. They also, by their very nature, damage our world.

ENVIRONMENTAL DESTRUCTION AND POISONINGS

At 1 am, local time, on 3 December 1984, Champa Devi Shukla witnessed deadly clouds of dim brown gas flood his poor suburban street. People panicked as those around them fell, dying. They started a stampede, killing even more. Children's hands were wrenched from their parents', families whirled apart.[51] Over half a million people were estimated to have been exposed to the gas; over 3800 were killed almost immediately, over 20,000 premature deaths were reported as a result of the exposure over the subsequent two decades.[52] It was the worst industrial accident in history, over 40 tons of methyl isocyanate gas leaked from the Bhopal pesticide plant in India thanks to lack of necessary maintenance from cost-cutting by multinational company, Union Carbide. The tragedy of the poisoning at Bhopal is but the tip of a huge iceberg of environmental contamination and pollution resulting from the workings of empire. Large corporations—corporate empires with government support—are polluting the world and contributing not only to the premature death of tens of thousands of people but also to the destruction of pristine habitat.

Collectively, industries in the US alone, released more than 3.54 billion pounds of toxins in the environment in 2016.[53] That is the equivalent in weight of over 2800 fully loaded jumbo (A380) passenger jets![54] Mining corporations are clearing once pristine lands in large open cut mines, and other mining companies are contaminating ground water by pumping high-pressure water, sand and chemicals into the ground known as hydraulic fracturing—fracking—to mine natural gas. Over 137,000 fracking mines have been drilled since 2005 with over 14 billion gallons of toxic wastewater produced in 2014 alone.[55] The international not-for-profit agency Pure Earth indicates over 200 million people worldwide are affected by pollution, with tens of thousands poisoned and killed by it each year, including our children.[56]

Large companies as part of hybrid empires (with government support) are destroying our world and essentially poisoning us.

They have a very smart strategy to ensure it continues. They learnt a very clever technique from the East India Company.

You will recall one of the reasons the East India Company was so powerful and successful for so long was thanks to its lobbying of British parliament. They used enticements such as gifts. Interestingly, they even helped train future members of parliament to further their cause. Current corporations have learnt from them and gone much further.

In *Global Spin: The corporate assault on environmentalism*, Sharon Beder explains that in response to the rise in influence of environmental groups between 1965 and 1970, and a rising distrust of big business, corporations organized themselves to counter regulations—such as Clean Air Acts, and Clean Water Acts—that were being imposed on them and threatening their profits. Two waves of corporate activism arose out of all this, in the 1970s and in the 1990s to counter the environmental movement. Part of this involved increasing business lobbying.

According to Beder, in 1971 some 175 firms were lobbying in Washington. By 1982 this had risen to 2445 firms. In 1980 there were over 12,000 lawyers representing business for federal regulatory agencies, 9000 lobbyists, 50,000 trade associated personnel, 8000 public relations specialists, 12,000 specialized journalists, and 1300 public affairs consultants. Businesses united and started co-operating to counter the interests of environmentalists and public interest groups. Business Roundtable organizations were established—in the US (composed of chief executives of almost 200 corporations), and in Australia (composed of chief executives of over 20 of Australia's largest firms)—to crank out 'smooth public relations messages', and ensure senior executives were effective in dealings with politicians and bureaucrats. These measures and others—such as hiring private consultancy firms—increased corporate influence and power in governments and in society. They even took to the media to re-educate the population.

By the hiring of PR firms, the corporations spread their message. One of their aims was to discredit the environmental groups. Another was to educate the public and change public opinion. One of these ways has been to develop and distribute 'educational' materials to schools so they could improve corporate image and shape environmental perceptions. They were so successful that a survey in 1992 revealed 51% of those surveyed agreed environmentalists had 'gone too far', where as one year earlier only 17% believed this was the case.[57]

Lobbying has become so powerful today that corporations and coalitions will provide staff to lawmakers drafting bills, and then help support the bill on every part of its journey until it is legislated. No private citizen could ever do that for any bill they proposed. The influence these companies have been able to muster would make the East India Company envious. Their aim has been simple and well-focused; to increase profit—build and maintain their empires—no matter the consequence to the health of the people or the environment.

It should be pointed out, this doesn't mean all corporations behave like empires and spread their destruction globally, many don't. Several corporations are becoming less hierarchical and recognize they can still make substantial profits without damaging the environment, or poisoning people in the process. Often these are co-operatives owned by everyone who works for them (we will learn more about them later).

Support and allow empires to exist and we show a flagrant disrespect and disregard for the land and water that sustains us.

The problem is, every day we have been supporting them.

HOW WE UNWITTINGLY SUPPORT EMPIRES

The first way we support them is by not reeling them in. We have been letting the major corporations control our direction and priorities; allowing them to write and promote their policies and agendas, making them more influential than our own. We have let lobbying, for instance, like that once used by the EIC, ensure empires rule and combine to form a dangerous and destructive alliance with our governments; hybrid empires. We have watched and willingly supported our governments as they sent/promoted companies into other countries to rob, exploit, and oppress them. We have—knowingly or unknowingly—supported the basis of war, poverty, starvation, terrorism and extremism; the very things we claim to abhor.

The second way we have been supporting them is by us personally not recognizing and caging the desires of our own inner beast.

Empires need strong desires for wealth and power for them to exist. They need the people within them to agree that wealth, power, and status are important, so the elite can justify and get away with what they do.

How can we criticize the elite when they are simply doing what we would like to do ourselves, to have the power, importance, and vast resources we would love to see in our own hands?

Consider it a moment, if we didn't let ourselves be consumed by the uncontrolled desires for wealth, power, and status, would we really allow the elite to rule over us, let alone build empires? Would we let them send our brave soldiers to fight and die on their behalf, convince them they are fighting for us when in reality they are fighting so the elite can maintain their power and privilege? The desires of our inner beast are immensely powerful, they have played, and continue to play, a fundamental role in the creation of a force that will forever threaten peace, unity, prosperity, and our survival: the empire.

How can friendship help us?

It can help disrupt every destructive aspect of empire, and dissolve empires themselves. We will see how next.

KEY POINTS

- Empires are formed out of brutal competition driven by our insatiable desires for wealth, status, and power.
- By supporting empires, we are contributing to our own mass misery and devastation, and possible extinction of all life on our world, often without being aware of it.
- Hybrid empires—some of the most powerful empires the world has ever known—are a combination of a sovereign state and corporations feeding off each other.
- The new corporate/government hybrid empire can now be commonly found in the US, UK, China, Russia, and Brazil.
- US and other hybrid empires learnt from the British Empire model. They found a way to conquer or have major influence in other lands without sending in their troops. Instead they sent their companies; saddling other governments with massive debt.
- **Empires by their very nature are destructive, inciting:**
  - wars and massacres;
  - terrorism and extremism;
  - mass poverty and starvation; and
  - environmental destruction and poisonings.
- **We support empires by:**
  - not reeling them in—letting major corporations control our directions and priorities through writing policy and lobbying;
  - not caging our desires for wealth, power, and status; by fuelling the basis of empires within us.
- The desires of our inner beast are immensely powerful and continue to play a fundamental role in the creation of a force that will forever threaten peace, unity, prosperity, and our survival: the empire.

PART TWO

The Friendship Key— Empowering Positive Change

Amid the war-torn uncertainty of 1943, at the height of World War 2, a secret meeting was held in Tehran between arguably one of the greatest presidents of the United States, Franklin Delano Roosevelt (FDR), the dictator of the Soviet Union, Joseph Stalin, and prime minister of the United Kingdom, Winston Churchill. The meeting was organized to consolidate the USA, UK, and USSR's alliance and strategy against Nazi Germany, and open a second front against a common foe; up until now the Soviet Union had been taking the brunt. It was an important meeting, with significant results, but perhaps one of the most extraordinary outcomes from this gathering was that FDR was actually able to make friends with Stalin!

In her book, The Roosevelt I Knew,[58] *Frances Perkins, a trusted friend and FDR's Secretary of Labor throughout most of his administration, mentions Roosevelt went to the meeting with the intention of liking Stalin and being liked. The meeting wasn't going so well until FDR tried a personal approach.*

The president began to make fun of Churchill and started teasing him about his Britishness. FDR described to Perkins, 'Winston got red and scowled, and the more he did so the more Stalin smiled. Finally, Stalin broke out into a deep hearty guffaw, and for the first time in three days I saw light. I kept it up until Stalin was laughing with me, and it was then I called him "Uncle Joe". He would have thought me fresh the day before, but that day he laughed and came over and shook my hand.'

In this amazing meeting were two men from completely different backgrounds, and countries, with very dissimilar beliefs and styles of leadership—one ruling with an iron fist and brutality, the other with conciliation and goodwill. At a time of enormous distrust and global tension, FDR chose not to go in all business-like but rather to try to build friendship. He could have approached with an attitude of disdain and contempt, but friendship was his way, and it helped consolidate an important alliance and special union in a terrible time.

What can we learn from this unexpected meeting?

Many things. Perhaps most telling: if two men so completely different, at a time of massive global tensions with their own people dying in the tens of thousands, and having every reason to be distrustful, can be friends, what's stopping the rest of us?

CHAPTER 5

Friendship: Prosperity, Peace, Respect

PEACE AND FRIENDSHIP WITH ALL MANKIND
IS OUR WISEST POLICY, AND I WISH
WE MAY BE PERMITTED TO PURSUE IT.

—*Thomas Jefferson*

At first glance it can seem odd, how can a single person—like us—satisfying a few simple desires have a much bigger influence? How can prioritizing time for people we care about, for example, and some we don't, help prevent the enslavement of a child in Haiti, for instance, where one in every 48, mostly children, become slaves? How can prioritizing respecting and taking the time to listen to those around us help rid the world of refugees drowning at sea, their children dying on a beach, or families suffocating with poison? Or stop people we may know from dying in wars, from terror, starvation, hate, and poverty? The notion seems absurd, ridiculous. Until we look at the basis behind it all: ourselves.

Human exploitation and enslavement, the devastation of the clash of empires, climate change, and the problems we see in our communities, towns, and cities, all have one common denominator: us.

Our actions and choices created it all, consciously, or otherwise. These have been governed by a combination of, and competition between, our basic human desires and motivations; we don't 'do' anything without them, they define us. Why can friendship, just meeting a few basic human needs, then, be so influential?

It gets to the core of who we are and offers to answer it in a more functional way. By its very nature friendship helps us eliminate slavery, empires, and create a lasting prosperity and peace, offering us a powerful way to instigate real change and hope.

How does it do it?

Let us consider the main issues from the last two chapters in turn and see. Then, before looking at how to apply the Ten Desires, pose a practical and powerful question that can help us begin to foster real and powerful positive change. A single query that can begin to substantially transform our lives and the world.

COUNTERING SLAVERY

The Ten Desires of Friendship allow us to counter each of the three fundamentals behind slavery and exploitation. It begins with a simple notion: friends share.

Reducing Wealth and Debt's Power

We know from the Ten Desires that we care for, protect, and support our friends. In other words, if they are in trouble we help them, such as by sharing what we have. As nature has made abundantly clear, human beings do better if we help each other. Sharing helps counter the importance, and power, of wealth and debt. There are many ways this can work. One way is lessening the power of debt with the help of friends.

Back in the 1970s, during the time of the war in Indo-China, Australia accepted many Vietnamese refugees. Most of them arrived with nothing but the clothes on their backs, and horrible memories. Soon, however, many Australians became very annoyed with them. Within years they saw them driving in new cars and owning property while many Australians were struggling to make ends meet. How did they do it? They pooled their resources, and shared.

It would start by renting and finding work. Several families would share a rented house to cut back on costs. Combining their incomes, and saving where they could, they soon had enough for a deposit on a house. They then all moved into the house and everyone worked to pay it off. Then they did the same with another house, they all worked to pay that one off and so on. Many families living in cramped conditions had a common goal in mind; to help each other. Before too long all the families had houses of their own, all paid off, and cars too. Through support, caring, and respect for one another, they were able to make debt less powerful. People became the priority, not individual wealth or debt. This contrasts with the approach many of us are taught.

How common is it for us to take out a personal loan for a car or house? They are often large loans where we try to pay them off ourselves or with just the help of our spouse or partner. It is what we just expect to do; everyone else seems to do it. And we all work extremely hard long hours in the process. How many hours a week do you work to pay off your loans? Our debt becomes a chain shackling us down, holding us back from spending more time with each other and enjoying our families, friends, and the human contact part of our life. At no point, however, do we consider joining with other families to reduce this burden, like the Vietnamese have done; working together as a community of friends.

Another way friendship also helps disempower wealth and debt is by lessening our desire to show off; for flamboyance.

When friendship is our priority there is less point in having the flashier car, being seen in designer clothing, owning the bigger mansion, or always having the latest gadgets or phone. Let's be honest, a large part of what we buy is to show off, to show people our wealth and status. But friends already value, validate, and respect each other; there is no need to prove it by showing off. The more we focus on friendship the less we have to impress and the less we feel pressured to take on debt to do it.

By its very nature friendship takes away the power of wealth and debt by making it less relevant.

Friendship has another wonderful way of helping reduce the power of wealth and debt: it can drive us to create a common wealth we can all use so we all feel more secure, like the Ancient Inca once did.

Before the Spanish invasion the South American Inca—the builders of Machu Picchu, the breath-taking city high in the Peruvian Andes—would build large storage facilities for surplus grain above their valleys and farms. It is believed they did this for the common good, as a resource to be shared by all in a time of need. By placing it so high they didn't just keep it safe from flooding—if that was a risk—but also, quite likely, as a highly visible reminder of the support of their community, and state. It was a shrewd tactic of the Inca elite. By allowing a common wealth it would not only keep the locals happy knowing they felt secure in tough times but also lessen the chance of them wanting to take the wealth from those higher in the hierarchy; reducing the chances of uprisings.

There are many ways to apply this Incan idea of pooling resources into local common wealth so we all feel more secure and less driven for greater wealth and higher debt. For example, we might choose to create a regional reserve fund in our neighborhood, town, or suburb, which individuals and families can tap into when we are doing it tough. Or pool our wealth into a local bank run and owned by the communities, not with the main aim of making huge profit for a few but to help local families and businesses. Or, as we have in many countries around the world, ensure we have a sturdy and well-funded social security system so that when people lose their jobs, or are severely injured, they have resources to fall back on. Mind you, we need less common wealth if we are a close community and share more from the beginning, as friends are wont to do. We can even create and share more common areas in our local communities that provide food.

For example, we can create community market gardens, areas communities set aside so that everyone can help grow food for their community—so they can reduce their cost of living and debt burden. This idea is currently taking off in Detroit among the poorer communities now that many large companies have taken their production elsewhere, and the jobs with them.[59] A similar approach is to farm the urban footpath, as practiced in some suburbs in cities of Australia and North America.

In many suburbs of Australian cities, such as Sydney, Melbourne, and Adelaide, ornamental trees, shrubs, or just lawn, are planted on the council-owned land between a person's residence and the street. This was recognized as a waste of good, productive, land. So, some suburbs planted edible plants and trees that bore fruit instead. Being public land, anyone could harvest the fruit,[60] once again reducing household expenditure and debt, and increasing a community feel to the suburb in the process, allowing people to share more, to be better friends.

When we choose friendship first—make it more important than wealth, power, and status—we are driven to find ways to build greater security together. United by friendship we automatically reduce the power of our desire for wealth, and the power of debt, reducing the influence of at least one of the fundamentals behind slavery.

Friendship also helps us find beliefs that allow for greater equality and reduce hierarchies and exploitation.

Reducing Hierarchies

Imagine a belief system that promoted equality, where everyone was important and no one person—or group—was considered a ruler or better than the rest. A way of believing that promoted your individuality; that encouraged you to be yourself. A belief system that meant everyone had an equal say, where no one person or group had control over another. One that automatically promoted the value and respect of everyone. Would you like to live among a people that had such a belief? Surprisingly, until relatively recently, this is exactly how it used to be.

Before we created farms, towns, and cities we lived in close contact with the land. We gave trees, animals, rivers, the sky, even the land itself, qualities of spirits, like the Shinto religion of Japan today; we gave nature human-like qualities to make it easier to predict and understand. We created rich spiritual stories—beliefs—that told of us living among beings different to us but not too unfamiliar. We lived among equals; there were no rulers—no great all-powerful spirits who dictated our lives. This belief was reflected in our tribal structure.

To live in a nomadic tribe is to live among consensus. Unless we were at war—needing the quick decisions of a leader to guide us—we all had an equal say and would compromise so we could agree on matters affecting all of us. Consensus is a show of respect, and indicates we are a valuable member of our group. It allows us to find validation in our ideas and find a show of support. It allows us to come together as friends.

For perhaps tens of thousands of years or more—since we could speak—consensus played a major part in our lives. Many examples still exist of native people believing in spirits and walking among equals, from the jungles of the Amazon, to native tribes of Asia, Europe, and the Americas before European invasion. Before farming we held beliefs that helped reinforce our friendship with each other and the land; not surprisingly, as mentioned earlier, slavery and exploitation were very rare.

The fact we blatantly exploit each other, and that slavery still exists today, tells us something profound about our current beliefs.

Perhaps it is time we reassess what stories and beliefs we live by and consider changing them to those that no longer promote hierarchies, give validation to inequality, and to treating other people as inferior.

Ironically we, of the 'civilized' nations, have long held we are superior to the native tribes we have been so quick to wipe out and ignore as 'primitives'. We have found good reasons to disregard them; our technology is better than theirs, what could they possibly teach us? However, when it comes to having beliefs that promote friendship, equality, and unity, we could do much worse than to learn from them. They had beliefs that were far more conducive to promoting friendship and reducing the disrespect and exploitation of other human beings than we do.

Promote friendship and make it a priority and we can expect our beliefs to change accordingly. By simply choosing to put friendship first, ahead of the desires of our inner beast, we help eradicate another of the fundamentals that permits human exploitation and slavery, and prevent our children, and generations to come, from suffering its damaging effects.

Friendship can also prevent the powerful desires for wealth, power, and status unleashing untold brutality upon the earth.

Countering the Beast

One of the biggest problems we have with the desires for wealth, power, and status, is that they can easily get out of control, as they have in India, China, and as occurred with the Spanish during the conquest of the Americas. We have seen how these desires become insatiable—stronger—the more insecure we feel. The more powerful these desires the more likely we are to exploit other people, even treat them as animals rather than human beings. Friendship helps counter these effects in several ways.

It begins by helping us reduce our insecurities.

As we have seen, friendship helps us feel secure in food by pooling our resources—such as creating a common wealth, to share. We can take this further by ensuring everyone has food and shelter, such as through government housing and social programs, charities, and community donations and support.

In other words, the more we share rather than hoard, the more security we bring to everyone, including among the elite.

The majority is less likely to want to take what the elite have if the elite are more prepared to share. That doesn't mean giving up ownership as part of some communist manifesto, it can be just letting people borrow what we own, and more often. What's wrong with helping our neighbors out by sharing, like sharing our mower, or feeding their kids with our kids once in a while? Friendship also helps us feel secure against threats.

Focus more on meeting each other's friendship needs and we make less enemies, increasing our sense of security. We will learn in later chapters how to make more friends in general but also how the Ten Desires of Friendship can help bring about peace between neighbors, communities, and governments. As we shall see, dialogue, listening, respect, caring, and searching for commonality, all go a long way towards friendship and peace. There are circumstances, however, where a friendship approach can work against us. A good example is when one nation or community has superior technology.

One consequence of having a society driven by the desires for wealth, power, and status is improved technology, especially weapons. Feeling so insecure, and in the quest for greater wealth and power, these are communities or states regularly at war. War puts pressure on the people to develop better weapons; the state with the superior technology and weapons has a better chance of success. This works against the society that has found a way to live in peace, it will leave their weapons and technology less advanced and ripe for conquest by the technically superior force.[61]

We saw a classic example of this with the Spanish in the Americas. Being at war for so long in Europe the Spanish developed steel, armor, and guns. The Aztecs, a stable empire for some time, without many other empires to fight, only developed primitive shields, arrows, and spears. A group of a few hundred Spanish could conquer millions. Similar examples occurred all around the world when the more technically advanced Europeans, such as the Dutch, French, Portuguese, and English conquered great lands in Asia, the Pacific, Australasia, and North America. The Europeans, all developing a similar level of technology by regularly fighting each other, were far better prepared for modern warfare than the people isolated from these advances on the other side of the world living an overall more peaceful existence.

Today, thanks to the wonders of transport and communication, developed countries have similar levels of weapons technology. The world is in a much better position to let friendship take hold and end the out-of-control desires of our inner beast. Today friendship can help unite us in ways power and conquest never will, through peace and good will. By doing so it reduces the strength of our out of control desires for wealth, power, and status globally.

At a very basic level friendship can help rid us of all the fundamentals that ensure slavery and exploitation persists, and with it racial prejudice and hate. It can finally allow our societies to heal, and stop us treating each other like property, or inferiors. Wouldn't it be great if in the future our children didn't have to know the disrespect and abuse of being treated as less than a human being?

Friendship can also help eliminate one of the most destructive forces that our inner beast ever created: the empire.

COUNTERING EMPIRES AND THEIR DEVASTATION

Friendship, by its very nature, disrupts the damaging effects of empires and robs them of the very forces that fuel and drive them.

Countering War and Massacres

Make friendship our priority and the basic needs for war and conflict go away. Friends don't fight to conquer or kill each other. If we don't seek to conquer each other where is the need to take over other states by force, like the Qing dynasty did by uniting many constantly warring states through conquest to create one, temporarily stable, empire, the one we now know as China. At a most basic level by reducing conflict friendship prevents the development of empires. It also eliminates the core fuel that drives them.

By being personally driven to satisfy our desires for wealth, power, and status you and I are fueling the empire.

As was alluded to earlier, empires can only exist if enough people put wealth, status, and power ahead of people and thus friendship. These desires of our inner beast legitimize and empower the elite, the builders of empires. Want to personally do something to stop the wars, the refugees, and the massacres? The first step can be to make friendship a priority in our lives (we will look at this more in a moment).

We can also use the Ten Desires to help us structure our societies and change our governments to make them more friendship-friendly. This too breaks down empires by decentralizing them, and making them more transparent and accountable to us, the public. We will learn how we can build such societies and create such governments, using the Ten Desires as our guide, in Chapters 10 and 11.

We don't need to continuously learn of a new war and new mass deaths and suffering.

Countering Terrorism and Extremism

When our basic human needs are met there is no reason for terror and extremism. We do not meet each other's desires by focusing on our differences.

The Ten Desires teach us, as we will soon see, that if you exclude us, make us seem different to everyone else—such as focusing on the differences of our clothes, culture, language, or beliefs—we create a potential enemy or threat and divide our society by making us afraid of each other. The more fear we create the more we huddle together with people who seem like us and the more we can notice the differences in those outside our group. This makes us even more wary of any differences and want to exclude these people even more. This not only breeds fear but hate.

Focusing on each other's differences rather than what we have in common creates the very thing we want to rid ourselves of: terrorism and extremism driven by social exclusion, fear, and hate.

This is great fuel for empires.

When faced by terrorism and extremism empires have someone to fight, and a need to exist. Creating 'a war on terror' would be ideal for an empire so it can become even more entrenched. This war would fuel even more terrorism and extremism as people try to oppose the empire's oppressive force. It would create an enemy that needs to be wiped out, one that threatens our peace and safety, one the empire can offer to eliminate, perhaps put troops in the country where they come from so they can exploit their resources too. The ongoing terrorism and extremism ensures the people behind the empire continue to let the empire exist and increase its influence and power.

So, if we want to get rid of terrorism and extremism we should work to make everyone feel like a friend. To put special effort into focusing on our similarities and not our differences; unite and embrace each other as human beings and ensure each other's basic human needs are met.

This fundamentalist and extremist nonsense can stop.

Countering Poverty and Starvation

Empires do not want to share, friends do.

We have just noted, the more we share, the more we ensure no one goes without, the more secure we feel. Do this in our families and communities and we are more likely to want to do it internationally as well—we will be more open to helping others less fortunate and be motivated to eliminate poverty and starvation once and for all—globally. When we treat each other as friends then nations and people all over the world look more like potential friends, people we are prepared to get along with and help for help's sake, not just to use as a way to make more money and have greater influence.

Personally focusing on friendship eliminates the greed within empires that creates exploitation and prevents sharing internationally.

With friendship we prevent many of the reasons behind poverty and starvation. No longer will we feel guilty not giving enough to the destitute and impoverished, there won't be any.

Countering Environmental Destruction

It is hard to treat the land with respect when we don't respect each other, or ourselves. Friendship is founded on respect; it is a key component of the Ten Desires. It is hardly surprising we so easily destroy the natural world and treat it like a slave to use at will since that is how we treat each other.

When friendship is a priority its power extends beyond personal friendships, to treating the natural world as a friend too, much like ancient tribes once did.

Beliefs matter here. As alluded to earlier, if we believe in gods, or a god, then we create the idea we can be like a god and control all things, rather than treat them as an equal. Friends treat each other as respected equals. Treat nature as a respected equal and would we really be so quick to rip it up for its minerals, and poison it so readily?

Empires are not friends with the natural world; the desires that drive them—the desires of our inner beast—don't allow them to be. Friendship can help us change that. It can help us stop empires ruining our precious world and harming everyone on it.

Friendship, by its nature, counters the destructive effects of empires. It gets to the heart of what drives it, fuels it, and creates it in the first place. It dissolves empires from within and prevents them being created again and perpetuating mass misery and destruction. The friendship we prioritize and meet for each other is a very powerful anti-empire and anti-slavery force. It can also be a powerful drive for great prosperity, as we will soon see; a source of hope and promise for our children and the generations to come.

But for all its promise friendship comes with an almost fatal flaw. It is weak.

Too easily friendship desires can be subdued, overpowered, even ignored.

Look around your life right now, how often do you put status, wealth, and power ahead of friendship? How often do you work the extra hours to pay for the extra stuff you don't need just for the status, to appear you are being successful, instead of spending the time with family, neighbors, or friends? It is common, almost all of us are doing it. Our society and economies are built on it. After all, if we weren't after the status, wealth, and power, would we really work so hard and so long in the first place, let alone buy so much that doesn't make us feel any less hungry or uncomfortable? Of course not. And this is where friendship runs into a big problem. It is competing against whole societies driven and consumed by the desires of our inner beast.

It is well and good to want slavery and exploitation to end. It is even better to want empires to dissolve and to live on a healthier, less polluted, less war ravaged, planet. But while we just go about business as usual none of that will change, and neither will our relationships, families, communities, and governments. Yes, we might learn how to meet the friendship desires for each other—and we will do this soon—but if we don't continue to make friendship a priority in our lives it will be just a matter of time before we can expect things to go back to the way they were, as they have done for thousands of years; the desires of our inner beast, as we've noticed, are very strong.

So, what is the solution? How can we give friendship its best chance of rising and staying prominent and influential in our lives, so it can continue to provide all the positives we know it is capable of?

One way is to begin by continually asking ourselves just a single, powerful, question.

THE POWER OF A SINGLE QUESTION

One of the main reasons our desires for wealth, power, and status have been so influential and powerful, and been allowed to see the rise of slavery, empires, and potential destruction of our planet, is they are sneaky; the desires of our inner beast have remained hidden. Our inner beast relies on us not asking questions but just acting on impulse, on instinct. By remaining out of our conscious thoughts it can rule unopposed and dominate our lives, and the world. As we have seen, it has done this extremely well; how many of us have even considered these three desires even existed, let alone that they oppressed friendship and wreaked havoc upon the earth?

If friendship is to ever have a chance this won't happen by us just letting nature take its course; the desires of our inner beast are too strong. It will require us to bring the beast into the light, so we can expose it and rob it of its greatest strength, its stealth.

How do we do that?

A very simple way is to repeatedly, and persistently, ask just one simple question:

Am I putting friendship first?

It is the perfect weapon against our inner beast. With one simple question we remind ourselves: are we putting our desires for wealth, power, and status first, ahead of our desires for friendship and people? Are we putting stuff, and our need to feel superior, ahead of being appreciated, respected, valued, cared for, safe, secure, and loved? A single self-inquiry makes us instantly aware of what is driving our actions and choices in the moment and allows us to choose our consequences, our future. It brings the beast into the light for us to decide if we want it as our master.

Are you putting friendship first?

Before we look at some of the circumstances where we could ask this friendship question, let's see how much the desires of our inner beast have a hold in our life. Let's see which way we have been leaning; towards friendship, or the inner beast.

I'd like you to take a little quiz. Try to be honest and answer according to how you would normally react or have reacted in the last months or years. For every statement you agree with give it a score of one. If you don't agree give it a score of zero. We will tabulate the scores and offer an interpretation at the end.

THE FRIENDSHIP PRIORITY QUESTIONNAIRE

STATEMENT	SCORE (0 OR 1)
I would rather spend time at work than with friends or family.	
Wealth, and having a more comfortable lifestyle, is important to me.	
Having a more expensive house in a better suburb is worth working weekends for.	
I'm more than prepared to move away from my family and friends if my new job pays me more or offers a promotion.	
I must work hard to maintain or improve our standard of living, it is expected of me.	
If they want what I have they should work harder, like I did.	

I don't like to be bothered by other people unless it's urgent, I'm too busy.	
I don't have time for losers.	
Winning is everything, I keep score by how much I have.	
Work and my career are the most important things in my life.	
TOTAL	

How did you score? If you scored zero, then perhaps friendship is important to you—perhaps you should be writing this book! If you even scored just one out of ten, then that suggests that friendship isn't a major priority. The higher the score the more confirmation we have that the desires of our inner beast are prominent in our life.

But what if I like it this way, what if this is how I want to live my life?

That is our choice. The aim here is not to dictate what you or anyone else must do, but to make us conscious of our choices. To help us decide our own path rather than just blindly doing what we did before, like running with a blindfold towards the edge of a cliff and doing it because it was what we did a moment ago. If we still want to take a running jump to our demise, fully knowing the outcome and what that will be like, that should be a conscious decision not a blind one. So far, we haven't even realized we have had a blindfold on. This question helps lift the cover.

Suppose we do want to make friendship a priority, and give it the best chance of transforming our future, what then?

Then we start by asking the friendship question as often as we can and learn—as we are about to do—to satisfy the Ten Desires of Friendship in the different aspects of our life. The key, is to keep asking this question even as we are working to meet more and more of our friendship needs. That way we ensure we give friendship its best chance and reduce the possibility of our inner beast, once again, suppressing it.

The following are some examples and suggestions of when we might want to use it, so it can help guide us.

WHEN TO ASK THE FRIENDSHIP QUESTION
Major Life Decisions

Should I choose a career as an engineer or an artist? Should I have a family or focus on achieving success? Should I work overseas permanently and never look back?

When we are faced by major life decisions, those forks in the road that will forever change our destiny, we should always ask: am I putting friendship first? Why? To ensure we give ourselves the best chance of having our basic human needs met, including those of friendship. Will it really be worth it, especially if we have to sacrifice so much of our humanity to get it? Will the new job leave me feeling lonely? If I leave all my family and friends will I feel as cared for and supported away from them? Will it break my heart not to find enough time to spend with the kids? Whenever we make a major life decision we should always ask: am I putting friendship first?

Relationships

You don't know if he or she is the right person to share your life with, or whether you should break up. You are unsure if casual sex is a good idea. You want a family, but your lifestyle is so busy you never find the time to meet the right person, and you're not sure if you should keep being busy or make more time for others.

Relationships are often difficult at the best of times but helping us to recognize our priorities can guide us. This is where the friendship question can help. If our aim is to build as close a friendship as possible in our relationships—because friendship makes them more satisfying and stable—shouldn't we be making close friendship the priority, whether we can actually be close friends, rather than how much they earn, how sexy they look, or how well they perform in bed? Shouldn't we give ourselves the best chance of meeting someone we are attracted to and can be a close friend with?

We will look at how we can use friendship to help enhance all stages of a relationship, even help save them, in Chapters 7 and 8.

Work

Should we take the promotion for extra pay and work longer hours, or cut back to spend more time with our family? Should we work for people who don't respect us or others? Should we work for people who don't care or appreciate their workers' efforts?

Work is a competitive business, after all it is often primarily driven by desires of our inner beast. But we still have choices. Are the money and trimmings worth it if we are just plain miserable? Is it worth it if we barely have a life?

Asking the friendship question around work decisions can be invaluable.

Everyday Activities

Every day we choose to put friendship last, even with little choices. Here are other examples of when we could ask the friendship question:

- Whenever we buy anything—are we buying it to show off our status or how wealthy we are, such as the new phone, car, house, or clothes?
- Whenever we push into a line or queue—such as on our roads—is that putting friendship first?
- Whenever we tell someone else off, abuse them—are we respecting them? Could we have said it with greater care and empathy?
- When we are critical of others and say or write a harsh word—such as in a blog, email, or comment—is that what a good friend would do?
- When we exclude people or bully them—is that how friends treat each other?

- When we spread rumors, or lies—if friendship was our main motivation would we do it?
- When we step over people to get what we want—do friends do that?
- When we ignore other people's suffering—what friend would neglect another friend in need?
- When I sell a business for huge profit but put everyone out of work in the process—is that putting friendship first, or wealth, power, and status?

I think you get the idea. As a simple exercise, I'd like you to set the timer on your phone to go off—on silent vibrate if you prefer—five times in your day. When it goes off ask yourself the question: am I putting friendship first? Am I doing it at lunch by how I treat the counter staff and other customers around me? Am I doing it as I hurry to work and ignore others? Am I doing it when I buy the extra gadgets, play the new computer game, or get on social media rather than organizing to meet up with real friends in person? Am I doing it when I ignore my colleagues at work? Put the question up around your home and office to remind you.

They say the first step to changing a habit is to become aware of it; like admitting we are an alcoholic is the first step to beating the bottle, forever. The friendship question can be considered the first powerful step to helping friendship rise again to levels it once knew but we have forgotten, to be our new, functional, habit.

Because it is so weak friendship needs us to consciously pay attention and focus on it regularly. But it also needs practical insight and skills. If I was to say, go out and increase friendship in the world, would you know how to do it and what that meant? It is like saying, go out and make better cakes. Sounds good, many of us would love to eat a great cake, but what is a better cake, and what are the actual steps we should take so it is better? This is where the Ten Desires of Friendship help us, by offering both a practical insight into what friendship represents and how to increase it. They give us desires to satisfy and specific actions we can take to fulfill them to ensure friendship rises. There is a problem, however. We can't use a one-size-fits-all approach.

It would be wonderful if satisfying friendship desires was the same for every life situation and circumstance. All we'd need to do is meet the same friendship desires for everyone in all aspects of life the same way and everything would be rosy. Unfortunately, it isn't like that.

Why can't we meet the Ten Desires in some generic way; the same in all situations?

There are more desires wanting to be satisfied than just friendship desires. If we don't get the mix right we can end up with unnecessary heartache, disappointment, or even trouble with the law!

For example, suppose we try to meet the friendship needs for a customer, or a colleague at work, the same way we meet them for our partner. The customers or colleague might think we are getting a bit too fresh for their liking or take it the wrong way and think we have the hots for them when we don't. And if a woman treats her male partner like a girlfriend she could soon find he is sexually very unattractive and want to leave him. How we meet the Ten Desires, and the circumstances, are important.

The following chapters have been written to help us fine-tune how we can satisfy the Ten Desires, so we can gain the maximum benefits with fewer pitfalls. It will begin with the basics—how we might use them in general social encounters—then move on to how they can transform our relationships, work environment, businesses, communities, and governments. We will learn the difference between a casual and close friendship and why that is important—how it can keep us out of trouble and ensure our energies aren't wasted. We will learn the basics of how to be and, should we choose to, remain friends; the person others want to know and be with. Someone liked by many and disliked by few.

Wouldn't the world be a better place if it was filled with lots more friends, people who liked and supported us? People we could count on to be there for us when we needed them most?

KEY POINTS

- By its very nature friendship helps us eliminate slavery, empires, and creates a lasting prosperity and peace.
- **Friendship counters the fundamentals of slavery by:**
  - reducing the power of wealth and debt such as through sharing, pooling resources, reducing a need to show off our wealth and status;
  - adopting beliefs that see us as equals not inferior;
  - countering the desires of our inner beast through ensuring no one goes without, everyone has food and shelter, and we all feel secure and safe.
- **Friendship counters empires and their devastation by:**
  - opposing wars and massacres through controlling our own desires for wealth, power, and status—no longer providing the fuel for empires;
  - disarming terrorism and extremism through focusing on our commonality rather than our differences;
  - sharing at a local level so we are more likely to want to do it internationally, thus countering poverty and starvation;
  - treating nature as a friend like ancient tribes once did, thus circumventing environmental destruction.
- Friendship has the best chance of rising and remaining prominent and influential in our lives by us beginning to repeatedly ask ourselves a single powerful question: **'Am I putting friendship first?'**
- Because friendship compared to the desires of our inner beast is so weak it needs us to consciously pay attention and focus on it regularly.

CHAPTER 6

Using the Ten Desires Day-to-Day

> WISHING TO BE FRIENDS IS
> QUICK WORK, BUT FRIENDSHIP
> IS A SLOW RIPENING FRUIT.
>
> —*Aristotle*

Ever wanted to cook a delicious gourmet meal but never have? Taste the splendor, salivate in awe at your culinary skill? But what if you don't know the basics, like how to boil water, what the ingredients are, and how to prepare them? We can't just expect to make a top-class meal without some knowledge of the simpler stuff. It makes sense we approach friendship in a similar way; that first we work on the basics, then refine things later for better results. With that in mind we will begin by better understanding the Ten Desires and how to use them in general terms, then later in specific situations.

Before we do, it is worth clarifying two different types, or depths, of friendship; the close and the casual friendship.

CLOSE VS CASUAL FRIENDSHIP

It might seem obvious, but there is a difference between what we call close and casual friendships. At work, for instance, we would often have casual friendships while at home—hopefully—the friendships would be close. It is important we recognize the two main types to avoid thinking the depth of friendship we have for everyone should be the same when, clearly, they shouldn't. Besides, as you are probably already aware, trying to become close friends with everyone, even if we'd love to, is physically impossible.

What do we mean by close and casual friendship?

We can gain a better idea by considering the type of friendship we might find in a tribe.

In rugged, mountainous Papua New Guinea (PNG), north of Australia, many of the highlanders still live in tribes and farm their land, which they protect vigorously. Until westerners introduced rule of law and policing—in the mid 20th century—they took matters of justice (payback) into their own hands. For example, if one of our tribe accidentally killed a member of another tribe—such as in a motor vehicle accident—the other tribe would seek compensation, which could be many pigs and large payment. If it wasn't forthcoming then they could kill any member of your family or tribe at anytime, anywhere, without warning, as payback. This had a profound impact on what friendship meant for them.

A friend in the highlands of PNG is someone you can rely on not to kill you; they always have your back. They are also people who can help you survive. As Jared Diamond, professor of geography, points out in his book, *The World Until Yesterday* (Viking, 2012) the casual friendships we enjoy when we travel and get to know people for the first time, even catch up when we visit, were foreign and unfamiliar to the remote highlanders.

Common to tribes all over the world is they could rely on each other in the group to have their backs no matter what and be counted on to help each other survive. They bonded together strongly enough to want to do this. It is this tribal level of friendship that helps us define what we mean by a close friendship.

A close or deep friendship can be said to be a trusting friendship so close that we would give our life to protect the other person, and we could expect they would protect us, if they were able.

A casual friendship is all the other friendships, including people we are just friendly to, or who are just friendly acquaintances.

A close friendship would meet most, if not all, of our Ten Desires of Friendship; the more we satisfy for each other the closer the bond.

Of course, there are exceptions to the rule. Some of us may feel obliged to protect complete strangers, even at the cost of our life, but usually we have to know and connect with someone on a deeper level before we will do that, like our tribal cousins did.

This clarifies why it is physically impossible for us to be close friends with everyone we meet and shouldn't try. For starters, most of us live in big cities. It isn't uncommon we might pass or meet hundreds of people in a week; on the streets, public transport, and the people at work. Even if we did live less busy lives we aren't going to have enough time to satisfy their Ten Desires to the extent we can be and remain close friends. What is more realistic is we work towards meeting the Ten Desires for each other sufficiently that we can all be casual friends.

The good news is, whether we have close or casual friendships, are acquaintances, or seek just to be friendly, the Ten Desires we are seeking to satisfy are the same in each.

In this chapter we will focus on offering a more detailed introduction to what these desires represent, and how we can use them—in general terms—in our day-to-day life. In later chapters we see how we can meet them better in more specific situations, such as with our partner, people at work, and in our communities and governments.

TEN DESIRES OF FRIENDSHIP

As a prelude to using the Ten Desires it is useful to remember two important things: Firstly, attitude is important. And secondly, we should only work to meet these needs in others.

Why is attitude important?

It is next to impossible to satisfy someone else's Ten Desires of Friendship if we have already decided they mean nothing to us, or worse, we already hate them.

We aren't going to like everyone; that is true, and we don't have to. It makes it much easier to meet these needs, so we get the greatest benefit, however, if we also imagine, or at least try to imagine, them as friends already and want to like them, as FDR did with Stalin at Tehran, and Mandela seemed apt to do with many of the people he met.

We have already mentioned that to try to get someone to meet these needs in us is disrespectful. It is also critical we don't punish them if they don't.

Punishing someone for not meeting needs they might not even know about, let alone know how to satisfy, is futile.

It is easy enough to do; we just ignore them, yell at them, or abuse them in some way to let them know we aren't very pleased—as mentioned earlier. We can do it consciously or just as a reflex; a natural reaction to their behavior. But you wouldn't punish a dog you were training just because it couldn't do the trick you hadn't taught it yet, would you?

'Fido, fetch the ball, fetch! Bad Fido. Very bad. Go to your kennel! You'll keep going to the kennel till you bring me that ball, at my feet, after dancing on your hind legs, jumping through those hoops, and clean the ball in the water bucket!'

Better to lead by example; then others can learn from us—we can train them to be friends.

As we noted, this comes about largely thanks to our friendship desire for sameness; we tend to do what others do. The alternative is we all just go around punishing each other. How many of us are going to want to make friends with people who regularly hurt us?

It is important to recognize that at times we will get frustrated and lose heart. Why won't they meet more of my friendship needs for a change? Why am I always the one having to put in the effort? We must remember, not everyone is a fast learner, and some have been taught bad communication habits we will be reluctant to give up.

Meeting friendship needs in others requires patience and persistence. The rewards may not come straight away, but they will come.

Let us look at the Ten Desires in turn, then describe how we might use them. We will work on strategies to help us master and apply them in a moment. We shouldn't try to master them all at once.

Valued

We make people feel valued by giving them a pay increase, or buying them jewelry, regular flowers, or clothes—give them gifts or money. That will make them feel valued, won't it? Not really.

To give gifts or money isn't a show of friendship as much as a payment for services; it is trying to buy some kind of social response. It doesn't truly satisfy our desire to feel valued for a simple reason we mentioned before; it isn't wealth—or stuff—that satisfies our Desires of Friendship; it isn't how nature made us. So, what does satisfy our desire to feel valued? One simple way to satisfy this desire in others is with our time.

Let's go back to the example of how we satisfy this desire for a child, as mentioned earlier. How valued does a child feel if they are last on our priority list; everyone else comes first, and we only give them attention when all the chores are done? They don't feel valued at all! Neither do we.

If we want to make someone feel valued, we start by spending time with them. The same applies to being on time. If the other person can't even show up when they say they will what does that say about how important we are in their priorities? Not very important at all. How annoying is it when people are often late to meet us?

Powerful ways we can all show we value someone is to make time and be on time.

We also make a person feel valued if we listen to them, and help them feel heard. If I don't think you are important enough why would I want to listen to you? I wouldn't. Helping you feel heard helps you feel valued. Another simple way we can make others feel valued would be to ask their opinion.

If I never ask an opinion and instead just tell you what to do I am saying you aren't very important or valuable to me. Your opinions don't matter, you don't matter.

This reminds us of a fundamental feature of the Ten Desires we mentioned a moment ago; when we meet one desire we often meet others too.

Make a person feel heard, validated, approved, respected, cared for, supported, protected, noticed, and appreciated, and we also make them feel they are important to us.

To make a person feel truly valued to us all we need do is treat them as a good friend.

Another powerful way to make others feel valued is to give them something meaningful or important to do. Many teenagers these days are struggling to find their place and feel worthwhile. How can they feel worthwhile if we don't give them something meaningful, important, or worthwhile to do, if we do everything for them for fear of them making mistakes? The less responsibility we give them the less valued they will feel. Offer them important tasks and we increase how valuable they feel.

SIX STEPS TO MAKE OTHERS FEEL VALUED

- Make a prearranged regular time to meet.

- Be punctual.

- Do what you say you will do. If you make a commitment to someone follow it through as you said you would.

- Give people responsibility; important jobs, or tasks to do.

- Be a good friend and meet their other friendship desires.

- Take an interest, ask their opinion.

If we don't feel valued ourselves then perhaps it is time to ask how valued do we make others feel? Do you try to do everything yourself—be self-reliant? How is that making others feel valuable in your life?

Noticed

Ever walked into a store and none of the staff seem to notice you? Oh, they may be wandering around, even behind the counter, folding clothes, or working on something else. They may even be having a laugh together. Suppose you went up to them and they still ignored you, would you think they were being friendly?

Definitely not!

This desire is our brain saying, holy crap, no one knows I'm here; I'm not part of the group! That spells danger! We find safety in numbers, after all. It is hard to feel like we are among friends—and truly safe and secure—if no one acknowledges we are there.

We can make someone feel noticed in many ways, often it's very simple.

We can just acknowledge them as we walk by, such as look them in the eye, perhaps smile or nod, better still say 'hi' or 'hello', recognize them by name. Perhaps we might ask short questions like: 'How's it going?' or 'How's your day?'

Of course, we have to be culturally sensitive. In some cultures, for a woman to look a man in the eye, for example, would be almost criminal. To say hello would definitely be out of the question. Other cultures, such as in some Asian regions, prefer just a slight bow of the head without necessarily making eye contact. The aim is to be respectful of custom, but in a way that still conveys 'I notice you'.

If we are in a relationship we have more options. We can notice someone every time we go into a room they are in by touching them gently. We can say 'hi' or 'hello'. We can strike up a conversation. We will discuss how to meet friendship needs in relationships in greater detail later.

I remember a fellow working in customer service in the automobile industry once telling me they made it a rule that everyone acknowledged every other employee as they passed them. At the customer desk if a customer arrived at the counter and they were busy seeing to someone else they would still greet them and let them know they would be with them shortly.

He said this helped make work a great place to be, and the customers were happier too. We can meet peoples' need to be noticed almost anywhere, even, and especially at work (more about how to do that in Chapter 11).

The following suggestions are designed to help someone feel noticed.

SIX STEPS TO MAKE OTHERS FEEL NOTICED

- Acknowledge people around you—verbally or nonverbally—including as you pass them.

- Preferably notice the other person by name; this makes them feel more valued.

- Never ignore anyone, let them know you notice them no matter how important or trivial they may seem.

- Never punish anyone by ignoring them.

- Be culturally sensitive to how you can meet this desire in others.

- Be a good friend, meet their other friendship desires.

It goes without saying if we are making people feel heard, appreciated, respected, cared for, protected etc we are noticing them.

Can noticing others come with drawbacks?

Sure.

Others may misinterpret our attentions.

For instance, if you are at the gym or at work and smile to a person of the opposite sex they may think you really like them and want to know them better, might be interested in a relationship, or sex. This can get complicated, especially if that isn't what we were trying to convey. Being friendly is so rare these days just a simple hello and a smile can be taken out of context. It can even make people very suspicious and wonder, 'What's this person up to?' 'What are they after from me?' 'What is their agenda?' Hopefully as more of us learn to meet friendship needs in others and they become common we can all begin to see there is no 'hidden agenda', others will be less suspicious, and less inclined to take our intentions of being friendly in a way other than intended.

I grew up in a large country town. Noticing each other with a nod or a smile as we passed on the street was second nature. Driving past others on the road we would always wave. The country people were friendly and weren't suspicious if you noticed them. When I moved to the city to study it was an enormous cultural shock. Friendliness was hard to find and seemed often to be taken the wrong way. I later learnt it was those who approached you with the most friendliness in a city that often had other intentions, like signing you up or selling you something.

Appreciated

I had a guy recently tell me his wife says he doesn't appreciate her. 'How can she say that?' he asked. 'When she is tired and working too hard (often for the kids) I tell her to go and rest while I take care of it, but she never does. And she says I don't appreciate her! Does it sound like I don't appreciate her?'

Appreciation can be a hard desire to satisfy in others. The problem being, we often don't really appreciate someone until they aren't there any more, only when they are gone for long enough, perhaps forever, do we realize what we are missing and how important they were. We get used to them.

Getting used to someone and just expecting them to do what they do is like ignoring them; they don't feel valued or important, worth protecting and keeping around.

We all like to feel we play an important and meaningful role in other people's lives—that they'll miss us when we are gone. Much of our own self-worth is determined by how others regard us. Feeling appreciated is essential.

How do we make someone feel appreciated?

Suppose I told you, anyone could do a better job than you, or you are easily replaceable, would that make you feel appreciated?

Definitely not.

We help someone feel appreciated by letting them know their help is/was really useful and needed. We can inform them what an important job they are doing and thank them. If their help was indispensable, let them know—say it. In short, we give them reason to feel they are important to be around.

The following steps can help make a person feel appreciated.

SIX STEPS TO MAKE OTHERS FEEL APPRECIATED

- Let them know you notice their efforts.
- Offer a genuine 'thank you'.
- Make them feel special/indispensable; like they are the only person who could do it.
- Let them help you so they feel you need them and that their help is important.
- Give them important jobs or tasks to do (see Valued).
- Be a good friend, meet their other friendship needs.

Let's face it, in a world full of hierarchies, where we feel someone is better than someone else, it is easy to take those who we feel are lesser than us for granted. In fact, we can 'expect' those lesser than us to do things for us, as if they are our slaves. We don't have to thank a slave, they must work for us and do our bidding, or they get punished, or go without—they must be our doorman, or footstool, and not complain or we don't pay or feed them. In terms of meeting friendship needs this attitude is clearly absurd and doesn't work.

If we want to make people feel appreciated we never exploit them, treat them as inferior, and never take them for granted as if they are our servant or slave.

A friend is never our slave.

Heard

Have you ever noticed someone look at their mobile phone, or media screen, while you are talking to them? Perhaps you noticed them yawn, or turn their heads away whilst you were speaking, as if bored? Maybe you noticed people ask a question that indicated they didn't hear a word you said? In any of these circumstances did that other person make you feel they were really listening and truly got what you were saying? Of course not, because they weren't listening. It was as if you weren't even there.

Helping others to feel heard is an active process.

People involved in counseling/therapy use this technique all the time; it is called active listening. This requires we pay attention; we focus our attention solely on the person talking, no distractions from phones, computer screens, TV, other people, or events. It means looking at the person and participating such as nodding our head to show we get what they are saying, paraphrasing to give our interpretation of what they said so we are sure we get it. It requires us to try to empathize.

Empathizing means trying to put ourselves in the other person's shoes. We try to imagine what it might be like to lose our home if the person we are listening to lost theirs. We try to understand what it might feel like to break up in a relationship with someone we really cared for if they just did. We try to visualize what we would feel like dangling from the top of a 50-story building by a single rope when we know they did it in spite of having a huge fear of heights! Of course, to do this takes time. We can't fully appreciate what someone is saying to us, especially if it is a complicated story, in just ten seconds. 'Sorry, you had your ten seconds; time's up!' And sometimes we need to continue the conversation later or agree to meet at another time. So, if you know you can't listen properly now let the other person know what they are saying is important, you'd like to hear more, can we arrange another time, 'How about Thursday, or what time best suits you?'

The following suggestions are to help ensure a person feels heard.

SIX STEPS TO MAKE OTHERS FEEL HEARD

- Make time to listen properly, don't do it half-heartedly.

- Give your undivided attention to what they say; take an interest, don't let yourself be distracted, especially by mobile phones, computers, or TV.

- Actively listen, nod, ask questions, paraphrase, seek clarification.

- Try to empathize; put yourself in their shoes to try to imagine what they have been going through.

- If you don't have time to listen now make another time and stick to it.

- Be a good friend and meet their other friendship needs.

Letting someone feel heard is more listening and less arguing—keeping the ears and mind open and the mouth more shut. If we try to impose our views on them it makes theirs seem less validated. It's like saying, 'Who cares what you think, clearly, it's wrong, let me tell you the way it really is!' By pointing out what we can both agree with we not only make someone feel heard but also satisfy their need for sameness—to be like each other; at least two desires satisfied at the same time. Protecting their concerns for confidentiality, if that is what they want, is also a sign of respect and shows we value them—we wouldn't risk the friendship by breaking a confidence, another way of meeting more than one of the Ten Desires at a time.

An important note:

We can both agree to disagree; letting someone feel heard doesn't mean we must share the same views as much as try to understand and accept their views may be different to ours.

Making someone feel heard doesn't mean we have to give up on our own ideas—lose a sense of self in the process. It means respecting our differences and trying to understand them better.

In terms of social media, trolling, telling people they are wrong, or abusing them, certainly doesn't make them feel heard. Perhaps we need to ask more questions and try to understand their point of view more clearly before we are quick to rubbish theirs and shout out our own. We could all do with being friendlier on social media.

Making someone feel heard works particularly well with teenagers. They don't want to be told what to think or feel; they aren't children anymore. Often what they want, especially from parents or important role models in their life, is for someone just to be a good listener, empathize with them, show they understand and that they are ok; they often just want to feel heard and validated.

How well do you find people make you feel heard? Does it annoy you when they just fob you off or their attention seems to be elsewhere? Then how well do you meet other people's desire to be heard? Are you being a good example?

We could all do with more listening and finding more time to do it.

Sameness

Have you ever noticed you have most in common with your closest friends? These people can dress like you, talk like you, have a similar education and morals like yours, similar ethics, and views about life. It is wonderful to be able to just speak your mind with a close friend because you know they 'get' you; you aren't that different. Oh, there are bound to be some differences. We aren't, for instance, going to dress like identical twins—though we might—but in a close friendship the differences don't matter; they aren't what we focus on, are they?

Sameness, finding commonality, is a very powerful way of building very close and deep friendships.

It is also powerful in our lives in general.

How much of where we live, what we wear, how we cut our hair, behave in public, where our children go to school, what car we drive, and what suburb we live in is influenced by others; we do it because they do? The images we see in advertising often draw us in because we want to be like them, to have the stuff they do, to be happy like they appear to be.

Better still, sameness can be our most powerful tool and greatest hope for being better friends, for two main reasons. Firstly, we are all human, we all have the same basic human desires, so the more we focus on each other's common humanity the more our sameness can unify us as friends. And secondly, it empowers us with a choice to make people friends from the moment we first meet.

You may have noticed the first time you meet someone it is like our brain is checking to see if this person is friend or foe. It is looking to see how different that person is. From its survival point of view the enemy is going to be different so the more different a person dresses, speaks, acts, talks, or behaves, the more we are on the back foot and wary.

Have you noticed when you focus on the differences you have with someone when you first meet the more uncomfortable you feel around them? Our focus on the differences is often the reason why.

Now imagine choosing to only focus on the similarities, how do we see them then? Yes, more as a potential friend.

We might hate it, but this is where small talk comes in. Small talk, talking about the weather, gossip, news or sport, and any other piece of trivia or interest we can share is a great way to find agreement—show sameness. If I agree the weather is lousy, or a team we support needs a new manager, or we agree the car racing was exciting, then we have something in common and have gone a long way to satisfying our need for sameness.

The following suggestions are to make a person feel a sense of sameness.

SIX STEPS TO MAKE OTHERS FEEL A SENSE OF SAMENESS

- Look only for sameness—not differences—in everyone, especially when you first meet.
- Share the sameness by acknowledging what you notice you have in common.
- Avoid mentioning differences when they show up or you notice them.
- Share the common human experience: focus on us all needing family, a sense of safety and security, respect, caring etc.
- Even when you are afraid still try to search for sameness.
- Be a good friend and meet their other friendship needs.

We live in a diverse society with people of many cultures speaking many different languages. This can make us feel insecure, live in fear, or feel under threat. If we are made to be afraid by witnessing violence such as seeing it in the media then we will be drawn to focus even more on the differences of people around us. We will be looking to see who we need to be afraid of—those who are different—and those we can feel safe around—those who are similar to us. This can work against us.

Treat people like a threat and they will more likely act like one, feel different, scared, and vulnerable.

The more they act like a potential threat the more they validate for us they are dangerous or potentially dangerous and the more we focus on their differences still, wanting to isolate or marginalize them even more—like we mentioned with terrorism and extremism earlier. It becomes a feedback loop that only makes enemies, breeds fear, marginalizes people, and becomes a medium for hate.

This is perhaps one of our greatest challenges as human beings. When we are afraid and under some threat—when we feel most vulnerable—that is the time we need to look for sameness (the commonality between us all) the most.

This can heal divisions, avoid fights, and restore peace and goodwill. If we want to live in lastingly peaceful societies and countries, then increasing other people's sameness—emphasizing our similarities—can be our saving grace.

Abraham Lincoln was right, we destroy our enemies by making them friends. Focusing only on each other's similarities is perhaps our most powerful tool for destroying our enemies around the world.

Validated/Approved

No one likes to be called a liar, or not believed. Not many of us like to be told we are abnormal, or some weirdo or deviant. We certainly don't like to be told we are crazy! Do you? Whether we admit it or not, deep down inside, we all like to be validated and approved for who we are; we like to feel it is ok for us to be us. This is especially true when we are teenagers.

When the hormones are kicking in and we are starting to develop new sexual feelings nature drives us now, more than ever, to try to fit in with our peers; the social group we will have to live with. It does this by raising the strength of our Desires of Community Self; our Desires of Friendship. The result can easily leave us very sensitive to the words and actions of our peers, feeling self-consciousness, like we are strangers, and as if we are from some alien planet. This is especially true if our friendship needs aren't well met. Tribes had a great way to overcome many of the issues associated with this often-troubling and uncertain time: coming-of-age ceremonies.

From the native peoples of Australia, America, Africa and elsewhere initiation ceremonies would be held that taught the emerging adults what was expected of them in terms of roles and responsibilities as men and women. It welcomed them into the tribe as adults with adult responsibilities. It made it much easier for their adolescents to feel validated and accepted in a major time in life of self-doubt and testing boundaries. It helped them grow up.

Today such ceremonies are rare, though we can find one in Judaism in the form of the Bar Mitzvah. This lack of rites leaves adults, adolescents, and children alike struggling to know what is ok and not ok in a society of competitiveness and diversity of views, ideals, and beliefs. Yet we all just yearn to know validation and approval. Short of us all going through initiation ceremonies, and as a group reaffirming for each other how we should behave as grown women and men, something we may wish to reconsider and reintroduce, how can we satisfy this desire in others?

We can begin with empathizing, as mentioned earlier. Empathize with someone, agree we would think or do what they do in a similar circumstance, and we automatically validate them. We might not necessarily agree with what they have done, or how they were thinking, but we can validate them as a person. Trying to understand people, and ourselves, can help us here.

If I learn enough of your circumstance and know enough about myself and how I might react, I can find it easier to put myself in your shoes. I then have more to validate about what stories and feelings you might share.

Another important way to help someone feel validated and approved is to be less judgmental, less critical, and more tolerant of difference. This also becomes easier the more we understand ourselves and empathize. If I know, for instance, that I would be thinking and doing exactly what you are if I'd been born into your circumstances I become less judgmental and more understanding and in a much better position to validate you as a human being. This is something that comes naturally the more we know ourselves. It is hard to be tolerant and understanding if we barely know ourselves enough to relate to others.

The following suggestions should help a person feel validated and approved.

SIX STEPS TO MAKE OTHERS FEEL A SENSE OF VALIDATION/APPROVAL

- Validate the other person's concerns; let them know they are reasonable and legitimate.
- Agree with what they have done or think—if you do—and let them know.
- Empathize; try to understand their position and what they are going through and convey it.
- Be less critical and judgmental; let them know it is ok for them to have different views and ways of doing things. It is ok to be them.
- Take the time to know yourself, how you react to people and situations and where you learnt it; knowing yourself, you can better empathize and validate others.
- Be a good friend and meet their other friendship needs.

To help someone feel validated and approved we never put them down, or make them feel stupid, or inadequate. Disrespect is a quick way to invalidate someone and show we disapprove of them. A good habit in a conversation or debate can be to simply validate their point of view first. Then we can share ours and how it is different. That way we can debate and discuss and still remain friends.

Respected

If there were a golden friendship desire—one that is most precious and highly prized above all the rest—it would have to be respect. Respect must be at the core of every friendship or friendship cannot exist or survive. Despite all our differences respect must be the one desire we always look to maintain, no matter what, like Nelson Mandela did with all people he met.

Meeting other people's needs for respect comes with a big catch: it requires we first respect ourselves.

Have you ever met someone who doesn't respect themselves, perhaps they abuse drugs or alcohol, or just don't take care of themselves? Now suppose they give you a compliment about how you are looking, or about a recent success such as a new job, are you going to value that compliment as much from them as you would from, say, someone who took great care of themselves? If a person doesn't value and respect themselves why should we value and respect them? How can they make us feel valued and respected if they don't value and respect themselves? Showing we respect someone must come from strong self-respect.

Another major problem in terms of meeting other people's needs for respect are hierarchies.

Hierarchies by their very nature breed disrespect.

The fundamental principle behind respect is the treatment of someone else as an equal. Hierarchies create people who regard each other as superior or inferior. They draw people to disrespect those whom they see as lower than them. One of the ways they do this is by taking away choice.

Choice is the great equalizer. We give people we regard as our equals a real choice, to decide if they want to do what we suggest or not. We give orders—no choice—to people whom we regard as inferior, hence we give orders to slaves knowing they will be punished if they don't do what we say. Want to dominate someone, take away their choice. This is one of the ways hierarchies are created; by using power and disrespect to take away people's choices, by giving them directions and orders.

Want to show a person respect? Give them real choices.

In other words, allow them to say no without any punishment, such as a look of disappointment, an argument, or abuse.

I gave this advice to a wealthy builder once. He came back and told me it was the best advice he had ever received. By giving his contractors real choices—allowing them to say no, without any punishment or look of disappointment—he found they were offering to do some jobs, and offer some supplies, for free! It had a hugely positive impact on his business and how people treated him. Show people real respect and we are more likely to get it back in return, sometimes in spades.

Clearly, we never abuse those we respect. It is not what friends do.

To respect ourselves and others is to give us self-worth and self-value. It is to share a respect for all humanity and what it is to be a human being. It is a way of stating all human desires are important to all people, including us—to respect us is to respect the essence of all humanity. The more we all respect each other's needs and help each other satisfy them the more satisfied we can all be. Respect is key to lasting happiness and peace.

The following suggestions are to help make a person feel respected.

SIX STEPS TO MAKE OTHERS FEEL RESPECTED

- Act like we are equals; never look down on anyone, or raise them up on a pedestal.

- Say genuine 'please' and 'thank you'; value that others have gone out of their way to let you have your needs met.

- Let others go first—if there is time let others into a line, or in traffic—this indicates you respect and value their time too.

- Offer real choice—allow others to say 'no' to what we ask of them without punishing them, have a plan B ready that compensates for them saying 'no'.

- Avoid using titles unless it is part of the job.
- Be a good friend and meet their other friendship needs.

Many people think we need to call others 'Sir', or 'Madam' to show respect. This can indicate we think they are more important, or superior, to us—that is where the titles came from, and what they represent. A good example would be in the army where 'Sir' and 'Mam' would be used regularly—the military has a very clear hierarchy. Outside of the military the title itself can perpetuate the hierarchies of our society and hence the disrespect of others—unless we call everyone Sir or Mam in which case what is the point?

Kindness, caring, listening, appreciating, validating, empathizing, and noticing people, do far more to show respect than giving people titles.

Our aim when we meet each other's Ten Desires is not to rule over others as much as to live among the equality that is friendship.

Want respect? We must always show it—always, even and especially over the internet. Are you always respectful when you go online, or among everyone around you?

Cared For

Nothing speaks friendship more than caring. The touch of a gentle hand on our brow when we are sick, the hot chicken soup when we are stuck in bed with a fever, the concern and time spent being by our side to make sure we are ok. Every show of care is to be treasured.

In a society of divided, isolated, and lonely people there are plenty of opportunities to help others feel cared for. I have met many isolated lonely elderly people who come to me as a doctor just to know someone still cares. Will some people we care for grip onto us and never want to let go, be too sick, unwell, or demanding of us it overwhelms us? Sure, that is why we need more of us, as friends, to come together and share the load; it isn't for us to care for people on our own. Even medical professionals have supports or they too would be easily overwhelmed.

In a practical sense how can we make another person we meet feel cared for?

It begins by letting ourselves care in the first place. It begins, like friendship itself, with the right attitude.

An easy way to foster a caring attitude is to imagine the other person or people are a close relative we would hate to lose or see suffer.

Would we really let a mother we dearly cared for go through terrible pain unnecessarily? Would we really want them sick?

Caring is also easier if we take an interest in the person, have some form of emotional connection. So clearly if we get to know them and already treat them as friends we are also more likely to care.

The following suggestions aim to help make a person feel cared for.

SIX STEPS TO MAKE OTHERS FEEL CARED FOR

- Take an interest; see the other person as valuable, important, and worth caring for.

- Make the time; we can't show we care if we are never around to actually do it.

- Check on people and ask how they are and listen to the answer.

- Let them know you are there for them; give them your number and ask them to call if they think you can help and if you feel comfortable enough.

- Share the load, try not to take on too much by helping people on your own, better still form support groups for your neighborhood or work.

- Be a good friend and meet their other friendship needs.

To make someone feel cared for we can ask how they are going, then be prepared to actually stop and listen and find out. We can check to see if someone is coping ok; many of us don't think we are worthwhile enough to bother anyone else. If we take the time and interest in others we can satisfy the need to be cared for fairly readily as well. The more of us who meet each other's friendship needs the easier, less overwhelming, and more functional, caring becomes.

Don't find enough people care for you? Others will care more when we do. Try it.

Supported

I had a gentleman in his 30s come to see me with depression a few years back; he was unhappy with his life and had no real passionate goals or ambitions. So, I used the magic wand trick. I asked him, 'If I gave you a magic wand so you could do whatever you wanted, what would that be?' He said he'd dreamed of working in aerospace, with rockets and spaceflight. He didn't think he was good enough to do it though, and others in his family thought he should just keep with his steady job and buy a nice house. With a bit of support during our sessions—I have a general interest in aerospace too, which helped—he applied for a space camp here in Australia. He didn't expect to get in. Not only did he get in, when he was there he impressed the important people in the industry so much they gave him a scholarship to study aerospace in Europe. This was guaranteed to give him a job with one of the international companies he so admired.

Supportive counseling in therapy has been shown to have many positive benefits. Even if support doesn't come from a counselor or therapist when we have just a little support it helps raise our self-belief. Together we can achieve amazing things.

To support someone else is often one of the easiest of friendship desires to satisfy in others, often all it requires is encouragement.

If we want to offer material support—help them in a physical way, such as working with them—all the better. All support is important.

How is being supported different to being cared for?

We can support someone and not really care much for them; they may not be important to us enough that we care. It is like being at work. We can support someone to finish a project and not be close enough friends to care about them; we are just work colleagues. On the other hand, if we care for someone it is hard not to be supportive of them, especially in getting well. A little support is not to be underestimated. It is so rare these days, almost certainly due to our lack of friendships; any little bit is like a cup of cool water to a parched trekker in a desert. It can be life sustaining and give us motivation to keep going. How much better have you felt when someone believed in you and offered you their support? Even if it was just a few words, 'I think that sounds great, do it!' Or, 'How can I help?'

The following suggestions are to help a person feel supported.

SIX STEPS TO MAKE OTHERS FEEL SUPPORTED

- Offer encouragement for what THEY want to do, not what we think they should do.

- Offer assistance and see if you can help them. If you offer it be prepared to follow it through.

- Offer praise for a job well done or accomplished. It encourages and supports them to try something else.

- Offer support even among groups.
- The best support is usually given free of charge otherwise it is just business.
- Be a good friend and meet their other friendship needs.

Being supportive is about them, not us; it isn't forcing on them what we think they should do but rather supporting what they want to do. We may think their ideas or projects silly or foolish, but it isn't our call to make; it is their life and life-choice not ours. What satisfies our heart might not fill theirs, and vice versa. Besides, if it isn't going to be dangerous shouldn't we allow our friends to make mistakes? And if we are being too controlling we aren't showing much respect, are we?

Meeting someone else's need to feel supported should be a two-way street.

It feels good helping someone else, doesn't it? Why not let others enjoy the feeling of giving too? If we only offer support but don't accept it, we aren't being a very good friend; we aren't allowing them the ability to satisfy their desires to be friends.

Is there a risk this can backfire?

Sure. Others can turn around later and say, 'Why did you support me doing something so stupid and costly? I thought you were my friend!' Yes, and as a friend I let you do what you needed to do, and we discussed the options and possible consequences.

Ideally support should be given freely, without the expectation of support in return otherwise that is a business transaction and not an indication of friendship.

Friends share and offer support without expectation of anything in return.

Offering support as a group for one another can make the feeling of support stronger and more fully satisfy this desire in each of us.

When was the last time someone offered you support?

When was the last time you offered support to someone else?

Protected

There are two particularly compelling reasons we should all work to make everyone feel protected.

The first is, nothing leaves an emotional and traumatic scar on a young child's mind quite like that of not being protected from harm. Trauma to a child—physical or psychological—is a terrible breach of trust that can lead a person to never truly trust anyone again, and never allow them to closely bond with another human being.

Trauma, past and present, makes close friendships next to impossible, relationships difficult at best, and leaves us feeling like an outcast; alone, vulnerable, and forgotten.

It creates eternal doubt; if one person didn't protect us others won't either. It can mean our Desires of Friendship may never be truly satisfied as much as they could and make it very hard to satisfy them in others.

The second reason is, if it can happen to one of us it could happen to us all.

Your brain is the great generalist, when it sees something happen to one person it assumes it might happen to you too. If one person is belted to within an inch of their life how is your brain to know—with certainty—this won't happen to you? This is why if we want others to feel protected we need to work to protect everybody, no exceptions.

This can be hard to do in a society of competitors. We aren't going to care what happens to others very much, that is just one less competitor to worry about, better they are out of the way. But if we all fail to protect each other, even our competitors, who will protect us or our family when we most need it?

What we do to one person comes back to us.

How do we make people feel protected?

Consider the following suggestions.

SIX STEPS TO MAKE OTHERS FEEL PROTECTED

- When someone is being threatened act or speak up.
- Seek professional help; law enforcement where possible and needed.
- Gain support from those around you so you are less vulnerable.
- If you feel too weak or threatened record the details and report it.
- Ask the victim if they'd like help.
- Be a good friend and meet their other friendship needs.

The more we become friends and meet each other's friendship needs the sooner we can eliminate abuse, including domestic violence and childhood traumas. As friends spending more time with each other we will notice more quickly if someone is suffering. If we are among many trusted friends and relatives we will have more people to ask for help and protection. Haven't you ever wished someone had stepped in and protected you?

Should we put ourselves in harm's way?

Ideally, not. That is why we have the police. They are trained to protect people, we are not. But to not say a word when we know someone is suffering harm is the same as helping the person inflicting the trauma. Imagine you are that child, wondering if anyone loves them because no one is stepping in to protect them, wondering if they are a worthwhile human being because other people can be allowed to treat them like this. What would you like people to do to help you feel protected?

Helping others feel protected is one of nature's most important reasons for bringing us together as friends.

Let's use our numbers, watch out for each other, and make sure everyone feels as protected as our closest friend. Then we'll all feel safer.

No matter who we meet, every single person wants us to meet their friendship needs, just as we would like them to meet them for us. Looking for the friend in other people helps, like FDR and Nelson Mandela would do. So does understanding and patience; we can't expect instant results. To help you to master applying the Ten Desires I would recommend creating a friendship needs schedule.

For one week at a time try to meet one or two of the friendship needs in everyone you meet. For example, in week one try to help make everyone feel valued and respected. Make time for them, be on time, offer them choices—rather than give orders—and treat them as an equal human being rather than a superior or inferior. On week two practice meeting their needs for being heard, validated and approved. Take the time to really listen to, and understand their point of view and experiences, validate what you agree with and show your approval. You may wish to create a chart, like the one below to tick off every week as you complete it, to keep you on track.

FRIENDSHIP PRACTICE SCHEDULE

Week 1	Valued and Respected	Make time, be on time, offer choices, be an equal.
		Say please and thank you—no ordering others.
Week 2	Heard and Validated	Actively listen, empathize, validate and approve and agree when you can.
		Less judgment.

Week 3	Noticed and Sameness	Acknowledge people around you, focus on similarities not differences.
Week 4	Appreciated and Cared for	Recognize their efforts, that what they offer is special. Check if people are ok and need help.
Week 5	Supported and Protected	Encourage, praise, assist. Act or speak up if you see someone under threat.

If you find you need practice on helping meet one need more than the rest, such as showing appreciation, or listening, or making others feel valued, then focus just on that one for a week. The key is to be aware of other people's friendship needs and bit by bit try to satisfy them in everyone we meet as best we can.

The same approach can be used if we find particular friendship desires aren't being met in us. By focusing on meeting them in others we are more likely to get them back and have these needs satisfied by others. So if you aren't feeling valued and respected, for instance, now would be a good time to spend that week or two—or more—on perfecting meeting these desires in others. You may be amazed with the positive response.

The more we meet each other's friendship needs, the more we all become friends.

We now know some of the basics of meeting the Ten Desires. It is time to get more out of them, refine using them in specific circumstances. We will begin, in the next two chapters, by learning how to use them to help transform our relationships into something deeper, more stable, and satisfying, from before we meet, to helping enhance the ones we have. We will also learn why we shouldn't take friendships with the opposite sex lightly. As we shall see, get this wrong and we could be throwing our relationships unnecessarily onto the rocks.

KEY POINTS

- It is useful to clarify and distinguish two different types of friendship: the close friendship and the casual.
- A close or deep friendship is so close that we would give our life to protect the other person, and we could expect they would protect us, if they were able.
- A casual friendship is all the other friendships, including people we are just friendly to, or who are just acquaintances.
- Having a close friendship is ideal but it isn't always possible, or appropriate.
- Our aim is to meet the Ten Desires in others not expect or punish others for not meeting them for us.
- Practice meeting the Ten Desires regularly. Consider a practice schedule (see page 114).
- If you find particular friendship desires aren't met, practice meeting them in others.

SOME WAYS TO SATISFY THE TEN DESIRES OF FRIENDSHIP

1. Valued	Make time and be on time, ask for opinions, give important jobs.
2. Noticed	Acknowledge people around us and as we pass them.
3. Appreciated	Help others feel indispensable and important.
4. Heard	Give undivided attention. Actively listen and empathize.
5. Sameness	Look for and acknowledge what we have in common.
6. Validated/Approved	Agree when we can, be less critical and judgmental.
7. Respected	Offer real choice. More 'please' and 'thank you'. Be an equal.
8. Cared For	Check on people to see if they are ok, share the caring load.
9. Supported	Offer encouragement and assistance without expectation of anything in return.
10. Protected	Speak up and offer assistance when someone is threatened.

CHAPTER 7

Deeper, Lasting, More Satisfying Relationships

IT IS NOT A LACK OF LOVE,
BUT A LACK OF FRIENDSHIP THAT
MAKES UNHAPPY MARRIAGES.

—*Friedrich Nietzsche*

Tom and Jenny were in their early 40s, and parents to a lovely 8-year-old daughter. Jenny described her friendship with Tom as good; they'd talk, do family activities together, were rarely if ever abusive. The main reason she came to see me was she struggled to cope when he was away, she had few friends and virtually no social life so when Tom had to travel for a few weeks or months for his work she felt terribly down. Soon we discussed her relationship in more detail and in no time, she mentioned, disappointingly, she just didn't find Tom very attractive anymore; the spark, the physical desire had left many years ago, at times she found him repulsive. She felt duty-bound to stay with him; he was struggling at times too; he was a friend after all. Her face turned into a mix of anguish, sadness, and despair, as it soon dawned on her: she was lonely, and in a relationship that was contributing to both of them feeling miserable.

Tom and Jenny clearly remind us, there is far more to a satisfying relationship than just friendship, other factors are at play. Deny them and we reject the most successful and deeply satisfying relationship we are capable of as a human being; a bond worth truly keeping and embracing.

Sick of committing to losers and wasting time on them? Looking for a simple and sound approach to making relationships deeply satisfying, a way to both help fix and secure lasting and fulfilling relationships well into the future; strong enough to build a stable family? The Ten Desires can be invaluable.

To help us get the most out of satisfying the Ten Desires in relationships we will look at how to apply them over two chapters. In this chapter, we will use our understanding of human desires to make relationships simpler; to return to the basics. What hope do our relationships have if we can't even get the basics right?

We will begin by looking at relationships in terms of the greater whole, all the desires at play seeking to be balanced for us to feel truly satisfied. Ever wondered why we can have what seems like a great relationship but still feel miserable being in it? Perhaps feel it is all our partner's fault when often it isn't? As we shall see, being in a relationship isn't just going in as a prospective partner, we are going in as a human being—we need a balance in our lives, to satisfy other parts of who we are, or even with the best relationship we won't feel satisfied in it. Then we will look at the relationship proper, and what makes for a successful relationship.

A successful relationship has two distinct components: successful attraction, and successful compatibility. We will see what they mean, and how and why we need to maintain both. The Ten Desires play a critical role here (we will learn what that is in a moment). Then we will learn why it is so important some of the Ten Desires need to be met with our partner differently to how we might satisfy them for a same-sex partner, or other friend. As we shall see, seven of the Ten Desires are gender-sensitive. Don't account for this and our increasingly close friendship can tear our relationship apart, as Jenny and Tom managed to do. But that isn't all.

At the core of any fulfilling and stable relationship there must be respect.

In the next chapter, we'll learn how to satisfy the critical desire for respect in a relationship and more. Perhaps your relationship is one that could do with some serious patching up? Here we will learn how to use friendship to help fix the relationships that need it. We will also learn how to avoid sabotaging the closeness we have so diligently grown—stabilize the close friendship and relationship we have built. Then we will learn how to make relationships easier for us all.

Relationships shouldn't have to be so hard. Friendship can make them so much easier at every stage, even before they start. We will see how simply focusing on friendship can make relationships easier for us all, now and into the future. Wouldn't you want your children to find it easier to find and keep 'the one' than we did?

Along the way we will learn of the damaging role our inner beast has played and continues to play in our relationships. Nature played a nasty trick on us in terms of relationships, it left us with a vulnerability our inner beast could exploit. As we shall see, desires for wealth, power, and status are toxic for women promoting oppression, disrespect, and abuse. They also lead to us doubting our sexual roles and identity, leaving us confused, and make it harder to feel truly satisfied with our partner.

Our inner beast poisons relationships. Thankfully, friendship can counter its damaging effects here too.

We know our relationships are in trouble. That up to three-quarters of us would have an affair if we didn't get caught, and that the average relationship lasts only seven years, speaks volumes. Far too many of us just aren't satisfied, like Tom and Jenny, or are finding our relationships way too much hard work.

Before we continue, it is worth considering the problem. What's going on?

From a human desires point of view, it's simple; we just aren't having our needs met in our relationships.

Study relationships, read widely, and they can appear impossible to understand; there are so many studies, and so much expert advice can overwhelm and confuse us. Yet deep down, if we look at relationships through the lens of our human desires, there is a simplicity to them: if our basic human needs/desires are met—and we see how they will be met in the future—we feel deeply satisfied, even content, and want to stay. Why leave if we are truly, deeply, fulfilled where we are?

In the end, it comes down to basics. The large numbers of failed relationships, and high levels of dissatisfaction even when we are in them, clearly indicate the basics are missing.

Unless we get the basics sorted we can't expect any lasting, positive, relationship success.

What are these basics, and where do the Ten Desires fit into all this?

You will recall we briefly introduced them early, they are represented by the Balance of Self Model.

DESIRES AT PLAY IN RELATIONSHIPS

We have already come across all the basic desires at play in any relationship, they are those that satisfy our life; the desires represented in the Balance of Self Model. In this model we see an overview of all our desires at play in all relationships.

You will recall from the Balance of Self Model our basic human desires were broken into three main groups: Personal Self, Family Self, and Community Self. The Family Self desires are the only ones we need to meet for each other in relationships; the ones we need our partner to satisfy for us and vice versa. But in any relationships, we also have Desires of Personal Self and Community Self. Take the example of Tom and Jenny introduced earlier.

Tom had clear evidence of a low Personal Self. He had let himself go; was overweight, unfit, often tired, and refused to get proper help or do anything about it—clear indications of low self-respect. He made no time for himself, meaning he no longer knew what he liked anymore and would often ask Jenny to make decisions for them both—he had lost a sense of self. A strong Personal Self makes us attractive and Tom had let his appeal slide.

The problem is our partner cannot increase our Personal Self, ultimately only we can do that. They can help by giving us our space and be respectful—more about how to do that in a moment—but in the end only we can get to truly know who we are inside, maintain, and then express it; only we can truly get to know and be us. And our partner cannot satisfy all our Community Self desires, only other people can do that.

As we have mentioned several times, human beings are social. It takes more than just our partner to fully satisfy these desires, to make us feel valued, appreciated, etc; to satisfy our Desires of Community Self. Our partner might tell us—and believe—we are the best person in the world, but we won't necessarily believe it until others also show their support and validation.

How do we feel truly satisfied in any relationship? Recognize friendship—and the Ten Desires—are part of a greater whole, the basics, all deserving our attention.

Where exactly do the Ten Desires fit into that whole?

They are a critical part of the essentials and basics we can recognize in any successful relationship: successful attraction, and successful compatibility.

BASICS OF A SUCCESSFUL RELATIONSHIP

You set eyes on the hottest babe or guy on the planet and you instantly want to be with them. You summon up enough courage—heart racing, palms sweating—and you meet, more than once. The chemistry sizzles! But does that mean the relationship is going to be all wine, roses, and sparkling rainbows? Unfortunately, not, as many of us who have learnt the hard way know all too well; successful relationships require much more!

When we look at relationships in terms of the desires seeking to be satisfied it can get confusing to see how they all fit in, how they work together. There are desires to be physically attractive and noticed, desires to be an individual, desires to fit in with our peers, and among all of these the physical desires such as those for intimacy and sex; desires all competing, swirling around inside like an emotional soup. Seeing our relationships in terms of successful attraction and compatibility can bring clarity to the turbulent mix. It can also help us more clearly see what we need to make them work, and where a close friendship fits in; a vital aspect we all too commonly neglect or ignore.

SUCCESSFUL ATTRACTION

The sizzling chemistry, our heart skipping a beat being near them, a desire to be close, this is lust personified; physical attraction; wanting to hold, feel, embrace the other person, and more! It is nature talking, bodily, and direct. It is shouting to us through desires of attraction to fulfill many essential human basics, what it needs from us to be human. We should clarify; attraction here means far more than just looks, though looks seem to be what our society tends to focus on. For example, as we noted earlier having a strong Personal Self is attractive, so too is a person's personality. In the end many factors combine to make someone attractive to us, many we may not consciously notice or realize, in the end just leaving us with that feeling, that magnetism, that draws us closer. Every relationship needs, to at least some degree, desires of attraction; being repulsed by our partner, or prospective partner, won't do. Ideally, we want mutual attraction, enough pull on both our parts to bring us together. If nature didn't give us these desires we'd never have sex. No sex, no babies. It can be seen as nature saying, this person is worth considering having a family with, go for it! If we lose that attractiveness we lose an important part of the natural connection of our relationship.

When is attraction considered successful?

If attraction is sufficient to get us together to begin and maintain a lasting relationship we can call it successful attraction.

Attraction, however, doesn't just serve to bring us together, the introduction, it also contributes to keeping us together. To keep that attraction helps us continue to meet important relationship needs—it keeps us satisfied. It doesn't have to be as strong as when we first met—that is often built on idealized dreams anyway—it just needs to be enough to keep us wanting to physically be around each other. It definitely shouldn't be the opposite: revulsion, like Jenny was feeling for Tom.

There is a hurdle when it comes to attraction, though; there are no guarantees, especially at the start. Not everyone likes bananas.

SUCCESSFUL COMPATIBILITY

Like it or not, as mentioned earlier, there are some people we will just not get along with. It's like some people don't like bananas, or mangoes, or pineapples, and no matter what we do we can't make them, even if we do. That doesn't mean there's something wrong with them, or us, it just means we are different. We always need to remember: there will be people we can be attracted to who are so different it becomes impossible to truly satisfy each other.

In terms of relationships, compatibility means having like-minded dreams, ideals, morals, ethics, and direction in life. It means weeding out the deal breakers; the things we know we just couldn't tolerate in our partner, such as infidelity, smoking, taking drugs, being an alcoholic, a liar, and so on. It can mean one of us wants children and the other doesn't, one wants to live overseas or in another city and the other doesn't. It can mean one person has to dominate the other, be controlling.

Yes, we can be the best-looking couple in town, start off great in bed, but just be on different journeys. Unfortunately, at some time—perhaps months or more—the incompatibility will show up, then our relationship will fall apart, as it was always going to do.

When is compatibility successful?

Successful compatibility is when we feel satisfied with each other long-term; over many years or decades.

Where do the Ten Desires fit in?

As you have probably guessed, to be compatible means being able to be close friends—being able to satisfy the Ten Desires for each other so we become close. If we can't be this close then we are not truly compatible.

To put it another way, the Ten Desires solidify the compatibility component of our relationship, they validate and consummate it.

To create the most stable and fulfilling relationship we need to be, and remain, mutually attractive close friends heading in a similar direction.

We also need to continue to work to satisfy in us the desires our partner cannot, so we bring a satisfied individual into our union, a person who is meeting their Personal and Community Self desires we mentioned earlier.

Compatibility in a relationship is paramount if we are to stay together, but so is attraction. Unfortunately, nature threw us a curve ball; it found a way for us to become friends and destroy our mutual attraction at the same time. In other words, it made the one thing that is supposed to bond us closely over a long period of time, friendship, actually tear our relationships apart by making us unattractive to each other. Unless we are careful how we satisfy our Ten Desires we can become like Tom and Jenny, friends, just not very attractive to each other anymore. We might then feel a desire to leave.

Look at the Ten Desires from a relationship perspective and we can recognize seven gender-sensitive or specific desires among them. We will consider them in a moment, with recommendations of how to satisfy them in our partner. Before we do, it is worth pointing out this is just an introduction and summary of suggestions based on applying the Ten Desires, it is not intended to be comprehensive. The aim is to help learn basic principles, so you can adapt and apply some of your own yourself. To learn more about Personal and Community Self, and how to satisfy and raise them, consult the relevant chapters in *A Balance of Self*, as these are beyond the scope of this book.

So, how can we be closer friends in our relationship whilst enhancing the attraction to each other? We can begin by learning from a wise and ancient people whose practices were refined over 60,000 years.

APPLYING THE TEN DESIRES IN RELATIONSHIPS
Gender Differences Matter

The Australian Aboriginal culture, before European settlement, had an interesting approach to male and female relations. Many of them practiced what was termed secret 'men's business' and 'women's business'. Certain ceremonies would be held in sacred places, stories would be told, and rituals performed, the other sex was never privy to. When it came to helping men and women remain attracted to each other it was a brilliant solution.

The men would be among men and learn to be true to the desires of being a man, the women would be with women and learn how to be true to the desires of being a woman. Why was it brilliant? Deliberately, or otherwise, they recognized basic gender-specific qualities inside each of us that the other sex finds attractive.

Nature had to make certain features of women attractive to men and vice versa.

By now some of you may be thinking gender-specificity in friendship is all nonsense; friendship is friendship. It is like saying there are gender-defined roles, when in effect they are nothing more than a creation of our culture, our society; men and women can take on any role they choose. It is being sexist, pure and simple, right? Yet I continually see many women wishing men would 'grow a pair', complaining of their men as too weak and effeminate; a real turn off. And I also see many men longing for the feminine in women; a softer, caring side—not weak, but nurturing—rather than trying to be tough and compete with them in ways other blokes do. The struggle going on in our society to define our sexual place in the world is leaving many of us confused, unsatisfied with each other, and unfulfilled in our relationships. Begin to understand some of the reasons and we can see why recognizing the gender-specificity of some of the Ten Desires is so imperative. Our inner beast has played a fundamental, and destructive, role, especially for women.

How Gender Roles and Identity Became Confused

As we are learning, nature drives us with desires and motivations that reflect what we need to do as human beings to survive. Friendship desires, for example, are a reflection of our need to come together to form groups—such as supportive tribes. It would be absurd for nature not to do the same when it came to our gender differences. It would be nonsensical, for instance, to make our babies need breast feeding and close and careful nurturing without giving women inbuilt desires to care and nurture the young. Similarly, it would be a waste to make men stronger and faster than women if it wasn't put to good use, such as to provide for and protect their family—bring home the bacon and keep the family safe from predators and attackers. Look at our physical differences and we can expect powerful desires in women to primarily care and nurture and—for most women—to feel deep fulfillment from it. We can expect desires in men to primarily want to provide for and keep safe his family, especially his children, and many men—though not all—get deep fulfillment doing it. But nature isn't stupid, it would have also had to create some adaptability.

Adaptability helps us survive, to change according to shifting circumstances. At times men will need to take up the caring and nurturing role, when a mother may no longer be around—they may have died. At other times women may need to take on the providing and protecting role, such as when the men are not around, and they need to protect their family from attackers or predators. In each of us there are desires found in each other, so our children have the best chance of making it. However, this very adaptability can lead to us losing sight of the primary gender-specific desires that define us, that live in our heart. Our inner beast has made, and continues to make, this adaptability work against us, playing a huge role in increasing gender confusion and, in the process, relationship dissatisfaction.

How have our desires for wealth, power, and status had, and continue to have, such a negative impact?

It's thanks to how nature made us to react to threat.

Put a tribe under threat, such as another tribe attacking, and the desires to provide and protect rise and the desires to care and nurture become less important in comparison; survival comes first. In the short term it works well, it's all-hands-on-deck to stave off the threat—protecting desires rise in all of us, even among women; as we noted, we can all protect each other and our children. Once the threat is gone we can go back to our previous roles—caring and nurturing can be given the immense importance it deserves, providing and protecting can go back to being the main preserve of men. However, keep the threat there long enough and soon the role of caring and nurturing isn't as valued as that of the provider and protector.

Maintain a threat or lack of food/resources and it becomes a man's world, where to be like a man is the ideal; being the provider and protector gets the greatest recognition and support. Keep the cloud of fear and threat around long enough and the only way women can get the recognition and respect they deserve will be to also become providers and protectors (fighters and hunters), giving up the crucial caring and nurturing role. Keep a society in fear and insecurity and we can expect many women to no longer want to be carers and nurturers, their desires to provide and protect will override their innate motherly/nurturing self. Soon they may not notice their innate desires to care and nurture and find them foreign.

Our inner beast makes this worse.

As we have seen, the desires of our inner beast make us competitors not friends. They don't foster caring, they breed conquest and control over others; to be superior and dictate terms. The desires for wealth, power, and status are, in fact, the antithesis of caring and nurturing. The competition they incite breeds fear and insecurity—we don't know who will take our wealth or power next. This further enhances our desires to provide and protect; they make us always on edge, always worried about not having enough. They don't promote a peaceful and supportive environment to allow caring and nurturing to rise and take a foothold. In the process, they drive more and more women to be the provider and protector, to earn more, have greater power and status, because if they don't they will all too easily be ignored, abused, and disrespected.

Look around us and we see societies consumed by desires for wealth, power, and status. We see many women wanting to match it with men on their terms—to be powerful providers and protectors. This is having a terrible side effect, the devaluing of mothers.

Living in a society dominated by desires of our inner beast undermines and devalues the vitally important role of being a mother, making it subservient to other forms of 'success' founded on greed and privilege.

In a society under the control of our desires for wealth, power, and status women are powerfully driven away from the caring and nurturing part of their hearts. They are left with an impossible choice.

If women primarily become carers and nurturers in a society dominated by the desires of our inner beast they will be treated as inferior, be oppressed, abused, disrespected, and treated as objects, props of status, accessories to the 'successful' who value wealth, status, and power above all else. After all, only the male dominant desires to provide and protect will be truly valued and respected in a male-desire-dominated society. If they respond by acting as providers and protectors, taking it to the men on their terms, competing with them for the status, wealth, and power, they can deny themselves contact with the feminine deep inside and the complete fulfillment of being a woman. No matter how we look at it, when our desires for wealth, power, and status dominate our society women lose. How many women have you met who are being torn apart to 'have it all' leaving them feeling unsatisfied, overly stressed, anxious, or depressed as a result?

As our inner beast tears women away from their hearts it also leads to an attack on gender roles, ruining our relationships.

When more and more of us are diverted from our traditional gender roles—those more consistent with what nature made us follow according to our biology—we can come to believe they don't exist, they are just an idea created by our society—we can want and try to do away with them altogether. Speak of women as carers and nurturers and you can be accused of wanting to keep them caged or oppressed—even though women can have enormous power and influence still in this role—we will learn how later. Speak of men as providers and protectors and you can be targeted as sexist—even though men who devote themselves to these roles can still treat women with great respect. Soon we can all struggle to know what it is to be a man or a woman anymore, let alone what our partner, deep inside, has been made by nature to find attractive—we can find ourselves pushed to be something else and confused. Our inner beast driving us away from our natural selves and what feels true to our heart, what we need to be truly satisfied by our partner.

Why is it important to recognize the gender-specific parts of the Ten Desires?

For two main reasons.

Firstly, it prevents us acting in ways that our partner won't find attractive; it helps ensure mutual attraction remains for us as men and women—we satisfy the gender-specific qualities nature wants us to find in each other. If we are in a same-sex relationship it can help us be aware, and true to, the masculine or feminine qualities our partner needs us to keep; what they were attracted, and remain attracted, to.

Secondly, it also helps counter the damaging effects of our inner beast.

As we just noted, the desires of our inner beast are the antithesis of caring and nurturing; it brings them down, suppresses them. However, the opposite is also true; caring and nurturing can also counter our inner beast.

We have seen when women are true to their heart they will tend to be more caring and nurturing. These roles help us all feel secure and safe; they encourage peace. With greater peace there is less fear and need for wealth, power, and status. In the peaceful world young women can grow up feeling true to themselves, not pressured to be providers and protectors or act like men. They can grow to be guides to their sons to teach them care and compassion, lessen their young men's desire for greater wealth, status, and power; lessen war and conflict. When women are true to their hearts they will also lessen gender confusion brought about by the effects of our inner beast, they can be our lighthouse, our beacon, to guide us from within, to teach women what it is to be feminine and caring and men how to be respectful people who can deeply satisfy women as men. When we satisfy the Ten Desires, taking into account our gender differences and what we need to be satisfied as men and women, women can be accepted and encouraged to be women true to their inner self so not only our relationships benefit, everyone does.

The reason the Australian Aboriginal peoples' approach is so appealing is that by men being with men in these ceremonies, and women being with women, they found a way to reinforce and validate the maleness among the men and feminine among the women. One of the effects was to keep them attractive to each other.

At the same time, helping them keep caring and nurturing alive; promoting peace.

Let us now look at seven gender-specific desires of the Ten Desires of Friendship and how to satisfy them.

Once again, it is worth pointing out, attitude is important.

Our aim is to satisfy these desires in our partner, not them in us. If we go in with anything other than the intention of nurturing and maintaining a closeness of spirit, we will struggle to find the closeness we are after.

HOW TO MEET GENDER-SENSITIVE FRIENDSHIP DESIRES

A key to success here is to try not to meet these desires like we might with a same-sex friend—girlfriend, or mate. Often, we only need to tweak these desires with a few gender-specific differences in mind.

Valued

Sick of your partner showing up late, or not showing up at all? Sick of them putting everyone and everything ahead of you?

So you should be.

You will recall, we make others feel valued by giving them our time and being on time. The same applies here, we aren't making our partner feel valued if they are last on our priority list, or we are always late and never do what we say we will do. We also don't make them feel special if we spend more time with one of our friends than with them. If your partner put their friends ahead of you, even broke off your meeting in preference to meeting with them, would that make you feel important? Me neither.

Close friendship in a relationship is about prioritizing our partner—making the friendship more special and exclusive than with other friends. It means not neglecting the time together but prioritizing it, no matter how busy we might be, especially if we have children—no excuses.

Gifts will never help us bond as close friends. We must spend sufficient quality time together.

What is sufficient, let alone, quality time? It can vary, some of us need more time together than others, but if our partner is hinting, or telling us, they aren't feeling very special or important to us then that is a big hint we need to be giving them more. Quality time doesn't mean just hanging out together, such as being in the same house all day, or going to the movies, though these might be things we both enjoy, it means really talking, sharing our thoughts and dreams (see Heard, below), being intimate, and, most importantly, having fun together. Want to increase the closeness, in your special time together share secrets and thoughts you don't share with others.

Recommendations:

Make special and exclusive quality time for your partner compared to your other friends.

Make regular date nights once a week as a minimum to talk freely. If you have children get a babysitter.

Enjoy one weekend away together as a couple at least every month or two for friendship building time. The main point being, set aside time to be with each other to talk and have fun, then keep that time no matter what.

Treat time alone together as some of the most precious time in our life. Don't just hang out together because you have nothing better to do. Grow together, explore together, learn about each other what no one else knows; make it meaningful.

Don't be late. Unless there is a sudden zombie apocalypse you have no excuse. Calling to say you will be late—again—doesn't cut it. Better still, organize to be early.

Remember, we set the example for our partner in how we prioritize time for them. It isn't for us to force them to make the time for us.

Noticed

Ever been treated by a partner as though you weren't even there? How did that work for you?

As a rule, and especially in relationships, we always notice our partner and never ignore them, no matter how they have treated us—we never use ignoring them as a punishment or weapon. However, how we notice someone speaks volumes; we need to be careful.

For example, we might use touch to notice our partner, the touch being soft and intimate. If we used the same kind of touch on a friend—not our partner—it might be misinterpreted. If it is among other blokes, they might feel very uncomfortable and question our sexuality. If we touch a member of the opposite sex the same way we do with our partner it will set off a sonic boom if there isn't much intimacy happening in our relationship.

A hand on the shoulder, a pat on the back, a touch of passing hands, all speak volumes.

So too the nature of our smile, eye contact, and how we say hello. Noticing our partner, and how we do it, should be special and more intimate than with others, especially others of the opposite sex. If they are around us we should always make the time and effort to ensure our partner feels noticed.

Recommendations:

Get to know how your partner likes to be noticed best—discuss it.

When you are in the same room notice each other, even if you pass in the corridor.

Instead of punishing each other by ignoring the other person make time to sort out any differences, talk and compromise, empathize, and listen. (See Heard, below.) Ignoring each other, especially as a punishment or after an argument or disagreement, is never ok.

When your partner notices you acknowledge it; notice them back, never ignore it or take it for granted.

Notice the differences in your partner's appearance you find appealing, especially if you know they have put in the effort. The more you notice it the more they will do what you find appealing again.

Don't notice people of the opposite sex in a more intimate way than you would with your partner, even if your partner says they are ok with it, deep down they almost always aren't.

How we spend the time to notice each other presents enormous opportunities for intimacy. Intimacy helps keep the flame of attraction alive.

Heard

Ever felt you were talking to someone imitating a brick wall, or a log? What was that like?

Active listening and empathizing are the name of the game, but we need to consider men and women satisfy this need for each other differently. What we talk about with our same-sex friends—in general terms—should not be discussed very much with our partner.

For example, many women will talk about emotions and feelings, how people behave or misbehave; the talk is often people-focused. Most of the time men will not talk about such matters. In fact, such talk may make many men feel uncomfortable. We can recognize good reasons why. For instance, if men talk about feelings they are sharing what can be used against them. Since they are competitive and protectors this can reveal potential weaknesses others can exploit. If women persist and make them reveal these weaknesses it can backfire. If the man hasn't sorted these issues then the once confident man can appear weaker in a woman's eyes, less able to be the confident provider and protector she needs and lead him to becoming less attractive in her eyes. Yes, it might make him more 'human' by revealing his vulnerabilities but at a price to the relationship.

Similarly, men can't expect women to talk about lots of things they like to talk about such as cars, mechanical things, power, wealth, and competitiveness such as in many sports. This might provide a common interest, and make her a great mate, but can also make her appear less feminine and attractive to him, depending on how far she takes it. Different men will have their own idea of how bloke-like they are prepared to accept their partner before it becomes a turn off. Unfortunately, they might not realize it has gone too far until it is too late.

Recommendations:

Rather than talk about what you would talk about with your same-sex friends talk about what you both share that affects both of you. For example, what you want to do together and your future, the tasks and topics that will affect your family and future together; the topics that are important to you as a couple.

Encourage your partner to share their experiences so you can empathize and validate them (see Validated/Approved below).

When listening, actively listen, and always try to empathize. Don't just nod, ask questions; clarify to be sure you understand what has been said. Try to understand their point of view.

Always, always, always give undivided attention—no phones or computers to disrupt you. If they start talking to you get off the phone, computer, or turn off the TV, make real eye contact and listen.

Be less judgmental, more attentive and try to understand. We don't feel heard—or validated—if we feel someone is constantly critically judging us.

Don't expect your partner to listen to your gossip; gossip is often different between the sexes.

Don't try to make your partner into your girlfriend if you are a woman and a bloke if you are a man.

It is worth noting, men and women have different ways of meeting this need for each other. Men tend to be problem solvers; tell them a problem and they will solve it. This isn't what most women want to hear. We will discuss this more under Validated/Approved in a moment. To help our partner feel heard we need to consider the differences of what satisfies this need between the sexes.

Sameness

Ever met someone who looked the goods only to find you had absolutely nothing in common, except being human, of course? Did that huge difference bring you closer or further apart?

Sameness creates some of the strongest feelings of closeness but if we become too alike we actually become less attractive. Like two north poles in a magnet, we can repel each other. Besides, who really wants to live with a clone of themselves? It is boring and uninspiring, and it doesn't help us learn about ourselves and the world and develop as a human being. Being too different doesn't work either.

What we want is a degree of similarity in the Goldilocks zone—not too similar, not too different.

This is especially true when it comes to gender characteristics or behaviors. If you are a woman attracted to a man and he starts to behave and dress like you as a woman he will often become less attractive. You might become good friends, just lose the attraction towards one another. Similarly, if you are a man attracted to women and your partner starts to get all macho, dressing like a guy, and trying to be tough like many guys try to be, then that can be a turn off. Oh, you might still have sex, and share lots in common—be good mates—but that doesn't mean he will find you as attractive and still want to be with you as much as when he knew you as a more feminine woman. He may even find himself drawn to women more feminine than you.

Recommendations:

Focus on the similarities between you, never the differences. For instance, focus on similarities in beliefs, dreams, ideals, ambitions, morals, and ethics. Look to be with someone of similar status to you in society—such as similar intellect, wealth, and level of attractiveness. These commonalities can make our relationships more stable.

Share the simple things you both like or don't. If you both like or dislike a TV show, movie, a color, a food, a politician, share that you do. Don't bring attention to what one person likes and another doesn't.

Focus on what you both like about her feminine side, so it enhances it. Focus on what you both like about his masculinity, so you enhance that too.

Keep your identity as a man or woman. Spend more time among men who are manly if you are a man and women who are feminine if you are a woman; like the Australian Aboriginal people did.

Don't spend all your time only with each other as a couple. The more we do the more we take on the other person's traits and become like them. It might be ok for the friendship, just not the attraction.

Work to maintain your Personal Self, as mentioned previously. A strong Personal Self—remaining our genuine selves—is attractive and keeps us attractive. It stops us being so alike that we annoy each other.

Relationships work better if we are two people rowing in separate boats beside each other, heading in the same direction. Rather than being two people rowing in the same boat.

It is critical to remember, being different, having varying interests, friends, and tastes is a good thing—we don't have to give up our individuality to be close in a relationship. If we must be someone other than ourselves, to like what we don't, to try to create things in common that we don't agree with or like, just to find or build a common bond then we were probably never compatible in the first place. Losing ourselves for a relationship doesn't work.

Validated/Approved

Ever been told you are full of it, and haven't got a clue? Was that good for you?

It stinks when others invalidate us; we all want to feel validated for who we are, gain other's approval and acceptance. We help enhance the bond in a relationship by especially validating and approving the gender differences and different gender roles—validating the parts we find attractive in each other.

For example, by validating women as feminine, sensual beings, in touch with their feelings and intuitions, treasured as carers and nurturers, we enhance them. By validating men as providers and protectors, confident, able to keep us all safe and well provided for, we enhance these qualities in them. Similarly, by validating and approving the respect for the differences in each other and the vital role each of us plays we build a foundation that allows us to feel most satisfied, safe, valued, and respected among each other; we recognize the gender differences, but validate these are ok. What we validate and approve guides our behaviors, actions, and determines how satisfied we feel in each other's company.

Wouldn't you, as a woman, for instance, like a man to validate, approve, and even encourage your femininity, rather than ignore or oppress it? Wouldn't you, as a man, prefer a woman to validate and approve you as a man contributing in a substantial way to your relationship and family, to validate and encourage your maleness, rather than put it down or try to ignore it? The key is respect (we will discuss this more in a moment).

In gender wars, no one wins. Validating, respecting, and approving the gender difference between us helps end that war and bring us closer, as satisfied, mutually respected, friends. We don't need to deny gender roles to bring about peace, we can embrace them with respect.

Recommendations:

Validate each other's concerns regularly, recognize your partner's view as reasonable and legitimate.

When you agree with what your partner says or does, let them know.

Always try to understand your partner's point of view (see Heard, above).

Validate that they don't always have to agree with you and vice versa. We can agree to disagree and still get on just fine.

Be less judgmental and critical and more understanding so it is easier to validate and approve them.

When discussing topics, always validate the other person's view first. Never call them stupid or say their ideas or views are ridiculous.

Validate and approve any gender-specific behaviors you want to see more of in your partner.

Guys: don't try to solve your partner's problems unless they specifically ask you to!

You have probably noticed if you tell a guy your problems he will come up with a solution; it is what most guys do. It is also how guys bond. Guys bond by doing stuff together, such as building things or working as a team to get jobs done. This solutions-focus doesn't help us feel validated. It is like saying 'That isn't a real problem or concern, because all you need to do is take these steps, one, two, and three, and it's fixed!'

To feel validated and approved we aren't after a solution. We simply want to know the other person gets where we are coming from, what we are going through. We want them to show they are like us.

To simply dismiss a concern with a solution doesn't do that.

So, a hint for guys; listen more, empathize, try to understand, and keep the mouth closed unless you are doing these. More hugging, less solutions, would be good. If in doubt, check with your partner, to see if you are on the right track.

Supported

Sick of your partner being unmotivated and spending too much time on the couch, or in front of the computer playing games? Want them to get active, and do something worthwhile? Support can help.

We can all do with support in following our heart's ambitions. Even a little support can make a huge difference and see us do things we never imagined we could. By especially supporting activities and plans that enhance our gender-specific desires we also help each other remain attractive.

For example, we should pay special attention to supporting women in activities that are high on caring and nurturing and support men in their ambitions and activities to provide and protect.

When we support women as carers and nurturers, not only our relationships benefit, so do our families and societies—caring and nurturing can transform and improve them. When we support men in their ambition to provide and protect we give men pride inspired from their heart. If they can be providers and protectors while still focusing on friendship—rather than the desires of our inner beast—then their pursuits can be beneficial to all of us and far less destructive.

Recommendations:

Offer regular encouragement for what your partner wants to do.

Listen to what and why they want to do it. Validate their desires. Talk and compromise if the family is suffering as a result. For instance, if the ambition is to be a successful writer or artist then do they really want us to fund that or are they prepared to still contribute to paying the bills?

Offer assistance, see if you can help them achieve what they want or feel they need to do. For those who seem particularly unmotivated why not offer to get involved with them, as you would help a child clean their room to get them to do it rather than trying to get them to accomplish it on their own.

If your female partner wants to do a job or task that is driven by caring and nurturing give it great support.

If your male partner wants to provide for the family and keep them safe, support them, if you think it is at all viable.

If you can both afford it, let them learn from their mistakes, and remind them that the people who have succeeded the most were those who grew from every setback.

Don't be too surprised if your man has little motivation to provide and protect if you are doing it for him. Unless his contribution becomes important he may not feel a desire to do more.

Always give support and take support and assistance when others offer it. Support is a two-way street. To only give or only take denies our partner, and ourselves, the satisfaction of having this desire fully met.

Many of us have learnt that there is no point doing anything worthwhile because it never works or is much harder than we thought. So, we give up. But if even a small spark exists it needs lots of encouragement, care, and nurturing, to grow into a motivational fire. Do you care and nurture your partner's ambitions and interests or throw water on them before they even get a hearing? Keep putting our partner's ambitions down and we can grow apart, or they develop deep roots on the couch or in front of a computer.

Finally, don't forget to be the example. We can't expect our partner to get motivated and be active if we aren't. It is hard to support plans or activities that haven't even been sparked yet. Hounding people to find that activity you'd like to support won't help them find it. Showing them how to, by finding and following your own, might.

Protected

Has your partner ever made you feel unsafe, perhaps threatened you? Did that make you want to run to them and become even closer? Would we expect it to?

Safety is not negotiable, it is a human necessity and right. It is absolutely critical we feel safe in our relationship. Satisfying our desire for protection does that. We can all provide it, but who primarily provides protection in terms of gender roles can affect how attractive we are to our partner.

Let's be clear, women can be great and effective protectors, especially if they are specifically trained. However, by doing this they can take away the role of protector from the man and can leave him weaker, less confident, and less attractive in many women's eyes, threatening the satisfaction of their relationship.

Ultimately it is a woman's choice if she takes on strong protective functions such as in combat and frontline policing roles.

As long as we recognize that by doing so we can threaten the closeness, satisfaction, and stability of our relationships.

That said, we should all be ensuring each other feels safe and protected—always. That can simply mean calling for support, preferably from those trained to best provide it—such as the police. It can also mean developing greater supports and closer community, so we can sort out any abuse, trauma, and potential threats early.

Recommendations:

Protect your partner always.

Call in trained support whenever possible.

Never abuse or inflict physical harm on each other; that is not meeting their needs for protection, or respect.

If you think your partner is being bullied—such as at work—ask if they need help, perhaps discuss the professional and work options. Seek professional help early.

If your partner ever discloses a previous trauma believe them, never judge them; empathize and listen (see Heard). Offer support, care, and be on their side.

Never test your relationship by seeing if your partner will protect you. That just indicates you don't value or respect them, let alone care for them.

Let a man help you to feel safe—take on the protector role—if you are a woman and you can increase your attraction to each other.

As you can see, we don't need to tweak the Ten Desires very much to satisfy them in a way to keep us mutually attractive, we just need to be aware and respectful of our gender differences. Also remember to be true to the gender attributes our partner found attractive in the first place, such as not making our guy into a girlfriend, or female partner into a bloke if we are attracted to the opposite sex.

Does that mean in relationships we should only focus on meeting the gender-specific desires, and ignore the rest? After all, they do ensure mutual attraction and promote caring and peace.

Not at all.

Meeting the other desires can make our relationship closer still—the more desires we satisfy the closer we can become. Some of the less gender-specific desires are some of the most important of all. Besides, satisfying these will also enhance our attractiveness to our partner, as a close and wonderful friend. Wouldn't you prefer to hang around someone who is respectful, caring, and appreciative?

KEY POINTS

- There is a simplicity to human relationships: if our basic human desires are met—and we see how they will be met in the future—we feel deeply satisfied, content, and want to stay.

- For us to be satisfied in a relationship requires we meet our Personal Self, Community Self, and Family Self desires. There are certain parts of us our partner can never satisfy, and it isn't their job to try.

- The needs and desires in our relationship can be easier to understand if we group them into those of Successful Attraction and Successful Compatibility.

- For the most stable and fulfilling relationships possible we need to be, and remain, mutually attractive close friends heading in a similar direction.

- Seven of the Ten Desires can be considered gender sensitive. If we aren't careful how we satisfy them we risk making ourselves unattractive in our partner's eyes and tearing our relationships apart.

- Our inner beast has contributed to gender confusion, reducing relationship satisfaction, devaluing the mother role, leaving women with an impossible choice. When the desires of our inner beast dominate society women lose.

- The gender-sensitive desires include: valued, noticed, heard, sameness, validated/approved, supported, protected.

- Our aim is to be true to the gender attributes our partner found attractive when we first met. If we are heterosexual that means not making our guy into a girlfriend and our female partner into a guy.

CHAPTER 8

Fixing our Relationship with Friendship

> OF ALL THE THINGS WHICH WISDOM
> PROVIDES TO MAKE US ENTIRELY
> HAPPY, MUCH THE GREATEST IS THE
> POSSESSION OF FRIENDSHIP.
>
> —*Epicurus*

A 2012 Pew Research Survey indicated most under-30-year-olds in the US aspire to an egalitarian marriage; a relationship that shares spouse work and is built on equal power.[62] It is a great start, a great show of respect. But only a start.

In this chapter, we will learn how to satisfy the desires for respect, care, and appreciation so we can make the friendship in our relationship closer still. We will then learn how to fix broken relationships using friendship, and finish laying important foundations; see how to strengthen them to prevent them falling apart. We will learn three simple rules: keep up the maintenance, keep the closeness exclusive, and keep the trust and secrets. Don't want your partner to be stolen by someone else at work, or over the internet? These rules can make the difference.

We will also learn how to make relationships easier in the future.

Sick of being single? As we shall see it is all too common, almost half of us are single these days, by choice or otherwise. We will learn how friendship can make it easier for us to find and keep a partner with whom we are compatible. It is time for difficult and unsatisfying relationships, even being uncomfortably single, to begin to become a thing of the past.

Friendship can turn this around. As will become evident, it can make a huge difference before we even meet.

Let us begin by learning how to satisfy the rest of the Ten Desires.

FRIENDSHIP DESIRES WHERE GENDER MATTERS LESS

We are going to talk about friendship desires for respect, appreciation, and to be cared for. Respect, as we all know, is paramount in any lasting and satisfying relationship. So too is not being treated like part of the furniture; something our partner doesn't mind having around but doesn't give too much attention to. We also need to feel our partner genuinely cares for our health and wellbeing; no one wants a relationship with an uncaring, unsympathetic, rock or we'd all have piles of rocks and stones littering our houses and watch over them diligently. It would be a mistake, however, to believe just because these desires do not help build mutual attraction they aren't valuable, they are still vitally important in relationships and increasing closeness. Actually, these are some of the most critical of all.

Respected

Do you like being ruled by a tyrant in your relationship; a dictator, manipulator, abuser, or regular liar? Does their behavior make you want to get closer to them; tell them your secrets, be physically intimate and closely bond?

Of course not.

Whether in a relationship or outside one, of all the Ten Desires this is the gold standard, the jewel in the crown, the rock upon which to build a magnificent home and life. Respect is a universal desire of all human beings no matter age, race, culture, belief, or gender—it transcends human differences. It is an absolute requirement in any close friendship. Just because our society has created hierarchies—for reasons already mentioned—doesn't mean they should ever be allowed to exist in our relationships.

We cannot have a close friendship with someone who is our superior or inferior.

In practical terms, satisfying this desire means you shouldn't put your partner—or prospective partner—on a pedestal, or next to you as a door mat. When you are in awe of someone, and it is a significant reason you are attracted to them, that is not a show of equal respect. If you are wanting someone to adore you, treat you as if you are the best thing since sliced bread, that also isn't a mark of equal respect.

Putting it another way, if we want to have close friendships we cannot have women or men treated as princesses or kings.

It's enticing, isn't it? In a society where the elite seem to get more of what they want than the rest of us, seem to be most respected, valued, and appreciated, it is tempting to want to be like them. Royalty figures, like princesses, princes, kings and queens, come to mind as people who seem to have it all. If only I could be treated by my partner as a princess or queen. If I only they would treat me as a king of my household we'd get on just fine.

No.

We can't meet each other's desires for respect if we treat each other as royalty.

We meet it by treating each other as human beings, equal in the sight of nature.

How does nature treat us? An ant, bird, tree, or lake doesn't bow down to us according to our gender or social standing—in nature's eyes we are all just human; we eat drink, pee, poop, breathe, and bleed.

Nature doesn't recognize a hierarchy in our relationship and neither should we, not if we want to satisfy each other's need for respect.

Remember, as mentioned previously, this also means we need to respect ourselves. If we don't then we can't make our partner feel respected either.

Recommendations:

Respect yourself, always.

Always treat each other as equals—no one is better, has more power, or is considered more important, than the other.

Never bring anyone down to dominate them. This means never abusing them, demeaning them, or oppressing them in any way.

Always offer each other choices—never demand or expect things to be done when you say so; no orders. This means allowing them to say no without any punishment, look of disappointment, or payback later.

Say a regular please and thank you. Their time is as precious as ours; they deserve thanks for devoting it to helping us.

Share your workloads, don't treat anyone as if you own them (see Appreciated, below).

Never try to change them into who you want them to be. If you can't accept and appreciate them as they are now you shouldn't be together. It is disrespectful to try to change someone else.

If you find you get anxious if you aren't in complete control of events in your relationship or family, seek a qualified therapist for help. Having to be in control just breeds inequality and disrespect. We need more consensus.

Respect is everything in a close friendship.

It is far more than just sharing decisions and the workload. Do you give your partner genuine choice, and say a regular and genuine please and thank you? Do you make sure you respect yourself and ensure you maintain that self-respect? There are no excuses.

Appreciated

Do you like to be treated like a coffee table, or an unpaid, unappreciated, servant? Neither does our partner.

It was mentioned earlier but bears repeating, we often don't appreciate someone until they are gone. In relationships when we take people for granted we ruin the closeness, it is like we turn them into a slave, or part of our regular surroundings. To not appreciate someone also makes them feel not valued, noticed, or respected, but it is easy to do. We are creatures of habit; we only notice significant changes, like hot when it is cold, or loud when it is quiet. This can work against our relationships if we aren't constantly vigilant.

Recommendations:

Work on increasing your appreciation of your partner every day. Imagine what it would be like without them, or with someone much worse.

Thank each other for cooking dinner, putting the kids to bed, taking out the rubbish, or cleaning up after themselves; all the tasks that make our lives together easier.

Never treat what your partner does as simply expected; they aren't your slave, no one is.

Remind each other how much harder or impossible things would be without them—how necessary they are in our lives, how they make a critical difference. This must be genuine, to lie is to disrespect them.

Let them know of the things they do for you that no one could ever replace.

Write a list for each other of what you most appreciate in your partner and share it, such as their warmth, tenderness, imagination, sense of fun, being a great parent etc. Stick it up on a wall, frame it, look at it regularly, especially when you are doing it tough together, that is when we need to be reminded of our appreciation for someone the most.

To be appreciated is to feel special, that we cannot be just swapped over, or replaced by another model. We should work to make our partner feel appreciated regularly.

Cared For

Suppose I walked past you when you were clearly sick; seeming nonplussed about how you felt and whether you were suffering and in pain. Of course, I wouldn't, I'm a doctor, but suppose I wasn't, would you want to know me as a friend? What about a close friend? Caring in relationships matters immensely.

Caring is the cornerstone of friendship and community. But it isn't enough that we say we care, we also must show it.

Caring is a show of love. Don't you like to feel loved?

Recommendations:

Take an interest in your partner's health and wellbeing—ask about it and listen.

Make the time to care for them, especially if they are ill; caring should then be the priority.

Let them know you are there for them, then when they do ask for your help be there.

Ask how you might best help them if they aren't feeling good, don't force your cure on them, that is disrespectful no matter how good your intentions.

Never expect someone to automatically know there is something wrong with you. Even our partners can sometimes be hard to read; we aren't mind readers!

Don't fake illness to try to get your partner to show they care for you, it creates dysfunctional co-dependency.

Caring, like helping people feel supported, should work both ways. We should care for others but also let them care for us, so they gain the pleasure of doing so. We should never fake an illness as this is also a mark of deception and disrespect. It can also lead to us being dependent on each other, feeling obliged that we need to be there. This doesn't create equality in the relationship it creates a savior and a victim. Playing a victim often fosters resentment and anger, obstacles to us being close friends.

I recall a piece of advice a female GP at an educational event said she was once told by her father. It was to not mix up feeling sorry for someone for being in love with them. It is sound advice. It reminds us that a close friendship in a relationship isn't about being someone's therapist, it involves being their companion, an equal who cares. Leave the therapy to the professionals!

Will some of us struggle to care for others, to empathize, or let others care for us?

Sure.

If we had a traumatic childhood, for example, we could have learnt to survive emotionally by learning to switch off our feelings; it is better than suffering the pain. This can also happen if we are abandoned by others we are close to, such as family, close friends, and other close relationships. We can then feel scared to care, or not want to as a way to avoid the fear and pain of future disappointment we are sure will happen. If we find we don't care for anyone, want to, but find we can't then we should seek professional help. If we don't we may find helping our partner to feel cared for very difficult or next to impossible.

Practice meeting the Ten Desires regularly, as we did when we set a schedule to master them earlier. For example, one week work on satisfying one or two of the desires in your partner the most, such as respect, by offering choices in the chores around the house, ask them if they would like to help then just move on if they say no. Offer choices in meals, date locations—let them decide—offer them a drink if you are getting one, and always say a genuine please and thank you. See how, over one or two weeks, you can perfect making them feel like a respected equal. Do it longer if you feel it is needed. If you find your partner isn't meeting certain needs for you then focus on meeting them in them first. Put up a list of the Ten Desires in the house as a reminder of what you are trying to achieve; your partner may be curious and ask what these are about, giving you the opportunity to discuss them and work to meet the Ten Desires together. It is much easier to be close friends if we are working from the same page.

Practicing meeting the Ten Desires with your partner helps you become closer, mutually attractive, friends.

Using the Ten Desires can do wonders for your relationship and close friendship. It can also play an integral part in repairing it when it is broken.

Suppose we or our partner are thinking of leaving; it is all too hard. Perhaps we hate what our relationship has become; the constant fighting, the horrible silences, the meanness, and want to improve or restore what we once had. What do we do?

We use friendship as part of an overall approach that ensures our needs get met; we help to ensure we grow closer together in a lastingly satisfying and meaningful way.

FIXING RELATIONSHIPS WITH FRIENDSHIP

There are three steps we can use to help fix our relationships using the Ten Desires—using friendship. They are not intended to be an all-encompassing or comprehensive set of recommendations as much as an introduction—it would take a book, or books, devoted to fixing relationships to do the topic justice. They are also not intended to replace a good couples therapist (more about that in a moment). The first step is an obvious one; first we have to recognize there is a problem.

THREE STEPS TO FIXING RELATIONSHIPS
STEP 1. Recognize it's Broken

If your tap is leaking that indicates a problem needs to be fixed. If your car is making terrible noises, struggles to start, or shudders when you brake, obviously parts of the car are in need of repair. These are all signs telling us something needs our attention. We can find similar signs in our relationships. What are some of the signs our relationship is either failing, broken, or in need of repair? These six signs of many give us a fair idea:

- long-term unhappiness within the relationship;
- aggression and abuse;
- our partner spends more time away from us than with us;
- we have lost the attraction;
- loneliness has set in;
- we argue, or fight, constantly.

As we noted, when our needs aren't being met in a relationship we won't be happy in it, we will feel emotional discomfort or pain indicating something isn't working; something is missing. We aren't talking about being unhappy for an hour, day, or a week, but over months or longer—we can't expect every day to be bliss and genuine smiles; we are allowed our bad days or moments. If the bad days outnumber the good, then that can indicate our relationship is failing. If abuse or aggression have appeared, then respect has been lost and our relationship is definitely faltering. If we prefer to be away from each other than together, and/or lost attraction for each other, and we feel isolated, alone, that our partner doesn't have our back, then we obviously have a relationship in need of repair. Aside from these perhaps one of the clearest signs our relationship is in trouble is in how we argue, disagree, or fight. Yes, couples disagree, they are supposed to if they are to remain individuals; to maintain a sense of self—Personal Self. However, how we do it is very telling, especially in terms of our friendship.

Using friendship as a way to improve relationships has already been well studied. For example, John M Gottman, professor emeritus in psychology, and his wife Julie have been filming and analyzing couples arguing for over 40 years and developed a friendship-focused solutions approach. Their work is well published and recognized; good evidence their approach has proven benefit. In the book, *The Seven Principles for Making Marriage Work* (Orion Publishing, 2000), John M Gottman co-authored with Nan Silver, they recognize six signs in an argument that can accurately predict marital demise: 'harsh start up', 'the four horsemen', 'flooding', 'body language', 'failed repair attempts', and 'bad memories'. As they point out, the outcome of a discussion is determined 96% of the time in the first three minutes of a 15-minute conversation. So, if it starts badly—a harsh start up—and we go in aggressively or on the attack, the outcomes won't be good. Similarly, there can be so many problems in our relationship it overwhelms us—flooding—which can easily lead to avoiding dealing with the issues—a trait to which men are especially susceptible. If we are all hyped up, adrenaline is racing, we are in fight or flight mode—physically alert to the max and can't settle down, waiting for an attack—our body language will indicate this and isn't a good sign. Who wants to solve a problem with someone behaving as a potential enemy who might attack us at any time? And if we can't repair the problems we know need fixing in our discussions or get so negative with our relationship even our memories together look bad then our relationship has real problems. However, in terms of the Ten Desires, the four horsemen are worthy of special attention.

What are the four horsemen?

They are named after the Four Horsemen of the apocalypse in the Bible and include: criticism, contempt, defensiveness, and stone walling. Consider them a moment in terms of what they can tell us about the Ten Desires.

Criticism is regarded as a broad attack on character and personality. 'I'm really angry you forgot to take out the garbage last night, again!', versus 'You just don't care; you're useless; you never do anything to help around the house!' The latter being a broader 'criticism'. From the perspective of the Ten Desires this immediately reflects a severe lack of respect and appreciation. But it also reflects a lack of feeling heard, valued and validated, supported, appreciated, and cared for. If we regularly expressed how we felt, in a respectful, non-judgmental, way, clearly indicating we cared for our partner and supported them, would they really have reason to attack us with such a broad brush?

Similarly, with contempt. Here we hold and accumulate long-fuelled negative thoughts about our partner, about being fed up with what they do or say. As an act, contempt demeans our partner. Such as, 'So you think running to the bathroom rather than helping will cure the problem?' Cynicism and sarcasm are both types of contempt and this question has both. If we spent the time listening, showing we cared, appreciated, and validated our partner's concerns, and respected them as an equal, a valuable person in our life, would we really want to hurt them by showing contempt or our disgust? At least half of the Ten Desires aren't being met for us when our partner shows contempt.

When we get attacked by our partner we naturally defend ourselves. Research indicates this can work against us thanks to us saying—in effect—the problems isn't us, it's you. It is also a sign of weakness and will bring on more attacks. For example, 'When haven't I mowed the lawn when you told me? Of course, I do.' It puts us on the back foot, admitting then protecting our perceived fault. This, again, immediately reflects a huge lack of respect. To act like a victim is to behave as an inferior, like we are living in a hierarchy and trying to defend our position. If we listened, validated, and empathized more, we wouldn't need to feel defensive from the start; we'd sort out our problems much earlier as equals. Defensiveness is a clear indicator many of the Ten Desires aren't being met. Then we have the worst of them all: stonewalling.

We all know this one. This is when we tune out, don't pay attention, or just don't engage; no discussion, nothing—acting like a stone wall. We often know it as 'the silent treatment'. It usually arrives later in our relationships, after the first three horsemen. It is a particularly bad sign. In terms of the Ten Desires it is by far the worst. To stonewall is to not meet ANY of the Ten Desires; how can we satisfy any desires if we are doing an imitation of bricks and concrete?

How we argue or disagree speaks volumes as to the level of the closeness of our friendship. The Four Horsemen are sure indicators our relationship is heading for the rocks. They clearly indicate the Ten Desires are being cast aside and the relationship is in need of major repairs.

If we aren't disagreeing in a way we are still close, or closer, friends at the end of it, if we can't put it behind us and still be close, then we know our relationship—and friendship—has significant problems.

Now consider your relationship. Do you feel lonely, unattractive, unhappy for months or more, are you the perpetrator or victim of abuse and aggression? Does your partner want to be away from you more than with you? Do they prefer to be at the office, for example? Do you start your arguments or discussions harshly, go in for the attack? Are you guilty of criticism, contempt, flooding, negative body language, being stuck in bad memories, of failing to fix the issues or problems you both try to sort out? Are you guilty of stonewalling?

The first step to fixing a problem requires we recognize it. The six signs can help us see our relationship definitely has a problem. It should be pointed out, just because we have one or more of the six signs doesn't mean our relationship is over, just that we need to work at it, taking us to Step 2.

STEP 2. Stepping Up

I have had many people present to me with marriage or relationship problems complaining it is all their partner's fault, 'If only they'd make the effort, if only they would listen, if only they were more decisive, and would stop trying to change me! Even taking out the garbage would be good!' So, when it comes to saving the relationship they would often ask, 'Why should I have to do all the work?' You don't. But when it comes to relationships if we each blame each other, if we each continue to place the burden on the other person to change, what chance do we have things will substantially improve?

Buckley's!

The Ten Desires are our wakeup call.

As we noted from the outset, the Ten Desires work properly by us satisfying them *in others*, not by us trying to force, or coerce others to meet them for us. They require *us* to be the example. They require *us* to step up. That means stop blaming and start changing—us.

I get it, we shouldn't have to do the majority of the work to save our relationship. But if it is worth saving is it really worth wasting our time and energy on focusing on the anger and blame?

Until we give up punishing our partner, trying to get them to constantly change and be the example ourselves, we can expect more of the same discontent we have suffered already.

Would it be better if both were working to meet the Ten Desires for each other together?

Ideally, yes, of course. And ideally, if we need it, we could do well to seek out a good couples' therapist—see below. However, that might not happen, and we can't expect it to. I have met several couples where the other partner is so overwhelmed by the relationship problems and fears—flooding—they feel incapable of wanting to participate. Many don't think there is a problem. Over time, as we show more respect, care, value, and appreciation, they too can come on board, often simply by mimicking what we do thanks to our common desire for sameness; we are more likely to do it if someone else does it too.

When we stop acting like their enemy and more like a friend they will start treating us like one.

Saving and improving a relationship begins by us proudly, and strongly, taking the lead.

STEP 3. Fill the Holes

Fixing a relationship requires a holistic approach; we don't just work to fix the friendship, we fix ourselves and the priorities that let it get this way. No point filling the leaking holes in a water tank if we keep drilling new ones. Filling the holes means:

- improving Personal and Community Self;
- prioritizing friendship—countering our inner beast;
- satisfying the Ten Desires.

When a relationship is failing it is important to remember it wasn't just the lack of friendship that led us here. For example, if we had a strong sense of self—Personal Self—we'd have maintained our self-respect and self-worth and demanded more of ourselves and the relationship; we wouldn't have taken so much crap for so long and let the relationship fall to its current state. It would have also meant we'd stayed more attractive. If we didn't let ourselves be isolated we'd have more friends to offer advice and support so we didn't only share our burdens with our partner and overwhelm them. Or we wouldn't have let ourselves feel trapped; too scared or insecure to leave because we didn't have anywhere else to go—because we had a low Community Self.

Fixing any relationship isn't just about fixing the relationship itself, it is about repairing ourselves and what is out of balance in our lives (see The Balance of Self Model, page 6).

Increasing our Personal and Community Self should be a priority, as mentioned previously. But we also need to counter the desires of our inner beast if our relationships are to have any chance at long-term success.

As we have seen, we live in societies almost completely dominated by our desires for wealth, power, and status. While they remain so strong, we can expect them to continually work to tear our relationships apart; ruin our friendship. We have seen how it can affect gender roles and negatively impact on women, but it can do so much more. For instance, we could work on satisfying feeling valued, try to find more time together, but if we continue to prioritize that bigger mortgage and we need to slave longer hours to get it, good luck finding, and keeping, sufficient time together to feel special, valued, validated, cared for, supported, or even appreciated. If our desires for wealth, power, and status remain our priority we will find loads of excuses not to talk, catch up, discuss what is important, have fun time, and just appreciate each other's company.

Fixing and improving a relationship long-term requires we counter the destructive forces of our inner beast. Thus we must put friendship first, or we can expect it to go back to the way it was in no time. The pressures that led to us neglecting our friendship in the first place will see us do it again.

How do we know if we have been letting the desires of our inner beast get in the way of our friendship?

We go back to asking the critical question: am I putting friendship first? (See Chapter 5.) We ask it in every aspect of our life. We face it head on and see just how much our inner beast has contributed to our relationship failing or falling apart. How has your inner beast been getting in the way of your relationship? Has the bigger mortgage and the better car helped keep you apart, has it really been worth your friendship? What about the promotion, being on the road for weeks at a time, or having to move cities or overseas to get it?

Until we put friendship first we might as well be swinging that axe at the water tank of our relationship continuing to puncture it with massive holes.

Ok, so we have made friendship our priority, what then?

We look at each of the Ten Desires and see if our needs are being satisfied by our partner, and whether we are satisfying them properly for them.

Try the following exercise.

Consider the list of Ten Desires below and the two columns. What I would like you to do is tick each box in the 'Met for You' column where your partner meets that need well—you feel satisfied in that area. Mark a cross where they don't. In the column marked 'Met for your Partner' do the same, tick the ones you feel you satisfy for them and which you feel you don't. For instance, if your partner makes you feel heard, they listen and you feel they understand where you are coming from, then tick the box in the column 'Met for You'. If you think you do a good job meeting this for your partner tick the box in the column 'Met for Partner', and so on. Try not to think about it, answer your best guess straight away.

Some clarification. To tick the box for sameness doesn't mean we have to feel perfectly alike, just that we have enough in common to help bring us together; we have similar morals, ethics, beliefs, general likes and dislikes that help us bond. If you think you do put a tick in the corresponding box, if not then a cross.

FRIENDSHIP DESIRE CHECKLIST

FRIENDSHIP DESIRE	MET FOR YOU	MET FOR PARTNER
Valued		
Noticed		
Appreciated		
Heard		
Sameness		
Validated/Approved		
Respected		
Cared for		
Supported		
Protected		

How do the columns compare? Do you think you are doing a great job, but your partner isn't? Actually, any crosses in either column are all holes in our relationship and all indicate they need to be fixed.

What do we do now?

We work to satisfy the missing desire for our partner. By fixing it for them we begin to fix it for ourselves.

Apply the approach we mentioned earlier, spend two weeks trying to meet just one or two of the desires for your partner and try to perfect it before moving on. Then try satisfying another one or two for a couple of weeks and so on. At the end of working on the Ten Desires do it again, and again, if needed. Practice makes perfect. Each time we try to satisfy a desire we will find a new or better way to do it for our partner. For instance, we might find after dinner is the best time to help our partner feel heard and truly listen to them, or straight after work if they want to debrief before dinner, or on weekends alone on a date so you can have a true heart-to-heart. No two people are the same. No two solutions or ways to satisfy the Ten Desires for our partner can be expected to be the same. The more we work to apply the Ten Desires the more we get to intimately know our partner, see them as a friend, and see ways to enhance the friendship.

What if, as we try to build the friendship, we find things we don't like?

That is normal. People rarely like everything about their partner. However, if we focus more on what we have in common, and what we appreciate and value in them and not what we don't, then even the foibles, the imperfections, can be wonderful, a part of the texture of a masterpiece we have grown close to and would never want to give up.

Friends focus more on what they enjoy and gain from each other rather than what they don't.

Focusing on what we have in common brings us closer.

Perhaps we need to alter our expectations too.

It is easy to get frustrated with our partner when they don't satisfy our desires, or we feel it is their fault we are unhappy—don't meet our expectations. Focusing on what we have in common can counter that, so too can altering what we expect. Sometimes we can expect too much, for us to be frustrated means we definitely are; we want our partner to change. But to focus on changing them, as we've noted before, just leads to disrespect. Better to be more realistic of who our partner is—not compare them to some character in a romance novel, or movie, for instance—so we can better accept and learn to appreciate them as they are. The fewer unrealistic expectations we have the less frustrated we become and the easier it is to accept their enjoyable qualities.

Disaster! Suppose you see crosses in every column, what do you do?

Don't panic!

It doesn't mean doom and gloom, it doesn't mean it is impossible to fix them all. It certainly doesn't mean your relationship is over, or not worth saving, or won't improve. Don't give up, don't let yourself be overwhelmed. They say a journey of a thousand miles begins with a single step. Every step we take to fill the gaps in our friendship is one closer to where we want to be.

What if deal breakers are involved? In other words, our partner has crossed the line of what we are prepared to tolerate, like cheating, taking drugs, or abusing us? We will consider such circumstances in a moment.

How long should we give our efforts, how long should we keep trying? **Expect change to take months or more in some cases.**

Remember, the friendly us isn't what our partner is used to, they are waiting for our old self to show up. Until we keep up meeting their friendship needs they may not respond much. Some may respond quickly; we are all different. As to when you actually give up after trying your best that is a decision we each have to make. If we consider it worthwhile would we ever want to throw in the towel? Not likely. That said, I have found many of us know deep in our heart if we should persist. If even just one of us no longer has their heart in working on the relationship—they know in their heart it is over and have emotionally moved on or shut off—then it is often an end-of-days sign. It's already a done deal. Until then, there is hope!

Suppose we aren't getting far, it's becoming too difficult, or things are getting worse, what do we do? Then we seek professional help: couples counseling. One example of the type of couples' counselor worth considering might be Gottman-trained couples therapists.

In 1996 John and Julie Gottman began the Gottman Institute, offering vigorous training to be recognized Gottman Couples Therapists based on their extensive scientific work. In terms of the Ten Desires, they use a friendship-focused method—trying to achieve the same result, close friendship, in a slightly different way than described here. Sometimes it is best to have a professional person we trust to help us; a couples' therapist can be the bridge we need.

It should be pointed out, couples' therapists use many successful approaches. I am not advocating one is better than an another, just recommending we consider one that helps enhance our friendship—this is the focus of my book after all.

So, we've put our relationship on a better course, patched up many of the leaks, and everything looks promising. Job done, right?

If only.

Without added care we could easily, and unwittingly, sabotage the very thing we have labored so hard to build; our friendship can struggle, or worse, our partner may be snatched away from us. It isn't enough we continue to fix our relationships, we also need to make sure we avoid throwing them off a cliff!

AVOIDING THE CLIFF

I recall a radio presenter recently struggling to come to terms with the idea that a close friendship with a member of the opposite sex wasn't very good for relationships. He told me his wife didn't mind that he had close female friends at work. Quite reasonably he asked, why should friendships with the opposite sex be any different to any other? Some patients who listened to the broadcasts told me, 'they just don't get it'; they knew from their own experience friendships with the opposite sex weren't as simple as that. I have had several women tell me they do mind their husbands having close friendships with other women, but they don't want to make a scene, or come across as looking too controlling.

Friendship with the opposite sex can come with a deadly sting in its tail. If we aren't aware of it we can undo all the work of building a close friendship in a flash.

We give the friendship in our relationship its best chance by following just a few basic rules.

RELATIONSHIP FRIENDSHIP RULES

To help the close friendship be, and remain, as good as it can be, remember 'The Three Keeps'.

The Three Keeps of Close Friendship:
- Keep up the maintenance.
- Keep your closeness exclusive.
- Keep the trust and secrets.

Keep up the Maintenance

It is true, with some close friendships we might not talk or see each other for months or years and still feel close the moment we meet. Friendships in relationships, on the whole, are not like this.

Imagine our relationship is the water tank we described a moment ago, only this one is prone to holes and cracks. Yes, we can ignore it, not keep up the maintenance and before we know it we have a leaking sieve.

A close friendship is not some medal of achievement we pin on each other's chests, or diploma on a wall, it is a long-term commitment.

I've met many parents who tell me they haven't had a night out together, alone as a couple without the kids, for at least four or more years! It's like the kids arrive and suddenly the friendship is taken for granted yet expected to thrive. That isn't how it works. If we don't put the time and effort into our friendships—the maintenance—of the type we did earlier as a couple, when we were still getting to know each other, then the friendship is going to suffer; holes and cracks will appear. Friendship needs good maintenance.

Meeting the Ten Desires is a commitment to satisfy these needs for each other every day.

It is being vigilant for the holes and cracks, the flaws in our friendship and relationship, and noticing them early then working on a fix. Prevention is better than a cure. Maintenance is better than a horrible break up, families being torn apart, and taking each other to court.

Keep Your Closeness Exclusive

Suppose you had a meal after work and forgot your partner had prepared one. You get home, but you are now not hungry. Would you want to eat the lovely meal they prepared? Well, we might like to as a show of appreciation, but we just aren't hungry anymore; our partner can no longer satisfy that desire for us. It is similar with the Ten Desires.

If a person of the opposite sex—other than our partner—is meeting one or more of the Ten Desires, it then satisfies that desire for us, meaning our partner no longer can.

The fewer of the Ten Desires our partner can satisfy the less close our friendship, and the less stable and satisfying the relationship. If the other person meets more of the Ten Desires than our partner does, then we can be tempted to leave and make the person who meets these needs our new partner.

I get it, this is not what many of us want to hear. With friendships so scarce, these days we can be drawn to find good friends wherever we can regardless of gender. We can be especially upset if anyone even hinted we should end them. But these rules aren't randomly made up, these are how nature created us. Nature made us to have a close friendship—as opposed to a casual friendship—with only one member of the opposite sex, and here is why.

Nature needs us to develop a bond so close to our partner they will never leave; a bond stronger than reinforced steel.

Why? Because our children survive better in the natural world with two parents, not one. If we don't stay together we threaten the children's chances. How can we create such a powerful and lasting bond? Well, sex won't do it; we can find someone else we are sexually attracted to very easily and be off in a shot. Looks won't cut it either; we can always find someone else who looks better too, and looks often fade, we might switch to a younger model before the children can make it on their own.

That leaves close friendship.

If we develop a really close friendship, and maintain it, then no matter how sexy or good looking the other people around us are we will not want to threaten something so close and unique as the bond we share with our partner. If we start to develop close friendships with any and every other member of the opposite sex we threaten the closeness and stability of our relationship.

I have seen it happen many times, perhaps you have too. The classic story is the husband spends long hours at work and develops a close friendship with a female member of staff. Since so little time is spent on the friendship with their partner their relationship becomes less close and falters. Then the other person steps in. It can even happen over the internet.

When we let other people of the opposite sex become close friends—as opposed to casual or professional casual friends—then we threaten the closeness, satisfaction, and stability of our relationship.

To help keep the closeness exclusive remember 'The Three Nevers'.

THREE NEVERS OF FRIENDSHIP WITH THE OPPOSITE SEX

- NEVER share what is emotionally important to you with a member of the opposite sex who isn't your partner, or you don't want to be your partner; share it with a same sex friend instead.

- NEVER share intimate secrets with a member of the opposite sex who isn't your partner and you don't want to be your partner. Share with a same sex friend instead.

- NEVER try to have your relationship needs met with someone of the opposite sex outside your relationship. You may as well throw your relationship into an incinerator.

It isn't like men and women can't be friends outside relationships, nor that we shouldn't be friendly, the problem comes when we cross the line by sharing what is emotionally important to us and what would help us bond closely with our partner. These are secrets we should share only with them.

Keep the friendship with your partner—or the person you want to be your partner—close. Keep all other friendships with the opposite sex distant, casual at best.

Keep the Trust and Secrets

It doesn't matter how much we meet each other's Ten Desires, if we break our partner's trust then we may never be close friends ever again.

We've mentioned it before; the brain is the great generalizer.

A breach of trust leaves a lingering doubt that festers and threatens our relationship.

If they did it once we immediately start thinking, they could do it again.

Some couples seem to deal with a breach of trust—such as infidelity or disclosing a deep secret—better than others. There can be many reasons we might give it a second try. But restoring trust is a bit like un-breaking an antique vase, we might patch it up, but it will never be as valuable as it was.

How might we restore trust if it is broken?

We can begin by creating a new history—making sure we do what we say and offer complete disclosure—no secrets. The more we do what we say the more we prove we are true to our word. If we do that long enough significant trust may be restored. If we don't do what we say—such as lie—then restoring trust and closeness is impossible.

Better still, never breach our partner's trust in the first place.

With regards to secrets, every secret we share only with each other helps bring us closer. There should never be secrets about illegal matters as to share such a secret indicates lack of care and respect. No matter how much we try to meet the Ten Desires for each other, to disclose a mutual secret of the relationship with someone outside it will still destroy the closeness.

What do we do if our partner has crossed the line we warned them never to cross, such as having an affair, or a deal breaker shows up we just can't tolerate, such as alcoholism, drug addiction, pornography or sex addiction, or regular lying? That is a personal choice that needs to be considered carefully, taking into account the reasons why and the implications for the relationship and any family involved. If children are caught up, we might be more likely to give our relationship and friendship more of a try. If not, we might just call it quits there and then. After all, if our friendship was close we, as a couple, would have worked to sort out our problems before one of us crossed the line. The fact the line has been crossed already tells us the friendship isn't as great as it could be. Then again, we all make stupid mistakes; do we end a close friendship just because one of us was exceptionally stupid? If in doubt discuss it with a professional therapist so you can properly consider your options and the likely consequences.

When relationships are important then close friendships are too. When close friendships are valued, relationships become powerful ways of experiencing a level of closeness, physically, emotionally, and spiritually, that we will struggle to find elsewhere.

But we need to be vigilant, as inside us, and pressuring us in our communities, are the desires of an inner beast that don't care for any of this. They make us doubt our sexuality and disregard each other. They turn us away from satisfying the basics. Thankfully, the Ten Desires, as part of a holistic approach, can help us counter these anti-relationship forces. Actually, they can help us do much more; make relationships easier and more satisfying before they even start.

FRIENDSHIPS MAKE RELATIONSHIPS STRONGER

Struggling to find 'the one'? Feeling desperate, angry, frustrated, depressed by the whole search? Maybe you've given up, or just accepted you will be single and have decided to make the most of it? You aren't alone. Whereas in 1950 only 22% of adults in the US were single, by 2014 it had jumped to a whopping 50.2%, despite the rise in online dating.[63] Yes, we may be pickier these days, but we are also living lifestyles with priorities that make relationships hard, not just to become close and satisfied, even just to get them up and running. Prioritizing friendship—satisfying the Ten Desires—can turn this around.

Imagine we lived in communities where friendship was a priority and what that might look like. It would mean families and children would regularly meet. We would become a people of shared similar backgrounds, of similar morals, ethics, beliefs, and so would our kids. Because we would talk to each other more and share these ideas and approaches we would be able to share ways to improve them—together. In the process, from a very young age, our children would learn how to be friends; when our community is close and unified children would learn from our example, be prioritized, not feeling left out, isolated, and forgotten. Their better friendship skills will mean they don't need to—or be so driven to—spend all their time on a computer. This would lay the foundations for strong relationships before they even conceive of having one.

Imagine it, learning to meet the Ten Desires before you are ten.

Without any special training, we would have already learnt how to be close in relationships—we would have practiced how to be tuned in with others in our community and within our family. We would learn from our parents the need to prioritize the friendship of our relationship, so we do it automatically on our own when the time comes. Study, having a career, making more money than others, would come second to how we developed friendships among respected, caring, friends; the opposite of what I was taught. Simply putting friendship first would also see us create a larger network of potential compatible partners and better opportunities to meet.

Meeting socially in groups is important when friendship is prioritized. Gatherings, festivals, celebrations, dances, telling tales can all bring us together like the Sundance ceremony did for the North American Lakota.

For the Lakota, ceremonies involving songs, dances, dressing in finery, telling of stories, connecting people to the land, animals, and others, played an integral part of their social life.[64] Ceremonies were held for all main events of life from birth, to consecration of service, to celebration of victory, though less attention was paid to war in these ceremonies than other parts of life.[65] Regarded as the greatest of all ceremonies was the

Sun Dance, a time when the Holy Woman, regarded as an emissary from Those Above, would spend ten days and ten nights declaring the laws and ethics by which Lakota would live. The four most important, she would shout: 'You shall not kill! You shall not lie! You shall not steal! You shall not commit adultery!' Great singing and dancing would be part of the ritual of the ceremony and bring people together, to mingle, be friends, and get to know each other. Regular social gatherings such as these made it easier to find a future partner. It was similar in Australia.

Indigenous Australian people would regularly gather and dress up, sing, dance, share stories, and connect with the animals, land, and each other through the Corroboree. Hundreds of people may be involved for specific sacred dances,[66] or just a few, teaching law, history, and ways of living. It too would be a wonderful way to meet future partners, through ceremonies that increased social connection and a bond with the land. When friendship is important social gatherings involving songs, dancing, self-expression, bonding, teaching law, history, and how to get along with each other and the world become wonderful opportunities to meet a partner we could share a deep and satisfying relationship with for life.

Just working together as a community on community projects can bring us all closer. We may already know our future partner very young and not know it yet, have played with them as children, known them or their family as we met and worked together as families, then finally realize our attraction for one another when the hormones kick in. Gone is the long and desperate searching, checking people's interests, having to go over a person's dreams and intentions with a fine-tooth comb to weed out the deal breakers; we are already set up to meet a compatible partner—they are nearby, ready for us to find each other. Then once we meet them we are already well versed in how to create the essential close friendship bond—we have had practice already.

If a close friendship is universally respected and highly regarded as pivotal to the stability and satisfaction of our relationships in our community then trust rises.

Yes, we might get the hots for someone else, but we'd recognize it for what it is, lust, without soul or the promise of compatibility—we would more easily dismiss it. When friendship is our priority there will be less infidelity, less trying to use sex as a way to improve our self-esteem or as a means to show how powerful we are, and less of it as a way to have our needs met elsewhere—they already will be better met. Our whole way of life becomes focused around building closer, stable, and more satisfying relationships—not threatening them, as it is now. We have much less reason to be worried about divorce, separation, and its effects on the kids. We can create the strong foundation of a stable and functional family and our children will be well adjusted—not traumatized by the separation—and more easily learn how to be the adults our community needs them to be.

It sounds ideal, doesn't it? Yet that is close to how it used to be.

When we were tribal, before we were farmers, we were already members of a close social group that valued friendship. We shared the same morals, beliefs, and ethics. We knew how to treat each other in relationships and our gender/relationship role. Yes, there would have been disagreements, even infidelities at times, but these would have been sorted out within a society built around unity not division, consensus not dictatorship, a society that needed to be a close community to survive.

Our relationships were made for close communities, to be among friends.

Sadly, today we seem to treat relationships as incidental; they will just happen and be great. The statistics, as we have seen, and our personal experiences, suggest otherwise. We have, without knowing or wanting to recognize it, been blocking and preventing our own relationship success at every turn. We have chosen to put friendship last and this has had far reaching consequences.

How do we make relationships the easiest they can be, at every stage, so loneliness can be rare; a thing of the past?

Perhaps it is as simple as prioritizing friendship and learning to continue to perfect how we satisfy the Ten Desires. Perhaps we need to learn to return to fulfilling the basics we know we have been neglecting for a very long time.

It is easy to get confused by all the advice out there about how to improve relationships. It is also easy to lose hope. Our inner beast has contributed to ruining our relationships and damaging them—just as it has everything else—making our relationships much harder and more unsatisfying than they need to be. The way we fix and transform them, make them better and easier at every turn, is by simply focusing on the basics. A crucial part of getting the basics right is prioritizing friendship and satisfying our Ten Desires whilst taking into account our gender differences. The key is to simply return to being true to ourself as a balanced human being; to being human.

KEY POINTS

- We should all be equally respected, appreciated, and cared for.
- Nature doesn't recognize a hierarchy in our relationship and neither should we, not if we want to satisfy each other's need for respect.
- Before we satisfy our partner's need for respect we need to respect ourselves.
- We are creatures of habit who only notice significant changes, like hot when it is cold, or loud when it is quiet. This can work against our relationships if we aren't constantly vigilant. We should work to increase appreciation for our partner every day.
- Caring should work both ways; we should care for others and let them care for us.
- **Three Steps to Fixing Relationships with Friendships:**
  - Step 1. Recognize it is broken—acknowledge the signs.
  - Step 2. Step up—be the example.
  - Step 3. Fill the holes—don't fix just the relationship, but also your life and priorities.

- **Three Keeps of Close Friendship:**
  - Keep up the maintenance—commit to meeting the Ten Desires in your partner every day.
  - Keep your closeness exclusive—follow The Three Nevers.
  - Keep the trust and secrets—breach your partner's trust or secrets and risk never being close friends again.
- Our relationships were made for close communities, to be among friends.
- We can fix and transform our relationships by simply focusing on the basics.

CHAPTER 9

Friendship, Better Pay, Jobs, Businesses, and Global Stability

A FRIENDSHIP FOUNDED ON BUSINESS IS BETTER THAN A BUSINESS FOUNDED ON FRIENDSHIP.

—*John D Rockefeller*

Struggling to make ends meet Zaida Ramos went from one short-term New York office job to the next claiming she was 'barely able to make enough in one week to satisfy what her family spent in a day'. When she joined Cooperative Home Care Associates she found a steady income, flexible hours, health and dental insurance, an active role in the business, and financial independence. It lifted her family out of poverty. It also helped her local community.

When Fritz Sennheiser founded his specialized German audio company, Sennheiser, in 1945 he believed 'that we should only spend the money we have earned … we try to avoid taking loans'. That idea helped limit exposure to bank financed debt, so the company not only survived the global financial crisis of 2008–09 but rose to become a hidden champion, a leading company in its field on the global stage.

Friendship is already making a positive impact in business, as these two examples highlight. It is helping people out of poverty like Zaida and her family, and businesses become stable, innovative, and adaptable, like Sennheiser; assisting in transforming them into competitive companies able to thrive on the global stage. Friendship offers many practical ways to make businesses successful, supportive of communities, and environmentally friendly, while at the same time offering increased, stable, congenial, meaningful, employment—better paid long-term jobs with better conditions.

Just meeting the Ten Desires in general in business isn't good enough, though.

Like with relationships we need to tweak how we satisfy them or we might destroy our businesses and our chance of better employment rather than increase it. If we satisfy them unprofessionally, for example, we might have to fight off harassment claims for crossing the line, lose client support, or be deregistered for corruption. Satisfying the Ten Desires in a professional way is imperative in business. In a moment we will learn to satisfy the Ten Desires professionally as managers, so we become more effective, get on better with our staff and bosses, and increase our employability and prospects for promotion. We will learn how to satisfy them professionally among work colleagues, so we make our work a better, happier, place to be, reducing infighting and bullying, as well as improving our people skills to further increase our chances of promotion and better pay and conditions; a better job. Then we will learn how to apply them to customers, the essential lifeblood of any business; no customers, no business.

Simply put: friendship sells.

But to think that applying the Ten Desires only has advantages in the workplace would be a big mistake. Friendship and satisfying the Ten Desires can spread positive change via our businesses far more broadly, into our communities and around the world. How? The main way: by containing our inner beast closest to its greatest source of power.

We have seen the unbridled damage from the desires of our inner beast: it automatically creates slavery, exploitation, hatred, prejudice, poverty, and destructive empires—including business empires, and the hybrid/government empires dominating our lives today. Business and commerce are some of the most fertile soils for unshackled desires for wealth, status, and power; they give them strength and nurture them. After all, most business and commerce is founded on competing desires for wealth, status, and power; the powerful desire for profit above all things. The East India Company is a classic example; the misery and death of millions was considered irrelevant so long as the insatiable desires of a few were satisfied.

If we can contain our inner beast in business we can counter all these tendencies at the seat of their greatest power, nip them in the bud before they get out of control. We can prevent the next Bhopal, companies drawing us into wars, taking over our governments, and tearing our communities and world apart. We can prevent the deaths of tens of millions, and us destroying the planet, and ourselves, in the process.

If there is one area where we need friendship more than any other, it is in the companies we create.

It isn't enough we treat each other at work as friends, as we are about to do; applying the Ten Desires to business also means applying them to its structure—who owns them, runs them, how they are run, and how the profits are distributed.

Why is this important?

It is a business's structure that determines how many jobs are created, how well paid the jobs are, the conditions of employment, the stability and long-term success of the business, and whether the business positively contributes to the communities around them or feeds off them like a leech. It also determines their impact on the world. If a business is structured purely for profit, for example, it will be prepared to do whatever environmental damage it can get away with to improve its bottom line (like Bhopal). By applying the Ten Desires to business structure we not only create better businesses we also ensure they help our communities and are less disrespectful of the environment.

This chapter will be broken into two parts. In the first part we will see how friendship and the Ten Desires can be applied to business structure. Even if we aren't a business owner this is still highly relevant to us. Why?

The simple answer is: choice.

When we buy from, work for, or create a business we are supporting that business but also how it treats its staff, its priorities (such as profit ahead of employment and people), and its environmental footprint (how much damage it does to the world and local communities).

By looking at business structures that already exist we can also glean what characteristics of business make them friendship-friendly, better suited to satisfying the Ten Desires. This can help guide us to create friendship-friendly businesses of our own, but also encourage and increase their number by us choosing to buy from and work for those that have these qualities in preference to those that don't. The more friendship-friendly businesses we create and support the more we reap the benefits we have already mentioned, including longer-term better-paid jobs. In the second part we will look at how to satisfy the Ten Desires professionally at work, as managers, workers, and with customers. We will learn, in practical terms, how to make that happen.

It is a shame, but not surprising, nearly all of the business structures we currently use or give preference to lean towards satisfying the desires of our inner beast; they are easily drawn to an anti-friendship focus. We find our greatest hope in the exceptions; profit and greed do not have to dominate economies at the expense of millions of people and the world.

BUSINESS STRUCTURE

Buy clothes or gadgets from a discount department store like Walmart or Kmart, and we have just bought from a typical corporation, a taxable entity that spreads profits among its owners; shareholders and CEOs come first. Have the unfortunate need of a lawyer and we may have just dealt with a Limited Partnership with several owners whose profits are shared among them in preference to, say, their workers. Call in a plumber, electrician, or carpenter, who works for themselves and we have just bought the services of a Sole Proprietorship, where the person who runs the business owns the business and doesn't have to share the profits with anyone, except the tax office, or maybe their husband or wife when they get home. There are many forms of business structure—the list is long—but of them all only two have a strong friendship-friendly focus, putting the needs of their workers, or the community, first.

In other words, only two types of business structure we currently recognize definitively put people ahead of profits; they aren't easily driven and consumed by the desires of our inner beast; wealth, power, and status for a few at the expense of everyone else. They are, non-profit corporations (non-profits) and the co-operative model, or co-ops.

But, I hear some of you say, government-owned businesses aren't driven to make a profit for a few, they work for us, the people, surely that makes them less driven by profit and power? Yes, but many of these jobs are hard to come by, they offer high prestige and often reasonable salary and retirement packages; wealth, status, a foothold into the power of government. This makes it is easy to get stabbed in the back or caught up in workplace bullying as people strive to get to the top. I have seen many patients working for government departments or businesses that have described this. Such entities are structured in ways that make them vulnerable to being consumed by the desires of our inner beast.

Does this mean all businesses that aren't non-profits or co-ops will necessarily be anti-friendship through and through, consumed by our nefarious desires? Not at all, and we will explore an important exception in a moment, one any business seeking to be successful—even globally—can learn from.

How can we be sure non-profits and co-ops are less driven by desires for profit, status, and power? That they are more friendship-friendly?

The non-profits are friendship-friendly almost by definition; their aim isn't profit but some other, often social, benefit. Consider the example of Bright Pink.

Lindsay Avner was just 12 years old when she tragically watched her mother fight ovarian and breast cancer. Knowing that both her grandmother and great-grandmother had also lost their fight with breast cancer before she was even born she underwent genetic testing at 22 years of age. The result was stark; she carried the *BRCA-1* gene giving her an 87% lifetime risk of breast cancer and 54% chance of ovarian cancer. Deciding on a proactive approach to her health, at 23 years of age, Lindsay became the youngest woman in the US to undergo risk reducing double mastectomies. Her experience highlighted a need for a warm and welcoming community that offered education and support, services she'd wished she had during her difficult journey. So, in 2007 she started Bright Pink.[67] Their mission: 'to save women's lives from breast and ovarian cancer by empowering them to live proactively at a young age'.

The fact most non-profits, like Bright Pink, put the needs of people ahead of profit and power alone makes them more friendship-friendly. Does that mean non-profits are the best business structure for meeting the Ten Desires? Unfortunately, not. Consider the example of the Wounded Warrior Project.

Founded in 2003, the non-profit Wounded Warrior Project was created in the United States as a charity to help veterans and service members who suffered physical and mental illness since September 11, 2001. It met a valuable need and touched people's hearts. It became so successful at raising funds that between 2003 and 2016 it raised over a billion dollars, $300 million dollars in 2014 alone.[68] However, in 2014 it also spent $26 million dollars on lavish employee conferences, elaborate events involving lots of alcohol. While other veteran charities had overheads of 10–15% Wounded Warrior Project was spending 40–50% and siphoning money away from the needs of suffering veterans for their own self-indulgence. The abuse of funds eventually saw their top two executives fired in 2016.

Non-profits, by their nature, can attract large amounts of money both publicly and from government, many receiving considerable government support; their tax-free status helps. Not being accountable to shareholders, as many for-profit companies are, can lead to lack of sufficient internal governance and oversight,[69] opening them to theft, fraud, corruption, and abuse of funds. The large wealth alone can act like a bright night light inexorably attracting moths from afar—enticing those driven by desires of our inner beast—to an environment ripe for exploitation. Although, on the whole, non-profits are more friendship-friendly than many other company structures they are far from ideal.

What about the co-operative model, the type that Zaida Ramos worked for, is it inherently friendship-friendly—does it encourage the fulfillment of the Ten Desires, perhaps meet them best?

Co-operatives are a special case worth looking at in greater detail, they have much to teach us about the potential for how businesses can meet friendship needs.

CO-OPERATIVES: FRIENDSHIP-FRIENDLY

What is a co-op? According to the US Small Business Administration (SBA) a co-operative is 'a business or organization owned by and operated for the benefit of those using its services. Profits and earnings generated by the co-operative are distributed among the members, also known as user-owners'.

How are they structured?

Typically, according to the SBA, a co-operative has an elected board of directors and officers who run the co-operative. Members become part of the co-operative by purchasing shares, but unlike in many other companies the number of shares does not affect the weight of their vote—just because you have more shares, or have more money invested, doesn't mean you have more say than any of the other members.

Co-operatives are democratic. They have regular business meetings and all members get a say.

How well do co-ops meet the Ten Desires?

To begin with, people are valued—paid what they are worth and given the time to voice any concerns about the business or the pay structure. They are made to feel heard; management must listen to them; they own the company. They are noticed and not ignored. They are respected, not treated as inferior; their flat hierarchy means people are regarded as equals. They are supported by the company, so it succeeds, and cared for by the company, so its members stay well. The co-op creates a better environment conducive to feeling protected—there is less reason to back-stab or bring someone down to try to get ahead—what is the point in climbing over equals? Their regular meetings and strict internal governance also help prevent abuse of funds such as lavish over spending and fraud found in some non-profits such as the Wounded Warrior Project. At the same time ensuring executives aren't paid exorbitant amounts compared to the wages of other workers as is more common in many other company models. They even help their community.

According to the International Co-operative Alliance (ICA), one of the established Seven Principles of the co-operative is to 'work for sustainable development of communities through policies and programs accepted by the members'. Since creating profit for a few isn't its main aim it can spread its success not only to its members but also into their communities, like Cooperative Home Care Associates did for Zaida, her family and community.

Co-operatives are commonly found in retail, agriculture, restaurants, healthcare, finance, and energy. Internationally, co-operatives are estimated to employ over 280 million people, and according to a 2015 study by the International Co-operative Alliance (ICA) the top 300 largest co-operatives were estimated to have a combined annual income of over US$2.16 trillion dollars, the equivalent of the ninth largest world economy.[70] They are not the current main business structure around the world by any means, but they are playing a significant role in world economies; they have been shown to work.

In summary, co-ops not only create an environment that positively enhances the satisfying of the Ten Desires—making for friendship-friendly focused companies—they also help foster community and corporate responsibility in a way that still makes a handsome profit, whilst at the same time preventing the uncontrolled rise of the desires of our inner beast—they cage our desires for wealth, power, and status within our companies so they don't get out of control and wreak havoc. The result seems clear.

As a business structure co-ops satisfy our Ten Desires best.

Does that mean all businesses must follow the co-operative model for us to have our Ten Desires met?

No. They can be met in all the other business structures, if they are deemed a priority.

For example, any company can create a flat hierarchy where there is less management and more decisions are spread among the workers—creating a greater sense of feeling valued, respected, and heard etc. As we have seen strict hierarchies are not good structures to help meet our friendship needs. Similarly, any company can decide to put the profits back into the company, increase the wages and conditions of its staff to increase their sense of wellbeing and loyalty. All company structures can ensure they pay the tax they should pay to help communities build hospitals, schools, and better roads and public facilities. They don't have to send profits offshore to shell companies, so their company runs at a loss on paper to avoid tax. Or give their executives huge pay rises through share options for the same reason; to avoid paying any tax.

If the will is there to put friendship—people—first all business structures can meet our desires of friendship and still be profitable.

Consider another successful business approach that works to meet many of the Ten Desires. It helped a whole country quickly recover from the global financial crisis (GFC) of 2008 without mass unemployment. It is called Mittelstand.

MITTELSTAND: FRIENDSHIP-FRIENDLY = GLOBAL SUCCESS

Mittelstand are a type of firm or business commonly found in German speaking countries such as Germany, Austria, and Switzerland. The term Mittelstand can be hard to define in English. It is often comprised of small and medium sized enterprises (SMEs) with annual revenues of up to €50 million and maximum of 499 employees. But it is also a term many larger firms like to associate with, having the positive connotations of nimbleness, flexibility, customer focus, innovativeness, social responsibility, a family-like corporate culture, and longer-term policies.[71] In other words, these are businesses with a strong family, worker, customer, and community focus. The specialized German audio company mentioned earlier, Sennheiser, is a classic Mittelstand company.

Mittlestand businesses are supportive of their local communities; most employees live locally. In Germany in 2015 some 71% of Mittelstand businesses were in small towns or cities of populations less than 100,000. Maintaining home-grown employment is a priority. Local businesses educate locals with the expectation of long-term employment. Youth unemployment is around 2.4% in Germany compared to Greece with 44%, Spain 43%, Italy 40%, and the USA with 16.3%.[72] Employment isn't just plentiful it is stable because the companies are stable thanks to a longer-term strategy.

Mittelstand companies seek long-term success not short-term profits as compared to many US companies.

That means when the business suffers a down-turn—like the GFC—it keeps its employees, often by negotiating with them to temporarily reduce hours. This contrasts with selling the business at the slightest downturn or opportunity, so the directors make a huge profit—short-term profits coming at the employee's expense, as regularly happens in the US. Mittelstand companies prefer to 'retain-and-re-invest' rather than 'downsize-and-distribute'. They also don't focus primarily on making a profit for the few.

Between 2003 and 2013, large American firms put 54% of profits into buybacks of their own stocks to increase share price and improve executive profits, 37% went to shareholders, and only 9% back into improving the business. In contrast, large family owned Mittelstand companies invested more into their own companies giving them equity ratios of 43.5%, meaning they were more financially stable, and hence better able to deal with sudden downturns like the GFC—they didn't have massive debts with the banks and have to shut their businesses down.

These are not companies driven by short-term profits at any cost—the desires of our inner beast aren't completely out of control—they have different priorities. A good example of this difference can be found in a quote from Robert Bosch, the founder of the very successful Bosch group: '… I have always acted according to the principle that I would rather lose money than trust. The integrity of my promises, the belief in the value of my products and of my word of honor, have always had a higher priority to me than transitory profit.'[73] Mittelstand companies are driven more by customer and worker loyalty, trust, innovation, and exceptional quality. They also have a flat hierarchy.

Because there is minimum management in Mittelstand companies, more open and direct communication occurs among staff. This allows for early resolution of disputes and disagreements, making for a smoother running company. It also means the staff can feel heard, valued, appreciated, and respected; all very important friendship needs.

These are families and communities working together with a primary aim of ensuring they all have well paid long-term and meaningful work. Their priority isn't short-term profit at the cost of people.

It is interesting to note that as manufacturing is closing in the US it is rising in Germany. By meeting many of the Ten Desires these companies have created a stable and powerful economically successful country with a high standard of living and lower unemployment. As we can see, there is more than one way of creating a successful business that still meets our friendship needs.

What does this mean for managers, directors, and owners of companies?

It means they don't need to be scared to choose to structure or restructure their business in a way that better meets friendship needs—our businesses can still be successful and stable—probably more so—if the Ten Desires become more of a focus.

What does it mean for workers?

It means if we are employees it is in our interest to choose to find and support companies that are better structured to meet friendship needs, such as co-operatives, and private and family companies with flat hierarchies that don't put profits ahead of people.

Friendship-friendly businesses can positively change our lives and the world. They can create a world where we can feel more confident, provide for our families and improve our communities. It is in our interest to create and support more of them.

How do we do that?

One way is to consider what characteristics in a business are more conducive to satisfying the Ten Desires, which are friendship focused. Then we can, as mentioned earlier, exercise the power of choice; we can buy from and work for businesses that preference friendship over those that don't, invest in and support them, and even choose to make these characteristics part of our business, helping friendship grow and spread into businesses everywhere.

What friendship focused characteristics should we look for? Consider the following brief recommendations gleaned from the above examples.

FRIENDSHIP-FRIENDLY BUSINESS CHARACTERISTICS
Flat Hierarchies

The more democratic the company the better. Flat hierarchies help us all feel more valued, respected, appreciated, approved, heard, supported, cared for, and protected. They help us feel like we make a real difference and have a real say. They can also increase nimble decision making and help improve innovation and future company development, as they do in Mittelstand companies.

Worker Loyalty

The staff's wellbeing must be a priority. This meets needs to feel cared for, supported, protected, valued, and appreciated, among others. It requires adequate health care, safe work environment, no bullying, being able to negotiate work pay and hours—being flexible—especially if the business demand goes up and down. It means putting in the time and effort to train and employ people with a long-term employment in mind, not dismissing them at the drop of a hat. The business that is friendship focused should work to maintain the loyalty and job satisfaction of its staff.

Customer Loyalty

Building customer trust and loyalty meets the customer's friendship desires for feeling valued, appreciated, noticed, heard, respected, supported and approved. In practice this can mean delivering on promises, keeping customers well informed, involved in future innovation, helping them improve their business (if your customer is another business), providing high quality product, getting regular feedback, working towards creating a long-term—professionally friendly—relationship (more about how to satisfy customers' friendship needs in a moment).

Greater customer loyalty ensures a growing and strong customer base: an assured income.

Shared Values and Goals

Staff working towards shared values and goals satisfies the strong desires of sameness; it unifies using commonality. It also satisfies desires for support, validation, the need to be heard, respected, and to feel valued. In practice this can represent monthly staff meetings informing everyone of current figures, goals, and progress (what has been achieved and our direction). It requires allowing everyone to have a say and share any suggestions. In effect, it is unifying everyone as a team.

Long-term Stability

We have recognized the primary aim of meeting friendship needs is to provide safety and security. Long-term business stability provides increased security of income, lifestyle, and community (social interaction). In practice this means learning from the Mittelstand example and ensuring high company equity to see the business through tough times, reinvesting in the company including in R&D, education of staff, constant innovation, improving staff conditions and pay, as opposed to siphoning profits to executives. It also means never letting outsider interests have a controlling share or interest in the company (outsiders are more likely to be interested in putting profit ahead of meeting friendship needs).

Family Focused

Companies that are family focused create an environment of support, care, protection, respect, validation, appreciation and being noticed. It is about treating staff as we might our family but also being family-friendly.

In practice this can mean having flexible rosters in case parents need to care for their children, creating child supports, organizing social events for all staff as we would a family gathering.

A family focused business is aware of the difficulties of modern family life and seeks to ensure work doesn't interfere with family any more than necessary.

Community Orientated and Environmentally Responsible

Companies that invest in their communities are people-friendly and responsible businesses. They help support communities knowing this makes for happier workers and families and hence staff less likely to get sick or take time off. In practice it can mean paying proper taxes, so the local communities get decent roads, housing, clean water, schools, hospitals, and power supply, or the company can build these for the community. It can mean building community halls for people to regularly meet, and parks and play areas for families. Instead of giving executives great pay rises the money may be given to the workers, so they can work less and have a better family, work, and community-life balance. With more money the locals can then support other local industries and increase local employment. Friendship-friendly companies will be environmentally friendly knowing a clean environment is better for everyone's health and wellbeing.

When desires for wealth, power, and status no longer dominate our businesses their structure and priorities change so we can better meet our Ten Desires at work, at home, and in our community.

Businesses are not islands; they don't exist unto themselves, they exist among people and affect people's lives, communities, and the world.

We choose whether they help improve our life satisfaction through meaningful, stable, people-friendly employment or decrease them through competitive, aggressive, selfishness aimed at satisfying insatiable desires that only ever make us isolated, lonely, and unfulfilled.

What type of businesses do you support? How many of the friendship focused characteristics of business exist in the businesses you buy from or work for? How many of them exist in the companies you have bought shares in? Choice is powerful. Every day, whether we are aware of it or not, we are determining if friendship becomes a priority in business and whether it improves all our lives or makes them harder and worse.

Ok, so we work for business that is more friendship-friendly, or maybe we just work for anyone who might employ us, what now?

We bring the Ten Desires down to the coal-face, onto the work floor; among the day-to-day interactions of people. We bring friendship and a better work environment to our working lives. Here we apply the Ten Desires in personal, simple, and practical terms.

Improving Work Environment

I have counseled many people about work related troubles over the years. Their complaints were all too common: victimization, being excluded, treated like property, disregarded, and undervalued like slaves. Some were in middle management, most were workers with families and expensive bills to pay. A few would talk of inspiring bosses who would always make time for them and listen, treat them with respect and dignity. Many described managers who didn't have a clue of the destruction they were causing. Whether we are workers on a factory floor, behind a computer, cleaning rooms, or in customer service, or managers, owners, or directors, learning how to apply the Ten Desires can help us get along and create a better, friendlier, effective workplace.

Key to applying the Ten Desires at work: aim to create casual friendships, not try to be close friends.

This means working to meet these needs in others as best we can but without the expectation of developing a close bond. Workplaces often contain people from many walks of life, it is unreasonable to believe we can all be close, especially in larger businesses or departments. What is reasonable, and achievable, is that all people will work to make others feel valued, appreciated, noticed, respected and so on. Ideally, we should aim to do it without being emotionally involved; being professional.

Whether we are a doctor, lawyer, dentist, nurse, CEO, manager, laborer, or general worker getting emotionally involved at work comes with consequences. For some it might mean being seen as too friendly, our intentions are misunderstood, or result in an affair that ruins our relationship (see The Three Nevers, page 164). For others it can mean letting our emotions influence our decisions. It is one of the reasons it is unethical for doctors, for instance, to treat members of their families; making the best decisions when we have so much emotional skin in the game is hard if not impossible. When it comes to satisfying friendship needs at work keeping it professional is often best.

There should definitely be no signs of favoritism.

Suppose we treat our spouse, sister, brother, uncle, father, or close friend at work differently by meeting more of the Ten Desires for them, for example, than other staff. This creates a hierarchy and makes others feel less valued, respected, noticed, appreciated, supported, and validated by comparison. Our family or best friend might feel great with us at work, but other staff can easily have a problem with us. This isn't good for unity and mutual support; for us working as a coordinated team. Our aim is to be impartial at work—even among relatives, or close friends—so everyone's friendship needs are met more fully and equally.

Below are suggestions of how we can do it as managers, workers, and with customers. All of us can learn something personally from each of them; they all have ways of satisfying the Ten Desires in a practical way we can apply at work. It can also help us as customers, allowing us to give feedback to the businesses we buy from so they can better meet friendship needs. Compare with your workplace, or the businesses, workers, and managers, you deal with and see how many, or how well, they satisfy these needs for you.

THE TEN DESIRES FOR MANAGERS
Valued

Making time and being on time are essential.

A manager or boss can help their staff feel valued by setting up regular one-on-one meetings. Then make sure the employee/staff member can have their say and share their concerns. Be on time to meetings and calls; being late indicates the other person isn't important. Always follow through on promises or commitments. Help staff feel valued by asking for their opinions and taking them seriously.

Noticed

Never ignore staff. Try to remember them by name and say hello when you pass them; this helps them feel valued and respected. Be careful not to breach cultural expectations. For instance, don't look them in the eye if it is not culturally acceptable. If they want to talk and you don't have time set up a meeting and keep it.

Appreciated

Remind people of how indispensable they are and that you are glad you are working with them. Let them know you trust them with this special project, assignment, or task. Avoid micromanaging them. Praise others for their work and effort, never tell them they are all hopeless, or useless. I recall a patient's story about how the company owner where he worked would bring everyone down, leaving staff on edge in fear of dismissal; he would regularly tell them they were all hopeless and he should just fire and replace them. This reduced productivity and left many people highly anxious and on sick leave, like the patient. Let staff know you have noticed their contribution and value it. Be especially appreciative of any assistance or help. Never take it for granted.

Heard

Take the time to listen. Practice active listening. Don't interrupt others until they have finished. Help them feel clear that you have understood what they have said. Ask questions to clarify, try to empathize and convey you would feel similarly if it was happening to you. Show an interest. Never dismiss someone while they are talking. If you can't listen now arrange another time so you can. Never talk to them while looking at a phone or computer screen; eye to eye contact is a must.

Sameness

Create group meetings so you can share common goals and direction. To help others feel comfortable around you engage in small talk such as the weather, the weekend, watching sport etc; things with which they will relate. Try not to fake it, people often tell. Talk about what you have in common, NEVER about any differences. You don't have to keep the small talk going for too long just long enough to indicate similarity. When you meet someone for the first time always look for similarities; something common in everyone. Common uniforms or dress codes can help create a sense of sameness, so too insignia; a mark we are a valuable member of the same team.

Validated/Approved

We all like others to agree with us, so do it where you can. If you like an idea, or a way a person does something, let them know. If they have concerns agree they are valid, never dismiss them out of hand. To make it easier to validate others make sure staff have clear job descriptions and then approve of their approach and work. If it isn't going so well, to help show respect, ask them how they might be able to do it better, then agree with their ideas if you think they have merit.

Respected

Respect is key in any business.

Always treat others with the respect of an equal—no matter their pay grade or job, like Nelson Mandela would do. Whenever possible don't order them around; explain the situation and offer them choices instead. Use a genuine please and thank you always. Never, ever, put others down, ignore them, or abuse them verbally, or ostracize them. Never lie or intentionally deceive anyone, that is a sign of gross disrespect and devalues them. Never intentionally embarrass anyone in front of others or set them up to fail. It goes without saying, never steal, that includes ideas of staff and presenting them as your own.

Cared For

Check on staff and pay attention to if they are struggling or in trouble regularly. Ask them if there is a problem and offer genuine assistance. Let them know you won't think any less of them if they divulge their issue or concern; it is better we work together and sort problems out. Keep their problems and issues in confidence, or they'll never confide in you again. Ensure your business or department is a safe and healthy place to work. A no drugs or alcohol approach at work should be mandatory. Not only do they harm us when we abuse them, but they also make work unsafe and inefficient. Many businesses will have random testing. It can show we care about the safety and health of our staff if we have such screening in place.

Supported

Supporting new ideas and innovations whenever possible is good for businesses that want to keep ahead of the rest. Show support by sponsoring people or being their mentor. Help them, where possible, to achieve their goals. If they don't have any goals, within the company or outside it, and feel they want some, help them to find direction, or recommend they seek professional help; if their goals fit in with company goals they will be more motivated. A little support to help a person move forward goes a long way to improve morale and performance.

Protected

Make sure everyone feels safe and secure. Bullying is to be reported and to be taken extremely seriously; never belittled or ignored. Most businesses these days have rules governing behavior, make sure they are enforced. Stand up for your staff and colleagues. The customer is not always right, not if customers abuse or threaten your team. Protected staff are more loyal.

To be able to manage staff well doesn't mean having to be everyone's best buddy, or worst nightmare. We don't need to invite everyone to our daughter's wedding or children's birthdays any more than we need to make them terrified of us through tyranny and abuse. In the end most of us simply want to be treated as if we are valued, appreciated and respected; this helps us work as efficiently and effectively as possible.

When managers—even CEOs—begin to perfect being professional friends then this can trickle down into every department and throughout the business proper—businesses reflect the priorities and behaviors of management.

If we want friendship-friendly businesses we'd do well to begin by ensuring all managers know how to professionally meet their staff's Ten Desires. We can put it in their job description if we must. How they actually apply it will be different with every manager and their circumstance; we all have our own style, priorities, specialties, and experiences to guide us; we are all unique, and how we satisfy the Ten Desires at work can expect to have its unique flavor too.

Of course, not everyone at work is going to need to manage others, have people that answer to them. Most of us will be workers. Here we can satisfy the desires in a similar way to make work a better place for all of us and potentially improve our promotion prospects.

THE TEN DESIRES FOR WORKERS
Valued

Being on time and doing what we said we will do is paramount for any worker, as it is for any friend. Never commit to a job and time to complete it if you know you can't. Be realistic and honest. Make time for other staff if they need it, such as to discuss problems, issues, or concerns. If you can't do it now acknowledge that their concerns are valid and important and make a time to meet. How valued would you feel if no one ever made time for you?

Noticed

We can apply the same recommendations for how to meet the desires to be noticed for managers, above. I know of businesses that make sure each member of staff greets each other as they pass them, usually by name; it is a good habit. No staff member should ever be made to feel excluded from the rest, either at work or socially. Helping people feel noticed, by the way, does not mean humiliating them in public; don't point them out in front of a group if it makes them feel uncomfortable.

Appreciated

Remind others of the good job they are doing and how working with them is a privilege, or honor. List the good qualities in each of them to make it easier to appreciate the people you work with; remind yourself of these qualities every time you are with them. Help others to feel important and indispensable. Welcome them to the team, and support them.

Heard

Engage in active listening, not interrupting them, asking questions to clarify, trying to imagine what you would feel like if you had gone through what they have. Don't let yourself be jealous; share their joy and experience as if it was your own. Practice what we learnt a manager would do to make someone feel heard. Make the time to ensure others feel truly heard. However, talking while working isn't always a good idea; it can be distracting and lead to mistakes. Better to set aside time between shifts or during breaks and help others feel heard then.

Sameness

When with other staff, always focus on what you have in common, NOT your differences. This can include a need to pay bills, take care of a family, or pay for a new holiday. Find a topic you both agree on and share and validate each other's views. Focusing on what we have in common can make others feel at ease.

Validated/Approved

Agree with people when you genuinely can; never lie, that is disrespectful. Approve of how well they are doing their job. Give encouragement. Never dismiss another person's views out of hand, even if you disagree, try to understand the reasons why they see things as they do and agree it is a valid view to take. We can validate each other and still respectfully disagree without trying to change someone else's views.

Respected

Always treat others with the respect of an equal; no matter their pay grade or job. Never order other workers or staff around, ask kindly instead. Always be polite, say please and thank you. Never bully or abuse anyone at work, no matter what they have done; disrespecting them just breeds more disrespect and abuse. Don't disrespect any minority group or people not at work, it only breeds division and lessens other people's respect in you. Others won't want to respect us if we are quick to morally judge, abuse, and punish others—they could be next! Never lie to others at work. And always treat yourself with respect. If you let others abuse you then you can't satisfy their desires for respect (for reasons mentioned previously). Speak to management or HR early to mediate a resolution to any conflicts or abuse if needed.

Cared For

Take an interest and care for those around you as if they are family. Offer assistance—never impose it; that is disrespectful, even if it is done with the best intentions. If people don't want to discuss private matters, respect that choice. Comply with job requirements of drug and alcohol screening; never come to work intoxicated or under a recreational drug's influence. Guide people to professional help if required; you can't be expected to be their doctor, nurse, or therapist.

Supported

Support colleagues around you, offer to help them if they need it. That doesn't mean doing their job for them. Encourage working together as a team to solve problems and issues. Work to unify the group of people around you not divide or fight among each other. Reminding each other we are working towards a common goal—such as the company's success so we have employment—can help unify us (see meeting sameness desires earlier). A common goal creates a sense of sameness around which we can build support.

Protected

We are stronger together. What someone does to one of us they do to all of us. No abuse, bullying, or harm should be allowed to come to any member of staff—to our work family. If we let it happen we are complicit; as if we did it to them ourselves. If we come together to protect each other we all feel safe and belong. We create a safe environment when we ensure everyone—no matter their job or title—feels safe and supported. Always help and protect those we see as most vulnerable. We don't have to like them, just help them feel protected and safe.

Working among people from different backgrounds, morals, and beliefs can be challenging. We smooth the bumps by being professionally friendly with each other; by satisfying just Ten Desires in everyone at work we meet. When we set the example, our colleagues are more likely to follow. Soon we have a happier and friendlier place to work for us all.

Of course, business isn't just about you, the worker, it is also about customers. Businesses can't exist without them. It is up to us to make their experience with us the best it can be.

When the customer is happier we have a job!

Here are some ways we can meet the Ten Desires for customers.

THE TEN DESIRES FOR CUSTOMERS
Valued

Customers feel valued when their time isn't wasted and is treated as precious. So too when a business goes the extra mile. For example, being prompt with service, providing products and services on time, providing a quality product as advertised. Customers feel valued if we put in effort beyond what is expected. For instance, if they are contacted personally—not as part of an automated system—to see if we can improve or help them further. Customers can also feel valued if we keep them up-to-date about new innovations and give them exclusive access. We do NOT make a customer feel valued by ignoring them (see Noticed) or leaving them hanging on the phone while a message says how important they are to our business. How valued do you feel if people ignore you and don't give you their time and effort?

Noticed

Customers should never be ignored, they should be acknowledged immediately, preferably by introducing ourselves. If we can't get to them straight away let them know. How many times have you walked into a store and been ignored, or not had your glass regularly filled with water by a waiter, or worse, left alone while they talk with other staff? Ideally, we should know our customers by name, especially any regulars. Noticing customers in a friendly manner is essential if we are to meet their Ten Desires.

Appreciated

We can help customers feel appreciated by treating them as special, as if they are most important of all and we would miss them—as people—if they left. This can mean giving them special service, gifts, or exclusive access to new products. It can mean special discounts and offers. It can also mean a courtesy call to see if all is well (see Valued). How appreciated do you feel if a business treats you like they don't care if you come back or not?

Heard

We can't help a customer feel heard if we don't listen, empathize with them, and validate their concerns or issues. It means making the time and having enough staff to set aside tasks to actively listen and offer this level of interaction. With so much loneliness in our society, for just one person to listen can make someone want to come back and do business with us above all others. In a time of computers and mobile phones it means making eye contact and never looking at the screen instead of the person. It means not cutting people off mid-sentence, or thinking we know their problem better than they do. We all want to be able to fully air our concerns and have them taken seriously. How do you feel when businesses just won't listen to you?

Sameness

Customers feel satisfied in their desire for sameness when we focus on similarities. This is where small talk can be useful, as mentioned previously. We don't have to ask them about their life—that can come across as prying, or being unprofessional—but we can share what we like in common, like taste in clothes, the weather, sport etc. If they are upset about how they have been treated, we can agree we wouldn't like it either if that happened to us. The more we agree with them the more we indicate we are like them and they feel happier with us.

Validated/Approved

Being honest always and validating a person's concerns helps them feel validated or approved. When they complain, begin by agreeing with them and validating their concerns first. This indicates you are on their side. Then negotiate any disputes or disagreements. Trying to prove you are right and they are wrong only shows you aren't empathizing or understanding their point of view and comes across as arrogant, superior, and disrespectful, and doesn't meet the Ten Desires.

Respected

Customers must always be treated as the most respected people. This means they are never abused, tormented, taken advantage of, or dismissed. They are also never spoken down to as if they are inferior no matter how they look, dress, speak, and treated with the same level of respect whether they are male or female. Some customers like to be treated as if they are royalty. It is up to staff to determine if this is the level of respect they wish to show, but by accommodating them it is important to realize you risk lowering the respect the customer has for you. If they see themselves as superior you will not be able to satisfy their desire for respect, only a higher person in the company will. Customers should never be allowed to disrespect staff. Firstly, no staff member deserves it. Secondly, they won't feel respected by someone who doesn't show they respect themselves by standing up for themselves, politely. If you find it helpful, role play how to deal with difficult and challenging customers who are not respectful and cross the line.

Choice also indicates respect; it is worthwhile offering customers options and choices whenever possible, better quality with higher price, for example, versus lower quality but lower price; the cheaper or more expensive options. Too many choices can be too confusing, just two or three can be good.

Cared For

Show a genuine interest and care for your customers and they care for you and develop a loyalty towards you. We don't need to pry as much as show we hope they are well and stay well. We can show genuine concern if they are sick or if a member of their family is unwell. Showing we care to a customer is a show of good will. If a company displays this level of care, it can create a very personal—though professional—strong bond with the client.

Supported

Supporting a customer is about helping them get what they want, not what we think they should have or need. It requires good listening (see

Heard) so we are clear about their expectations and desires. It requires satisfying all the other Ten Desires mentioned, especially respect, validation, and appreciation. If we, as a service provider, can help the customer achieve their objectives or exceed them we become a valuable ally and worthy long-term partner; see the Mittelstand companies example.

Protected

Helping customers feel protected is about ensuring they keep safe—that our products are not harmful, or any risks or potential dangers are explained—like how to operate machinery, for example. It also means keeping their information confidential and safe. In practical terms, it means not sharing details about a client with another client or anyone who doesn't need to know. In an age of cybercrime, it also means keeping all data about customers as secure as possible.

There are many ways to meet the Ten Desires in our customers; these are just a few suggestions. The bottom line is simple and worth repeating:
  We buy from friends not enemies.
  By meeting their Ten Desires we come across as being on the customer's side and working in their interest; as if we are part of their tribe. The more trusted, honest, and personable the relationship we have with our customers, the more we will attract and the longer we will keep them—the greater the customer loyalty. If we make getting money from them our primary aim our customers have no personal reasons to deal with us over someone else, so we can easily lose our customer base.
  It is important to recognize this chapter is only an overview with some general recommendations to apply to three different areas of business. To work properly will require adapting the principles and suggestions to each individual's business circumstance. That said, the general aim of satisfying each of these desires—in a professional way—should still remain our primary focus. How we actually do that we can adapt and fine-tune. To help apply the Ten Desires to every aspect of a business I'd recommend the following.

FORTIFYING THE TEN DESIRES IN YOUR BUSINESS

Print a list—or lists—of the Ten Desires and place it/them in prominent places around the office or workplace. Frame them.

Integrate meeting the Ten Desires as part of job outlines or descriptions.

Make meeting the Ten Desires part of the company objectives, business code, or company policy. Advertising these standards and objectives could be a useful way to gain more customers; it lets them know people come first.

Have regular staff meetings so recommendations can be made as to how to better meet the Ten Desires among colleagues, customers, and management.

Spread the idea of the Ten Desires among colleagues and management for them to consider if it isn't already policy. Sell the positives of how it will help the bottom line; most businesses will respond to that.

Set a timetable that focuses on meeting one of the Ten Desires for that week, so everyone can practice it—such as this week we will focus on noticing each other better, next week it will be helping each other feel respected, and so on. You can apply this individually yourself, much like we did in Chapter 6.

Remember the Ten Desires every time you buy from, or interact with, a business. If you refuse to do business with a company that doesn't meet these desires explain the reason why, such as an email explaining how you value respect, loyalty, and being heard and how they didn't offer this but might like to in the future, so they can perhaps regain our custom. Perhaps this will create some curiosity, especially if they want your business, so they too will learn how the Ten Desires work.

Imagine if businesses had put friendship first before the GFC of 2008. All companies would have had more capital; less debt exposure to banks. Banks wouldn't have been allowed to take on bad debt—such as from poor folk buying homes they couldn't afford—then selling the debt to put other banks or investment groups at risk. Businesses would have been more stable and employment more secure; like with Mittelstand. In effect, there wouldn't have been a GFC in the first place!

Prioritizing the Ten Desires isn't just good for us personally, or our businesses, it is beneficial to the financial markets, and stability of the world.

Friendship in business makes sense. It promises greater flexibility, innovation, adaptability, stability, and potential global success. It offers a happier and healthier work force—with less stress of internal politics and abuse, more caring and respect, and improved productivity. It promotes loyalty, from our staff—so we don't have to keep trying to replace them—and from our customers so we can build a stable income. It will also garner community support; our community will want to support a company that supports them. It is a win-win-win scenario. The business wins, the workers win, and the community and our families win.

Can we expect resistance to making friendship—and applying the Ten Desires—a priority in business?

Of course.

Let's face it, we are resistant to change, we don't like it; we prefer the familiar, even if it isn't ideal; change is scary. But as we saw at the beginning of this chapter, the Ten Desires are already being used in business, and they have proven to work.

Friendship makes absurd and out-dated the notion that to be successful we must be ruthless in business, need to be a tyrant or dictator to maintain order and company direction, that we need to pay the few directors and owners huge amounts at the expense of the workers and company. Friendship offers us the opportunity to bring commerce out of the age of the dinosaurs and into a new age of hope and prosperity, not just for a few, but for the majority.

It offers us a more equitable way of exchanging goods without the wars, slavery, fear, and hatred that has so far plagued our civilizations.

We live in a time when, as we noted, our wages have stagnated while the rich get pay rises. As we struggle to pay our mortgages, or even daily bills, the solution might seem simple: just get a higher paid job with fewer hours, and be around better people, get a better job.

But why sell ourselves short?

Why not make it all better; the jobs, the conditions, the income, the standard of living, the greater equality, and businesses that work with communities and families and care for our world? Friendship helps us do that.

But why stop there?

Why not also use the Ten Desires to unite communities and restore a sense of community spirit? Wouldn't you like to enjoy the peace and joy of a happier, kinder, neighborhood and suburb? Not have to worry about crime, or walking the streets at night? The Ten Desires can give us strategies to make this happen.

KEY POINTS

- Friendship offers many practical ways to make businesses successful, supportive of communities, environmentally friendly, while offering increased, stable, meaningful, employment; better paid long-term jobs with worker friendly conditions.
- Friendship sells.
- We can apply the principles of the Ten Desires to two main areas of business: business structure and improving the work environment.
- **Business Structure**
    - Only two business structures aren't easily driven or consumed by the desires of our inner beast: non-profit corporations and the co-operative model (co-ops).
    - Co-ops best satisfy our Ten Desires.

- ▸ The Ten Desires can be successfully met in any business structure if they are deemed a priority.
- ▸ An example of a globally successful business structure and approach that puts friendship—people—first is Mittelstand companies.
- ▸ Friendship-friendly companies can positively change our lives and the world. It is in our interest to create and support them by supporting those with friendship-friendly business characteristics, including flat hierarchies, worker and customer loyalty, shared values and goals, long-term stability, family focused, community orientated and environmentally responsible businesses.

- **Improved Work Environment**
  - ▸ When applying the Ten Desires at work remember our aim: to create casual friendships, not try to be close friends.
  - ▸ The Ten Desires can be applied to managers and CEOs. Friendship will then trickle down into every department; businesses reflect the priorities and behaviors of management.
  - ▸ The Ten Desires can be applied to workers to create a professional, supportive, friendly, effective team.
  - ▸ The Ten Desires can be applied to customers to build trust, loyalty, and satisfaction; stabilizing and increasing business.

- Prioritizing the Ten Desires isn't just good for us personally, or our businesses, it is beneficial to the financial markets, and stability of the world.
- Friendship offers us the opportunity to bring commerce out of the age of the dinosaurs and into a new age of hope and prosperity.
- Friendship in business makes sense.

CHAPTER 10

Bringing Back Community

SOCIETY HAS ALWAYS TO DEMAND
A LITTLE MORE FROM HUMAN BEINGS
THAN IT WILL GET IN PRACTICE.

—*George Orwell*

Whatever happened to community spirit?

I am often reminded by some older patients of a time when whole streets of people knew each other in the local suburb of Brisbane where I now work; where children played freely between houses, back yards, parks, and on the streets—they'd be on the lookout for cars. Of whole neighborhoods where neighbors regularly met, talked, and helped each other. Whatever happened to that?

Community spirit came under attack on many fronts. One part of the attack came from what we interact with daily, and many of us can't tear ourselves away from: technology.

Thanks to mobile phones, computers, and the internet we can communicate with people all over the world in seconds, and text or chat with them even at a bus stop. But when it comes to uniting and bringing us together technology is actually making matters worse.

A study by ACEVO, the Association of Chief Executives of Voluntary Organisations based in the UK, in 2016 reported 48% of 18–24 year olds said they often felt lonely. Other studies have confirmed similar results; even though young people are connecting on Facebook, Twitter, or many apps, it hasn't helped them overcome their loneliness—the technology on offer to the most tech savvy generation we have ever known hasn't stopped them feeling alone—why will become more apparent in a moment. When once we used technology, like telephones, to arrange to physically meet, to catch up, talk, and hang out, now we become lonely seeking to be 'noticed' among groups of people—online communities—we never actually meet. We are letting our technology bring us loneliness, we also let it divide us.

Gone are the days when we all read the same newspapers or watched the same TV shows and movies; something we could share in common. Now we watch different news and read from, or join online communities, our neighbors may not, sources of information specifically designed for select groups. A six-year study by the Proceedings of the National Academy of Sciences of the USA in 2016, for example, found if we are Facebook users we will only watch news from a select number of pages, creating an echo chamber reflective of our views.[74] Seeking information to simply validate our opinions rather than share differing points of view leads us to become segregated into smaller, intolerant, and narrow-minded online communities not interested in mixing with anyone who is 'different' to us. We become right-wing or left-wing, conservative or progressive, socialist or capitalist, no longer a community of just human beings. We have let technology drive us to focus on our differences not our commonality. It has become a powerful tool for division. Another source of attack came from us not staying in one area enough.

How many of us work all day then come home and crash? We might have to get the meal ready, put the kids to bed, then just flop in front of the TV or computer. Some of us poor souls get back to work! We work hard, often to have the better house in the better suburb. The fact the average American moves residence 11 times[75] speaks volumes about our priorities, and it isn't connecting with neighbors or building supportive, stable, communities. The almost obsessional focus on our hectic and upwardly mobile lifestyles is clearly driving us apart.

So is hate.

As mentioned earlier, hate crimes are tearing our societies apart. No one should be threatened or killed simply because of their race, color, sexual orientation, or belief yet they continue to be. The scars of slavery still see people discriminated against and oppression, dividing us. We are made to feel scared of minorities rather than welcoming of them. Consider the example of apparent 'African gang crime' in Australia.

In January 2018 the Victorian Police Minister, Lisa Neville, made a public statement claiming 'African gang crime' was 'out of control'.[76] The same month new Australian Home Affairs Minister, Peter Dutton, claimed 'people are scared to go out to restaurants of a night time because of these gangs'.[77] The media was portraying the existence of the 'Apex gang' of young African-heritage men terrorizing Melbourne streets. But there was never was a 'gang', as Victorian Assistant Commissioner Stephen Leane clearly pointed out.[78]

In March 2018 US President Donald Trump stated, 'Every day, sanctuary cities release illegal immigrants, drug dealers, traffickers, gang members back into communities. They are safe havens for just some terrible people.' He said this despite the evidence to the contrary; that immigration doesn't drive crime.[79]

Media and political agendas have left us afraid to unite, scared of the disadvantaged and minorities.

It is a sad state of affairs when we live in communities so scared and divided we lock our doors and windows, keep to ourselves, and hope no one will break into our houses or rob us on our streets. Sadder still, we have become so divided many of us fear for our children's safety.

Community division even seems to have infected the great city of New York!

In March 2016, a *Guardian Online* reader, David from New York, reported: 'I personally feel that NYC has become a more transient place rather than a community-building place. There's no real sense of community left ... Another life-long New Yorker I know once referred to the city as a 'five-star jail' which I found to be pretty accurate. What can be more lonely than a jail?'[80]

Community spirit and unity looks like it's died or is on life-support. We are suffering because of it.

So, how do we turn this horrible state of affairs around? Can we? Can we return to a greater sense of close community, of friends around us we can trust, of families that can revel in the joy of seeing their kids have fun together? Can we unite, and make society and community even better than our older generations fondly remember it?

I believe we can, and this where the Ten Desires come in.

The Ten Desires help us create a set of simple principles that promote united, supportive, communities.

Part of the solution is to use the Ten Desires to help us restructure our communities in a way that promotes community spirit; friendly unity.

MORE COMMUNITY, PLEASE

Watching societies being torn apart can make us want to take extreme measures, as Steve suggested we do earlier, 'let's blow it up and start again!' We long to go back to a simpler life, back to being nomadic tribespeople.

Yes, it seems a nonsensical notion but going back to this also makes some sense. After all, as we have seen, the Ten Desires evolved over millions of years for us to do just that; stay nomadic hunter gatherers; we evolved to meet these desires best in small tribes. So, if we are serious about meeting the Ten Desires in a long-term and sustainable way, being nomadic tribespeople is the optimal solution—we know it can work, it is has worked before among many tribes for tens of thousands of years, probably much longer. But is that our only realistic solution, the only one that might actually work?

We don't need to take things to such extremes.

Perhaps a better approach might be to learn from what nature intended when it gave us these desires in the first place and see how to make them work, to help us satisfy our friendship desires in communities closer to how nature intended, even in a technologically advanced world; a world of towns, farms, computers, phones, and cities.

How might we do it?

We can begin by garnering five principles from the Ten Desires to guide us, as we did with applying the Ten Desires to business earlier. Use our understanding of the Ten Desires to help us see what features we should encourage in our own communities and create in any new ones within future suburbs, villages, towns, or cities. As we are about to see, some new and innovative ways of restructuring our communities already work and meet many of these characteristics very well. We can improve on them further if we wish, no matter our country or culture. The following principles can be a foundation, a beacon, worth considering now and into the future.

FIVE GUIDING PRINCIPLES FOR UNITED AND SATISFYING COMMUNITIES
Group Size Matters

When we look up to the vastness of the billions of stars in the sky it is easy to feel insignificant, less than a grain of sand on a beach. It is similar being among many people. Among too many people we feel less significant, and less powerful. Nature made us feel this way for one important reason.

When we are one of thousands or millions our contribution isn't as important to the survival of everyone compared to if we are, say, one of 25 to 60, a small tribal foraging size. If we are in a small group, for example, it is more valuable and critical if we have a useful skill or talent, such as healing, finding water, or being a good hunter. If we are one among thousands there are bound to be others to take our place. It is harder to feel valued, noticed, and appreciated in a much larger group.

The lesson nature has taught us is simple:

The Ten Desires are number sensitive; if there are too many people to interact with we can struggle to have our Ten Desires met.

It is as if nature is saying there is an optimum group size for us as a species in the natural world. Go above this size and we feel unsafe even though, in theory, there are more people to protect us.

The Ten Desires remind us that the close bonds we share with others makes us feel safest of all; the closer the bond the more we can guarantee someone will be there for us; it isn't just about safety in numbers. But it can be hard to maintain that level of close bond when there are too many people to bond with. As our groups get bigger, at some point, we become less familiar and less important to each other, less close. The less important and familiar we become the less we can count on others to be there when we need them most. We feel less safe.

This idea of optimal group size for friendship is not a new one.

In the early 1990s Robin Dunbar, an anthropologist and psychologist currently at the University of Oxford, came up with what has become called the 'Dunbar Number'—a number representing the optimal size of human groups or amount of friends. It came about after he realized a correlation between primate brain size and the size of their social group; the bigger the neocortex—the frontal lobe in particular—the larger the primate group size. Primates include lemurs, monkeys, apes, and humans. Applying these observations to humans, and using a simple formula, he ended up with a number: 150.[81] Anything above that number for human groups seemed to be beyond our optimal processing ability. After exploring this number even more over the last 20 years he realized there were actually a series of numbers.

One hundred and fifty would be the number he says we would call casual friends, the people we would invite to a party—often it's more of a range between 100 and 200. The next step down is 50, the number he calls close friends—like dinner guests we might invite over. Then there is the circle of 15 we can turn to for sympathy and to confide in. The most intimate are a group of five, often really close friends and family members, who become our closest support group. The absolute limit of acquaintance level friends he considers to be 1500, the limit we can put a face and name to. He uses historical data to prove his point.

For example, the average group size of modern hunter-gatherer tribes, garnered from census data, was 148.4 individuals.[82] The professional armies of the Roman empire, 16th century Spain, and 20th century Soviet Union, had company sizes of close to 150, further broken down into smaller units of 50, then further subdivided to between ten and 15. The bigger battalions had companies joined into groups ranging from 550 to 800.

Does this mean these are the best numbers of friends and group sizes to meet our Ten Desires?

There isn't enough information to say.

It is worth remembering, the data he presented on close and casual friendships in our current society (according to his definitions, not those used in this book), are based on the levels of friendships observed in societies that are not friendship orientated; they are dominated by desires for wealth, power, and status, or influenced by them. Since we probably lived for perhaps millions of years in tribe sizes up to 150—mostly less than half that—without strong desires for wealth to divide us, it is quite possible we had more close friends then than we do today (certainly more of those we knew we had a close enough attachment to for us be sure they had our backs and we had theirs). Regardless of what we consider the optimum number of friends to be, we can still agree that group size is important; it will influence how well we meet each other's Ten Desires.

The bottom line, make our groups—the people we interact with—too big and we can have trouble satisfying our friendship needs. Make them too small and we can feel too unsafe and insecure—again not meeting our friendship needs.

Knowing this we can structure societies with these general numbers in mind to make it easier to satisfy our Ten Desires. How we might do that we will discuss in a moment.

Face-to-Face Contact Matters

If you could only have one friend, would you prefer to only have a virtual friend—a completely synthetic friend you could never meet—or a real one you could touch, and share experiences with—a real person you could physically engage and spend time with? It is true, when we are lonely almost any interaction can make us feel better, even one where we never actually meet, but long term, deep down inside, does the synthetic experience of friendship really satisfy us? The answer, not surprisingly, appears to be no.

According to John Cacioppo, the director of the Center of Cognitive and Social Neuroscience at the University of Chicago, a leading expert on loneliness, and author of the book, *Loneliness*, 'Surrogates can never make up completely for the absence of the real thing.' The 'real thing' meaning actual people, in the flesh. He says, 'The greater the proportion of face-to-face interactions, the less lonely you are.'[83]

Applying this to the Ten Desires this is hardly surprising.

We were made by nature to have many friendship needs met—the Ten Desires—by real people with real physical interactions.

Yes, we might meet a few of the desires on Facebook or Twitter for example, such as feeling validated so many people liked our post or picture, but that can never satisfy all the other ten. It is like chewing on a lovely chocolate cake and never being able to swallow; a hollow and incomplete experience. In the end, it takes real people to help us feel cared for and protected. We expect real people to come to our aid.

In practical terms this means if we want to build societies that satisfy our Ten Desires they will need to be organized in a way that encourages physical contact and social interaction, such as providing places to meet up. Preferably places where we don't have the distractions of phones, screens, or texts.

Regular Contact is Good

As we learned from relationships, it is next to impossible to satisfy our Ten Desires if we are never with each other. And as John Cacioppo pointed out, the more face-to-face contacts we have the less lonely we are. It is useful to note how we solved this problem when we were tribal.

Aside from the fact we were often around family and friends daily many tribal societies, from pre-Columbian America, to pre-European Australia, Asia, and the Pacific, had regular singing, dancing, and festivals, or gatherings of tribes, like the Sundance festival of the Lakota and the Corroboree of the Australian Aboriginal people mentioned earlier, though not necessarily so formal. Stories were told and shared. People renewed old ties. This was a time of laughter and fun organized on a regular basis, ways to unite and bring people closer, because they recognized they needed it. I recall a recent documentary on the Torres Strait Islander people north of Australia. They would still organize regular dances and performances as a way to bring people together and help them feel a closer part of their tribe and community. Regular face-to-face contact with each other in a society helps us satisfy many of our Ten Desires.

Does this mean we need to use alcohol or drugs to bring us together? No.

And we don't need *loud* music either. Though festivals, singing, and dances are to be encouraged—they satisfy many deep human needs—the loudness of music today is far more than the levels we had at festivals when we were tribal. It is hard to make someone feel heard if we can't physically hear them. That also means headphones are out, and shouldn't be used in public, they detract from opportunities to meet and talk to each other, not to mention they can be unsafe, especially when we are walking and are too distracted to know where we are going. We don't want to run into a pole, let alone an oncoming car!

When we build societies and communities, and consider how to arrange them, regularly meeting each other so we meet our Ten Desires more often is a component we should keep in mind.

Shared Facilities

Have you ever held a meeting at a person's particularly expensive and nice house (compared to yours)? Did you feel a bit uncomfortable, or maybe a bit inferior; they have so much great stuff!

It can be hard to feel of equal value and respect when we meet at places owned by others, unless our places are all the same.

This is where shared facilities become important.

When we meet in places owned by a common group of people—such as the community or state—we are meeting on neutral ground. It is similar to how several African tribes would talk under a tree—the talking tree. Ideally it would be a tree with low branches, so no one could stand up—everyone sat as equals. No one owned the tree, it was a shared place for meeting. It would help everyone feel of equal value and respect and allow them to all feel heard.

I recall a patient from the Solomon Islands once reminding me of their community orientated approach. He said everyone would share what they had, be it a truck, a tractor, or even their house. If it looked particularly expensive others were allowed to share in enjoying or using it too, for free. In terms of meeting the Ten Desires the sharing is a great way of helping everyone feel valued and respected. The 'owner', or custodian of the house or objects, could also take pride in knowing they were helping others feel good too—it could help them feel appreciated.

When we focus more on what a community has in common, such as what we share, we also feel a sense of sameness that unifies us.

Having shared facilities helps us satisfy many of the Ten Desires.

Walking Can Promote Talking

It is hard to feel heard, noticed, valued, respected, and appreciated if we spend most of our time in our cars. Even on public transport few of us chat these days. When was the last time you had a good conversation with a stranger on a bus or train? But if we walk around among people we have more opportunity to meet others, stop, catch up, and chat; preferably, once again, without headphones.

Many of us have a love affair with our cars; I know I like driving mine. We think nothing of driving to a mall and doing our shopping among a large group of strangers. We know all the things we need are in one convenient location, so we park in the big carpark or catch public transport to get there. It also saves time on having to go to many locations to find what we want, and we all know how busy we are and time-short. We might see teenagers hanging around a mall as a place to meet but, for the most part, malls and shopping centers are very impersonal and sterile, and not conducive to meeting people.

Want to meet more of the Ten Desires among people around us? Create an environment that requires more walking.

Of course, it will also help keep our weight down, and make us healthier too.

APPLYING THE FIVE PRINCIPLES

How might the five principles guide our community structure? Consider the following two examples:

Housing and Community Halls

Imagine housing arranged within close walking distance to shops, schools, and public facilities. Where walking is promoted more than driving. Imagine this as an eco-friendly place with easily available housing to accommodate people of varying cultures and income levels. This is part of the vision of New Urbanism, an urban design movement arising in the 80s in the US in response to a growing urban sprawl. Their Congress of New Urbanism was founded in 1993, and they have a Charter.[84] Here are some principles included in their Charter:

- To allow the independence of those not able to drive, especially the elderly and young, the activities of daily living should occur within walking distance. The interconnected networks of streets should be designed to encourage walking.
- Neighborhoods and districts should concentrate civic, institutional, and commercial activity within them.
- Neighborhoods should have a range of parks, from tot-lots and village greens to ballfields and community gardens distributed within them and have conservation areas and open land to define and connect the different neighborhoods and districts.
- To avoid concentration of poverty affordable housing should be distributed throughout the region to match job opportunities.

As an urban way of structuring a society how does this help meet our Ten Desires and the Five Principles?

From the outset it promotes walking, and hence puts us in a better position to meet other people. It decentralizes the shops but keeps them in walking distance creating a village-style atmosphere where people can get to know each other. It provides plenty of shared facilities such as parks, and community areas to meet. It facilitates face-to-face contact, and at the same time avoids a hierarchy developing with areas of poverty.

New Urbanism promotes friendship and can help us meet many of our Ten Desires.

Could it be improved upon to meet the Ten Desires even better?

Sure.

For instance, within the New Urbanism structure we could focus more on building community halls with public facilities that provide education, and social support such as professional counseling if needed for all ages. The hall itself can become the center of regular gatherings, much like churches are today, and be the hub around which a suburb supports itself and builds its sense of close community; like the African talking tree, but with greater back-ups. If we are to use the Dunbar Number, then community halls should support and unite no more than 1500 people. These would be active community meeting and festival locations spread among the suburbs with which we should be able to easily get actively involved. Ideally, we would develop a loyalty to one community hall that is the hub of our tribe of 1500 or less. We will discuss this more in a moment.

Another way to structure suburbs to help us meet the Ten Desires is the Honeycomb suburb. This organizes housing in a honeycomb pattern with houses facing a common area for kids to play and adults to meet (See Figures 10.1 and 10.2, below).

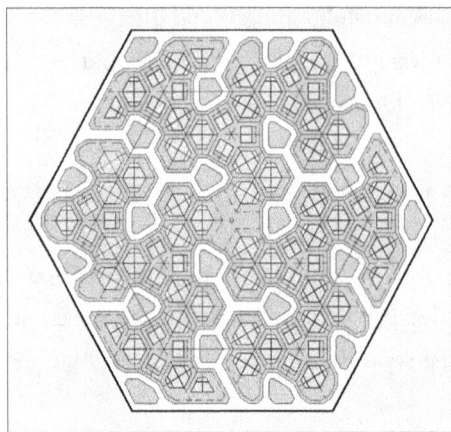

Figure 10.1
Plan of Honeycomb Neighborhood, tessellar, 2004, Creative Commons

Figure 10.2 Bird's Eye View of Hillside Honeycomb at Nong Chik, tessellar, 1 May 2008, Creative Commons

As Mazlin Ghazali, the architect of these suburbs and creator of these pictures recently informed me, four of these suburbs have already been successfully built in Malaysia. Clearly, they encourage a community feel and social contact, one of the main intentions of their design. They are also cost effective, offering a more affordable alternative to terrace housing and high-rise blocks.[85] If we wished to make them even more friendship-friendly we could, in addition, spread community halls among the suburbs as outlined above. The aim, like with New Urbanism, would be to promote a village atmosphere nearby where we can shop, catch up, and socially meet.

When meeting the Ten Desires becomes the priority in a society we can build our houses, shops, roads, and transport accordingly. Simple principles and understanding can guide us.

Suppose we live in a big city that isn't friendship-friendly and we can't just change the planning, how might we work to meet the Ten Desires better based on the Five Principles there? This is where forming smaller social groups can be helpful. It can even help among existing suburbs.

Organized Community Sub-Groups and Social Bees

The Ten Desires teach us that when we are among too many people we barely know, we can feel lonely, like David described about New York earlier. If we can't actually rebuild our cities according to a more friendship-friendly design—like New Urbanism—we can still find ways to break into smaller more supportive groups of people who can get to know each other. This can be done on a suburb by suburb basis, or even within city high-rises and local street blocks.

For example, Transition Bondi, in the Sydney beachside suburb of Bondi, holds regular events and meetings to encourage community engagement and meetings, such as Film and Feast the third Thursday of every month to eat and watch fascinating documentaries, a community garden with a Dig Day on the second Sunday of every month, and weekly meetings of Responsible Runners who gather just to clean up local waste left on their streets or beaches.[86] An even more specific approach might be to create and support a social co-ordinator role, perhaps starting with a social worker, to become the area's social bee (SB).

Let's face it, most of us are not good at meeting new people, even new neighbors. It is like arriving at a party of people we don't know; it can be awkward and painful for us to mingle. To help counter this so we actually get to know each other we can use socially-minded extroverts—familiar with the Ten Desires—to help facilitate our social contact. A bit like a common friend introducing us around at the party.

Much like a bee visits lots of flowers a social bee can visit lots of homes, get to know their family or household personally and well, and help introduce and integrate them into the local community through organized activities such as plays, dancing, festivals, barbeques, volunteering, and fundraising to help out other locals in the region.

Instead of spreading pollen they spread a sense of community, integrity, support, feeling cared for, noticed, appreciated, and respected.

It is much like in remote areas before we had phones, radios, or television. People who travelled, such as postmen, would visit locals to keep them informed and get to know them. Only this time they would also help bring them together, facilitate community, and help arbitrate minor disputes. If we truly value friendship then such a role would be one of the most esteemed in our community, and worthy of enormous respect.

The idea would be to create closeness among smaller groups. For example, among less than 150 to 200 who can come to know, care for, and support each other. Then many of these groups can form part of a larger group of less than 1500—like tribes did with their festivals—so we don't all see each other as competitors. If an SB can help create common goals, such as working to build new communal facilities, community vegetable gardens, or improving local housing for everyone for example, then they can also help create a unity through sameness (using common goals) and further facilitate the feeling among everyone. They can help everyone feel they are playing a valuable and meaningful role, including our youth.

It is a bit like the barn raising of the Amish communities and more common among rural America in the 18th and 19th centuries. Everyone comes together to raise a barn, but by doing so they help support the family they are doing it for, help give everyone a common goal and sense of purpose and a chance to catch up; a wonderful way to meet many of the Ten Desires.

Imagine how beneficial an SB would be for the elderly. Often their children's families are busy and as they get older, their friends die. This can leave them feeling particularly lonely and vulnerable. In our region volunteers and social services visit them, so someone keeps an eye on them and they have someone to talk to. Now imagine some of the benefits of the SB.

An SB can not only visit and get to know them personally but also help them get involved with others in social activities. They can help them find meaningful roles in their community. They can help the elderly feel valuable once again, noticed, appreciated, and respected. SBs can help the marginalized be part of a greater whole that cares for and looks out for one another. The SB could also become the core of a rapid reaction acute social support group, working on a roster.

A family member has died, we have lost our job, we are being victimized at work, we are debilitated by illness, we are too nervous to leave our home, our house suffers some major damage and we need help. If the community is not yet fully integrated to naturally help each other in such times, then a supportive acute reaction group can be a great help.

Tough times are part of life. To realize other people are there to call on when we need them most, can be invaluable. Co-ordinated by someone who knows us we trust—the SB—we can call on a few other people for the extra food, the bed, shoulder to cry on while others look after the kids, the working bee to fix up the damage until proper repairs can be arranged. Their job would not be to replace the professionals—fire and rescue, ambulances, the SES, or police—as much as supplement them, to give a personal touch, and show our community cares and is there for us. It could be a rotational roster so we all get a great opportunity to show we care. The added benefit being, when someone shows they will be there for us at our most desperate hour they reveal themselves as a true friend; they meet the Ten Desires in a way that might otherwise not happen, with gestures of a close friend we might not readily see.

Will some call on this service more than others? Perhaps look like they need it too much?

Yes, but we can accept this is one member of our group—our tribe, if we prefer—who feels their needs aren't being met. Clearly they are struggling to feel safe and secure more than the rest. Quite likely, they aren't yet convinced we won't abandon them as others have done in the past. It is like a young child, crying when they don't need to, doing the wrong thing knowing it will get a response and taking up too much of our time. All they want to know is we will be there for them, they are valued. Once they learn this, we prove it with our actions and persistence, the behavior improves, and the effort needed to care for them is less.

Think of being part of this reaction group as an honor, an opportunity to do something positive for our community, benefiting our neighborhood, and the safety, security, and fulfillment of our children. In fact, if we supervise teenagers and older children to be part of this group it can give their lives a greater sense of worth and meaning. It will help them feel they fit in (especially useful for teenagers). Mind you, it can also be another way for them to meet like-minded boys and girls of a similar age that doesn't involve alcohol, and it gets them off their computers!

I shared some of these ideas with a patient once. He was very supportive and said his local street already builds community support. He lives in a culvert—a non-throughway street—and the families, many with young children, have come to know each other well. How? He organizes regular BBQs for all the families to get together, usually several times a month. He is in effect already a version of their social bee.

Of course, to work properly the SB would have to be a full-time paid role, well paid for by the community, and they would likely need supports and trainees. It can be expected to be hard going at first—we are all so used to being out of social contact and can be set in our ways—but once the people experience the benefits of working and integrating together it can help most of us meet our Ten Desires better in a big city or town. No longer do our cities—or towns—have to feel like a jail. Maybe a paid SB is worth considering.

Ideally, we should organize all cities and towns to facilitate high levels of social involvement.

The Ten Desires are perhaps our greatest social instrument. They were, after all, built into us by nature to ensure we built communities, to not just be herds of animals who happen to stick together so we don't get eaten, unable to coordinate when we need each other most. It makes sense we use them as our guide to re-establish the communities they were meant to create. That doesn't mean having to go back to being nomadic tribespeople, it can mean adapting what we know to our modern technological way of life. It can mean using the Ten Desires and following principles founded on what we know will satisfy us most and structuring our societies accordingly.

We can recreate a sense of community. We can even make it better than it ever has been, more close, safe, and secure than at any time in history. Why? We now know what we didn't, or chose to forget. We know the value of friendship, and the components we need to make it work. Hate and intolerance, technology, and scars of a traumatic past, no longer have to divide us.

Having said that, communities need proper governance. If we aren't diligent and alert those who are driven most by desires of the inner beast will remain in control, negatively impacting on our lives and world. Thankfully, the Ten Desires can help us change that, as an individual, too. They can help each and every one of us create greater prosperity and a lasting peace.

KEY POINTS

- Community spirit has come under attack; technology, our priorities, and hate are dividing us.
- The Ten Desires help us create a set of simple principles that create and promote united, supportive, communities.
- We can learn from our desires and what nature intended to create closer communities in a technologically advanced world.
- **Five Guiding Principles from the Ten Desires:**
  - Group size matters: if there are too many people to interact with we can struggle to have our Ten Desires met.
  - Face-to-face contact matters: we were made by nature to have friendship needs met by real people and physical interactions.
  - Regular contact is good: festivals, singing, dances are to be encouraged.
  - Shared facilities: help us feel equally valued and respected and unify us through sameness.
  - Walking can promote talking: environments that promote walking are more conducive to us talking.
- **Examples of applying the Five Guiding Principles:**
  - Housing and community halls: such as New Urbanism and Honeycomb suburbs.
  - Organized community sub-groups and social bees.

- We can create a sense of community better than it ever has been because now we know the components we need to use to get it to work.
- Hate and intolerance, technology, and scars of a traumatic past, no longer have to divide us.

CHAPTER 11

Government by Us for Us

> THE CARE OF HUMAN LIFE AND
> HAPPINESS, AND NOT THEIR DESTRUCTION,
> IS THE FIRST AND ONLY OBJECTIVE OF
> GOOD GOVERNMENT.
>
> —*Thomas Jefferson*

It's embarrassing. We've had civilization for over 5500 years and our governments still don't work. They still don't satisfy our needs or offer us long term safety and security, and they are still dominated by special interest groups rather than being truly representative of their people. Do you feel your government listens to you and takes your opinions seriously? Do you feel it is making the best decisions to improve the lives of your family, neighbors, community, and the world? Or are they more interested in satisfying the needs of the most wealthy and powerful? We know billions are being spent by lobbyists; the numbers are staggering. We know government/corporate hybrid empires now rule and compete around the world at our expense. We know people are being executed, coerced, tortured, and imprisoned without trial under dictatorships and totalitarian regimes (just look at North Korea, one example among many). We see our parliaments struggling to pass even the most fundamental meaningful legislation; frequent deadlocks in the US upper house are a case in point. What an embarrassing, dysfunctional, mess.

So where does that leave us? We know the systems are broken, but can they be fixed? Can we finally get governing of the people to work for all of us? After all, many types of governing and governments have been tried, failed, and replaced. We will look at some of them in a moment.

Our knowledge of our basic human desires, and the Ten Desires of Friendship, can offer us a new perspective and a promising, and practical, guide. They suggest we can actually find the systems that serve us all best; governments we can all work towards and strive for to make our lives, communities, and the world a happier, and safer, place. They even give us the means to make it happen; they show us what we can do, empower us to do it, reminding us how one person does make a difference. We no longer have to feel powerless when it comes to governments to make real change.

When it comes to being satisfied by governments the rule is simple:

Being satisfied by governments is no different to being fulfilled in life; when our basic human needs are satisfied by them we are too.

In other words, the more of the Ten Desires our governments satisfy for us the happier we will be with them, and the closer they will be to working properly in our interests.

To help us find the best type of government, or governing method, we can use a similar approach here to what we used to help improve communities; we can garner a set of basic principles from the Ten Desires and use them to determine what we should aim for. Ever wondered if we should live under a noble king or queen, under a country ruled by science or business, or a compulsory system that gives us all a say? Let's see what satisfying our Ten Desires suggests.

Consider striving to meet this set of six guiding principles in any government.

SIX PRINCIPLES OF FRIENDSHIP-FOCUSED GOVERNMENT
Flatter Hierarchies Work Best in Long Term

You may have noted we have been giving hierarchies a hard time, and rightly so; they are not good at helping us meet our Ten Desires, especially those of being respected and valued. But that doesn't mean they should be treated like they're radioactive; avoided at all costs. In the short-term hierarchies can be useful. In the long-term they become a problem; they inevitably lead to growing dissatisfaction and the breakdown, or revolt, of an oppressed and dysfunctional society.

How can hierarchies be useful in the short-term but become toxic the longer they stay?

They work great when we need quick decision making or need to act as one.

Suppose you are in a battle with group of tribespeople similar in number to you. They act as an uncoordinated rabble, but you work as a well-oiled machine, finding their weaknesses, and using your numbers wisely to exploit them. Who is more likely to be victorious?

When we act as one we can be a formidable force, but this requires one person to coordinate the others, someone we listen to without question. In close combat the soldiers who question their leaders may hesitate and reduce the overall force's effectiveness. In active combat, where split-second decisions must be made, there is no time to develop a consensus. If quick decisions must be made—such as in times of war—to have someone with expertise to lead us can be a life saver.

Not surprisingly the military is built upon a hierarchy, today with generals and admirals on top trickling down to captains, lieutenants, sergeants, corporals, and regular soldiers, airmen and women, or seamen and women below. Each leader helps the others act as one, making each group stronger for it.

In the short term, while a threat exists, this hierarchy can work well, even in government. If we are under threat and have an experienced, knowledgeable, and strong leader to inspire the people we can rally together behind them to be victorious—united and coordinated under their leadership—like getting behind Alexander the Great of Ancient Greece, or FDR during World War 2. But in peacetime soon we find ourselves asking: 'Why aren't we getting more of a say?'

From a human desires perspective, while we are afraid our desires drive us to be around others of our kind—unite—and listen to one person we think best able to lead us rather than gather around for discussion.

The fear seems to suppress our other desires to be heard, respected, noticed, validated, and appreciated.

We don't mind if these friendship desires aren't met so long as we survive. When the threat and fear go away the other desires resurface and demand, once again, to be met.

This explains why tyrants and dictators can easily arise from times of war, upheaval, or threat, then need either fear or brutal suppression of the people to remain in power.

A great example of this were the inciting incidents leading to the rise of Adolf Hitler. After World War 1 Germany developed a fledgling democracy to replace its absolute monarch (the kaiser, or emperor). Because Germany had to pay impossible reparations to other European states, especially France, this left Germany under a state of constant threat—many people were starving and without prospect of work; they feared for their safety and that of their families. This left Germany open to a return to absolute rule; the people craved a powerful leader. Hitler obliged and created Authoritarian, and later Totalitarian, rule. He then kept them in a state of war and fear to ensure he remained in absolute power, as their 'savior'.

War or threat leads us to voluntarily give up our need to be heard and be as valued and respected as we know we would otherwise. We don't mind having leaders who can unite and protect us. But once the reason for the rule of a single powerful leader no longer exists—there is finally peace, and fear no longer reigns—then we start to want the respect, value, and to be heard back again. What the fear suppressed is set free, rises once more, and demands to be satisfied—nature once again wants us to be functional—fully satisfied human beings. The rise of these desires will soon breed dissent and can lead to a revolt against the government and leadership, unless they abdicate their central control.

Pain is a great motivator. Emotional pain of powerful unmet desires can make us go to extraordinary lengths to rid ourselves of discomfort and heartache. If the hierarchy doesn't return power and influence to the masses so their needs are met they will be driven to fight for it. It is a natural response to the pain. As the masses disobey and question the order of things the hierarchy are likely to either oppress them, misinform them, create a new threat or enemy, or instill more fear; they will not want to give up power they have spent so much time and energy to create, especially if they are strongly driven by the desires of their inner beast. Then we either have a revolt or revolution to topple the hierarchy on our hands, or temporary absolute rule—a tyranny—to suppress it. If the hierarchy isn't removed it will need to be increasingly oppressive, try to control our every thought and move, to prevent an organized and dissatisfied people rising up and deposing them, much like the totalitarian regime warned about, and well described, in the novel by George Orwell, *1984*. In this fictional dystopia Big Brother watched over everyone, oppressed them, and you could be incarcerated simply for having 'wrong' thoughts, which were described as thought crimes.

Why is absolute rule temporary, and why will it always remain so?

In the end no individual or organization can keep the human spirit and our deeper desires suppressed forever. We will keep fighting to satisfy our humanity—the truth of the deeper instincts nature placed inside us will always float to the surface and demand to be met.

Can you think of countries today where the leaders are exploiting fear, or creating new enemies, to try to justify their absolute rule; their hierarchy and privilege? In a time of terrorism, it is easy to be seduced by the idea that force and strong leadership are the solution. It is easy to make other countries, or religions, the enemy so that we unify against a common foe and keep the elite in power. Promote and build peace, however, and these despotic or dictatorial leaders no longer have power and influence, and we have a better environment to create a lasting peace and friendship.

When we create a government, we should keep in mind the effect of hierarchies on our basic human desires. Do we really want to live in fear and ongoing dissatisfaction? Do we want regular war, conflict, oppression, exploitation, and hate? Or do we want lasting fulfillment and peace?

Less hierarchy promotes greater long-term peace and more fulfilling lives.

Consensus is Fundamental

Consensus—discussion and compromise so we come to an agreed decision—was a fundamental part of how we governed our tribes for tens of thousands of years. One simple communal activity could help bond and unify us like no other.

Among a group of individuals all wanting what they want now consensus is the grease that lubricates society, smooths over our individual needs and differences, and binds us together as a greater whole.

It meets most, if not all, of our Ten Desires in a single activity. Unless we fear for our safety, as mentioned earlier, we all want to have our say, be heard, understood, validated, and taken seriously as an equal. Like under the African talking tree we want everyone to have equal say and respect.

Consensus is an imperative demanded by our Ten Desires.

Consensus has many useful functions. As well as unifying us though validation, feeling heard, and respected, it can further unite us around shared or common goals. For instance, if we all decide to work on creating or supporting a local business or businesses that help us satisfy our desire for sameness—we all have the same goal in common. Secondly, consensus can help us resolve disputes before they get out of hand. Everyone can contribute ideas towards a fair way of settling things, such as by offering an apology or compensation, and suggestions as to what form that might take. Consensus can provide an opportunity to be informed of what matters to our community, such as policy. It allows us to have a say in setting the rules and laws and the mutually agreed upon punishments, if there are to be any, through open discussion. Consensus allows us to create a peaceful, integrated, supportive group.

If we are to feel satisfied with our governments, we will need them to satisfy our need for consensus.

Group Meeting Size Matters

Suppose we have a town hall meeting and 1000 people show up. To help them feel heard we give them five minutes—uninterrupted—to speak, followed by discussion. That means we spent 5000 minutes just listening to everyone and trying to remember who said what. That is equivalent to 83 hours, a week if we only meet for 12 hours a day. Absurd.

We cannot create consensus if groups are too large; they need to be a manageable size.

Even groups of less than 150 will require 5-hour meeting times just to ensure everyone has their say if we only give each person two minutes to speak. We'd need to devote a whole day to meeting just so everyone felt heard. Then we have the issue of bonding.

A meeting of less than 150 makes for a more intimate experience and offers the opportunity to bond together as a people. We can begin to predict and know people well, and meet more of each other's Ten Desires, in meetings of this smaller size.

If we want to feel well represented, and heard, we need to remember to have regular meetings of fewer people. These groups can, in turn, send representatives to other meetings of group sizes that also aren't too large, so we can be sure our concerns have been passed on and taken seriously at a higher level. If we want our Ten Desires met in a government group meeting size matters.

Individual Liberties Need Respect

What is the point of having communities if all they do is make us feel unsatisfied, lastingly unhappy and miserable?

From the Balance of Self Model (see page 6) you will recall the concept of Personal Self, knowing what we feel and think in our own right; being genuine, and true to ourselves. A major reason for recognizing Personal Self is to remind us if we try to be like someone else we won't have our specific needs and desires satisfied—we will feel emotional pain and be unfulfilled. For example, if I don't drink when I'm thirsty but rather wait until you are then I might become very thirsty indeed, perhaps pass out! It is essential we recognize that within any group or community, individuals have basic human needs they require to be satisfied. We all may have the same basic human desires but the ones we need met at any point in time will be different among us; what I need to do to satisfy my desires may differ to what you do to satisfy yours.

A group is made up of individuals all seeking to satisfy their individual expression of their humanity. If the group—community—doesn't respect this, then it will make life more miserable for everyone.

This means the primary aim of any government should be to facilitate the satisfaction of the individual expressions of its people's humanity; to help them meet their basic human desires, as individuals, in a balanced and sustainable way. The more they restrict people from doing this, the more they cut off people's freedom to feel complete, the more unhappy, unfulfilled, and potentially restless, everyone will become.

In practical terms this means listening to and respecting minorities. It means, wherever possible, allowing them to express their individuality too so long as they respect other people's needs as well. When we start to disrespect each other's individual pursuit of satisfying our human desires we stop becoming friends and start to become enemies, or a threat.

Groups have struggled with the needs of the one versus the needs of the many for millions of years. If everyone only takes care of their own needs, then we don't work as a group and survive. If the group doesn't allow the individuals to have their needs met, then we create hostility and the group may fracture, and we don't survive. This is what the Balance of Self Model reminds us, we require a balance. But at no time should we lose a sense of our individuality.

Our basic human desires, including the Ten Desires, remind us that personal liberty is important and should be a major focus of any government worth having.

It requires the government to encourage and enforce personal and mutual respect; that no one's needs are treated as superior or inferior to those of anyone else.

How do we encourage and enforce mutual respect, the valuing of the desires of all human beings?

We have already seen that consensus can help us, so too do rules and laws.

Rules and Laws are Critical

Bite me and I'll bite you back! Though it might not be a physical bite.

We like to think we are higher beings compared to all the other animals of the world, but our desires and reactions tell us differently, especially our desire for payback.

In a pack of wolves when one wolf bites another what is the likely response? The other wolf will bite back. Why? So it prevents it happening again; so it gives the other wolf something unpleasant to remind it that it isn't a good idea to hurt me. If the wolf didn't bite back it would be bitten again, and potentially lose its status within the pack; its place in the pecking order. It is similar with us.

Hurt us and our natural instinct—if we haven't been taught otherwise—is to hurt someone back. It is a good way of us making sure we aren't walked all over by everyone else. It is effective to ensure we still get our needs met. We can hurt each other in many ways. Some are physical, like being hit or attacked, another is to prevent us having our needs met. Take away, or threaten to remove, something we want or need and we feel discomfort or pain; it creates emotional hurt—a very real pain experience.

We see it often in relationship fights. One partner ignores the other, making the other person feel the pain of not being noticed, valued, or respected. This creates emotional pain, so they retaliate by either abusing them or ignoring them too; they try to create a pain in the other person to prevent being hurt again. Soon we have a tit-for-tat exchange of us just hurting each other and our relationship falls apart.

We give this natural response to inflict pain in response to pain inflicted on us many names. Some of us might notice it as payback. Others call it revenge. In civilized society we often give it the name of justice. They are the same thing; the same desires drive them. Desires that try to ensure other people respect us and our basic human needs.

Let desires for payback run rampant and we create lots of conflict, even fear, war, and death. You will recall we mentioned earlier how the Papua New Guinea highlanders view friendship differently to us. A large reason for this, as we noted, was payback. It meant the tribes of the remote highlands lived in constant fear for their lives and were either always at war or on the verge of war.

How do we prevent such terror and chaos?

We have the rule of law.

To help prevent the tit-for-tat getting out of hand we created a set of rules or laws we can all agree to, and a policing force to act as the enforcers of the payback. We take the revenge away from each other and give it to a third party, so we don't keep ending up at each other's throats.

Aside from the desires for wealth, power, and status being of greatest threat to friendship, so is our desire for payback.

While we are constantly seeking to hurt people who have somehow hurt us we can't be friends. Unless we recognize this inner desire in each of us, what it wants—to ensure such pain is never inflicted upon us again—and ways to satisfy it other than through inflicting more pain and hurt, then we doom all chances of lasting peace and friendship.

Many nomadic tribes knew how payback threatened their peace and bonds of friendship. They would have their own rules and laws to help resolve matters quickly, and to help them respect each other's desires so they didn't constantly hurt each other—in more reasonable ways than the tribes of PNG. There were often strict rules about relationships, for example, so we didn't fight over each other's partners or wives. For instance, many Aboriginal Australians had such rules and laws, and nonfatal spearing of each other as forms of payback if the rules were broken. Knowing how powerful close relationships are and how many needs they meet it is hardly surprising; they would be a source of some of our greatest pain and require special rules or laws. A slighted heart can easily create powerful desires for payback. How much of the hostility we see in the breakups around us today are simply about hurting the other person because they hurt us—revenge? Sue them! I want them to suffer!

If a government is to help us meet our Ten Desires, it must have laws and rules that help us respect each other's human desires and means of preventing payback getting out of control—such as rule of law and impartial policing.

Impartial and incorrupt policing is essential, or our sense of justice will never be truly satisfied. Clearly consensus should play an important role—the more we discuss our differences and deal with how others have hurt us early—the more we resolve the emotional pain of loss, neglect, or disrespect—the less we need policing and the easier it becomes to remain friends. We don't need to go to the courts if we can sort it out ourselves in our social group.

Individual and Social Responsibility

Suppose everyone in a society said 'I don't give a crap, I'm going to do what the hell I want when I want! Screw the consequences!' What might happen to our society?

For starters, lots of people will get hurt. If we go around deciding to neglect the consequence of our actions then we will have sex with people already in stable relationships, take what we want from whoever has it, abuse people we don't like, and make a right ass of ourselves. It will make a lot of people want to either bash some sense into us or lock us up, and rightly so. To deny personal responsibility for our actions just leaves a tsunami of emotional pain and hurt in our wake.

Denying personal responsibility is a show of gross social and interpersonal disrespect—we disrespect everyone else's humanity, we treat them as inferior or inconsequential.

Personal responsibility within a society is essential if we are to have our Ten Desires met. So is social responsibility, in the form of good governance.

Former US president Ronald Reagan once said:

> We must reject the idea that every time a law's broken, society is guilty rather than the lawbreaker. It is time to restore the American precept that each individual is accountable for his actions.[87]

President Reagan certainly recognizes that personal responsibility is important, but to focus only on personal responsibility and deny social responsibility is a mistake. It is saying, in no uncertain terms, the government does not respect its people; it is above the people and should not be held to account for their social circumstances and how they react as a result.

The bottom line is, if people live in societies where their basic human needs are met fewer will be motivated to break the laws.

So, if the society is more friendship orientated and structured accordingly (see Chapter 10) there will be fewer disputes and conflicts, and less need to break laws in the first place. Social connection plays an important role here too.

If we are brought up in a close social environment we are going to be more empathic and aware of the pain our actions will cause. The outcast is more likely to hurt others without worrying about the consequences of their actions; the people not emotionally connected to us, not able to feel the emotional pain of the consequences of their actions because of it. Sometimes we know them as sociopaths. We can expect to create fewer sociopaths if we create a more integrated and friendly society and families; fewer people who don't give a damn about anyone but themselves.

Governments determine where funding is spent. They decide what priorities govern their decisions. Does it make them people friendly or greed friendly first? Does it put policies in place that help bring communities together—such as through council planning and creating social supports—or does it foster brutal competition? Does it promote ways of people integrating, unifying, and being more emotionally connected to one another and prevent crime, or promote hierarchies where people show they are prepared to do whatever it takes to succeed, including break the law?

Society is guilty every time a crime is committed. Every crime is an indication of priorities and approaches that aren't meeting the people's needs; a failure in the approach and application of governance.

The Ten Desires remind us not only that we must be personally responsible but that every government must be held responsible too and constantly and vigorously work to ensure crimes and disrespect of other human beings are prevented. To do otherwise is to create the basis of a fractured society that will keep falling apart rather than a united one held together with the glue of friendship.

These are just some principles the Ten Desires can help us to aim for, and demand, in any government. Principles that make it friendship-friendly.

Ok, so knowing these principles what type of governance or government should we be aiming for? Does it even exist, or do we need to create it?

THE BEST GOVERNMENT FOR US

As alluded to earlier, many forms of governments have already been tried. Are any of them particularly friendship-friendly, meeting the principles we have just distilled? Any we could put our whole support behind or aspire to?

It is beyond a book of this type to give a comprehensive list and explanation of all government types and how they function, but let's have a look at some main types and interesting examples.

Types of Governments

- Plutocracy—rule by the wealthy, heavily influenced by the desires of the rich.
- Kraterocracy—rule by the strongest and most cunning.
- Meritocracy—groups are set to rule according to their creativity, intelligence or wisdom.
- Technocracy—rule by the experts, such as scientists, doctors, or engineers.
- Autocracy—ruled by a single ruler who has all the power—such as an absolute monarch or dictator.
- Oligarchy—rule by a small number of people—but not a rule by class as in an aristocracy.
- Monarchies (Absolute, Constitutional, Crowned republic)—from ultimate rule as head of state to having ceremonial title only.

- Corporatocracy—rule by corporations—such as the rule of the East India Company in India.
- Bankocracy—financial institutions rule.
- Neptocracy—preferential rule passed on to family members.
- Kleptocracy—rule by thieves, such as the Mafia.
- Authoritarian Rule—a political system controlled by unelected rulers.
- Totalitarian Rule—a highly centralized and coercive rule regulating every aspect of private and public life—like the one described in the novel, *1984*.
- Democracy—all the people of the state are involved in decision making and affairs of state.
- Direct Democracy—where people represent themselves and personally vote for new laws and public policy.
- Liberal Democracy—founded on the principles of liberty and equality with separation of powers between branches of government and rule of law.
- Social Democracy—ensuring certain social rights are provided for, such as education, health care, child care, and public transport.
- Totalitarian Democracy—citizens vote for representatives but then have little to no participation in decision making or policy.

Among this list are only three types of government that don't have strict hierarchies or deny public consensus. These are the democracies, excluding the Totalitarian Democracy. The democracies that come closest to meeting the Ten Desires and supporting the six principles are the Liberal Democracy, Direct Democracy, and the plain old Democracy itself, as we'd expect.

According to the Economist Intelligence Unit's (EIU) Democracy Index, in 2017 almost half of the world's countries were considered democracies of some sort.[88] Many of you reading this probably live in one.

Can our democracies falter and be more authoritarian and hierarchical and take away the input from the people?

Sure they can.

As we have seen, once there is war, fear, or a sense of threat, we are more prepared to give up our personal role in decision making and leave it to those we consider better qualified.

Democracy is always under threat while hierarchies exist, there is turmoil in the world, and our desires for wealth, power, and status remain strong.

It is like democracies come with an inbuilt weakness or vulnerability; they can be hijacked or converted into another more authoritarian and less representative type of government quite easily. Money, status, and power can take away our say, the voice of the individual. In no time what was a hard fought for Liberal Democracy—like that of the US—can become more like a Plutocracy or Corporatocracy, run more by the wealthy and big business than by people like you and me. Worse still, it can fall to Authoritarian rule.

It is worth noting, in 2016 the EIU downgraded the US from a 'full democracy' to a 'flawed democracy'. In fact, 2017 was a bad year for democracy worldwide with 89 countries recording a decline when only 27 recorded an improvement, the worst performance since 2010–11 and the aftermath of the global economic financial crisis.[89]

While fear and division grip our countries we risk losing the very qualities in our governments that make us feel most satisfied and secure. We risk our governments being hijacked or drifting away from a proper representative democracy able to meet more of our basic human needs.

Do our current democracies meet all the six principles we just outlined?

No, they don't. Many of us still feel distanced from government, we don't feel active participants in the democratic process, and don't feel our opinions matter—there is insufficient consensus. We feel special interest groups with money and power have taken away the influence of our vote. We feel the governments don't really care for us, the common people, they are more interested in satisfying the desires of the elite.

Simply creating a democracy doesn't mean the government will automatically meet our basic human needs, especially if the desires for wealth, power, and status are strong.

A good example of this is how women have fared under the democratic system.

Democracy did not suddenly mean women would be respected or valued, able to feel heard, be noticed, and appreciated. We can see clear evidence from the fact that many of the early democracies wouldn't allow women to vote; women's suffrage had to be fought for and only became common later in the 20th century. Most of us live in democracies and we still don't value caring and nurturing and devalue women who focus on this role. As we noted when we looked at how to use the Ten Desires to improve relationships, we drive women to be like men, play the traditional men's game of pursuing power, wealth, and status, before we take them seriously. Then we still denigrate them once they are in office. Many democracies around the world fail the test of liberty for all individuals, a right to pursue the fulfillment of the human desires true to our heart and still play an active role in the goings on of our societies.

So far, our democracies have continued to fail women.

Can we have a democracy where women can continue to focus on being carers and nurturers and still play a major role in affairs of society; be authentic and have power and influence?

Sure, we can, it has been done before. We alluded to the system earlier. It is worthy of serious consideration simply for how well it meets our Ten Desires.

WOMEN-FRIENDLY DEMOCRACY

In the mid 1400s, in the region of current New York State, south of Lake Ontario and the Hudson River, five native tribes, the Mohawk, Seneca, Oneida, Onondaga, and Cayuga, united to form what the French called the Iroquois Confederacy. Under the inspiration of a man colloquially called 'The Great Peacemaker' and with the help of a great orator and leader, Hiawatha, five previously warring nations united and founded a council of 50 representatives. At the table sat only men, elected to office, to discuss and negotiate with each other ways to settle differences and threats. The remarkable part of their democracy was only the women could vote.

Among the Iroquois the women of the various tribes owned a seat at the council. They determined who represented them, not the men. According to the Iroquois Constitution, still accessible today, if a member of the council broke their laws, or didn't act in what the women considered the best interests of their tribe, the women could depose their representative and replace them with someone more appealing. They could only elect men. This was a brilliant system.

It meant women could discuss the matters of importance to their tribes and families among each other as they focused on raising their young to be the best members of society they could be; the most important job in the tribe. At the same time, they could help care for members of their community. In other words, they continued to be respected as women as carers and nurturers but also had an enormous influence on affairs affecting their nation. They could prevent men focusing purely on power and conquest and getting into unnecessary wars. They could temper the desires of the inner beast in all and promote peace, so their children didn't suffer or die without good cause.

Did this system of democracy satisfy all the six principles outlined earlier?

Yes, it did, including the pursuit of individual liberty, especially among women. I have never heard, seen, or read, of a democracy that has been better able to meet virtually all of our basic human needs than the model proposed by the Iroquois and The Great Peacemaker.

The Iroquois led a mostly peaceful existence for over 150 years. Then the Europeans and their hierarchy arrived, driven by the desires of their inner beast. They did not respect, or recognize, just how brilliant the Iroquois solution to democracy really was; democracy and respect were not their priority, they came from empires after all.

We have every right to be dissatisfied with our governments; authoritarian governments remain, and our democracies are not

meeting our basic human needs. **The desires inside us cry out for a better way.**

What can you and I do about it, here and now, to better our governments so they continue to improve?

Here are a few suggestions, based on satisfying the six principles of governance and our basic human desires.

HOW WE CAN IMPROVE OUR GOVERNMENTS
Prioritize Friendship: Ask the Friendship Question

The more we prioritize friendship in our life the more it spreads. Ask the friendship question regularly: am I putting friendship first? Work every day to meet the Ten Desires in people around us and others will follow our example. When friendship dominates the lives of people it will flow into the lives and priorities of our representatives, the people we elect or allow to lead us.

Vote and Be Active

If we, the ordinary majority, don't participate in governments then those with special interests will take it over and corrupt it to their ends. Voting should be compulsory, as it is in Australia, so the disadvantaged majority have a practical way of improving their lot by voting in people who will help them. If it isn't compulsory everyone must still vote, assuming we live in a democracy. If we don't, we can still discuss policy with our leaders, individually and as groups; ensuring our voice is heard. Dismissing government and politics as only for the politicians just helps reinforce the power and influence of the elite; we, the majority, aren't there to hold them accountable.

Form Local Social Groups

Identify the local street, suburb, or block that represents your 1500 people and the smaller group of less than 150 and get social—meet up. Work with your council to create festivals, dances, and meetings. Employ a social worker or some outgoing event organizer to go door to door to get to know everyone in your area and help you meet up—your social bee. Organize local working groups and meetings to plant trees, clean up areas, or grow vegies, and invite families along with a barbeque and drinks at the end of the day. Get to know your local tribe. The more we can meet the more we discuss what matters most, among friends.

Meet at Community Halls

Invite your local council, state, and federal representatives to regular meetings of your suburb or social group. Get them to inform you what is happening; what is being voted on, and what outcomes might occur.

The job of every representative should be to inform the people they represent of what is happening, so they can actively participate.

Encourage debate, discussion, and arrive at consensus. Hold our representatives accountable every day, not just before an election. Ensure the Ten Desires are met at every meeting—especially that of respect (allow for different opinions)—and to be allowed to have our say without being interrupted or abused, assign a chairperson to arbitrate and facilitate if needed. To improve our knowledge, we should regularly invite speakers with different views to our own.

Help the Marginalized and Disadvantaged

If we can help the people who are on the outer, who feel isolated and different, and make them feel welcome then we support each other's personal liberty, we promote tolerance and respect. We are all trying to meet the same basic human needs, but we don't all do it the same way.

If we don't allow diversity within the framework of mutual respect, we set up society to be intolerant of us and open ourselves up to abuse.

This means never abusing anyone, especially not over the internet. If you abuse someone, call them names, or wish them harm or discomfort, you set the example for others to do the same to you and ensure your Ten Desires will not be met.

Remember, punishing people for not meeting our needs, by hurting them or disrespecting them, doesn't make others want to meet these needs in us more, it does the exact opposite; even fewer of our needs get satisfied.

The more we promote respect, tolerance, and liberty the more our government will promote them too.

Create and Support a Village

When we create an environment where our Ten Desires are more easily met then friendship spreads, people talk, and we reunite as communities that can more fully participate in governments at all levels. As we have seen villages are great for that, they also support local business and employment, improve our health and wellbeing, and create a safer and more supportive place to raise our children. Villages help us form the social groups that allow for greater consensus and equality. They promote decentralization and more group self-reliance, reducing the need for government interventions or assistance; reducing the size of governments and thus having less interference by them in our lives. Don't go to the mall, create and support your local village instead, walk around and get to know the people.

Be Responsible

If we aren't personally responsible and respectful of the desires of others as equals, we invite governments to control us; we create the perfect environment for the rise of authoritarian and tyrannical regimes that rob us of personal liberties; we promote oppression. Payback is a natural instinct we can all learn to better contain and work out better ways to satisfy. When a crime is committed we seek emotional resolution. We want to know others can feel our pain or loss and care, so they won't commit the crime again. We need less punishment, incarceration, and policing if we can show we are caring and responsible friends. Sometimes a genuine, personal sorry to the victims can go a long way to taking individual responsibility and preventing payback.

When US President Abraham Lincoln gave the famous Gettysburg Address on that fateful Thursday, the 19 November 1863, at the Soldiers' National Cemetery in Gettysburg, Pennsylvania, he didn't just inspire the soldiers who had won a great victory just four months earlier and honor the fallen, he reaffirmed the principles of a nation and its government. In that simple two-minute address he recognized our human need to feel equal; to know equal respect. 'Four score and seven years ago our fathers brought forth on this continent, a new nation, conceived in liberty, and dedicated to the proposition that all men are created equal.' He also reaffirmed the fundamental premise of all democracies: 'a government of the people, by the people, for the people'.[90] A premise that reminds us of our calling.

We are the government. We form the government for us, to meet our needs. Unless we continue to do so we do not assure our own liberty.

Our governments leave a lot to be desired; they could all better meet our basic human needs. But they will only improve if we guide them, if we reassert ourselves as an active part of the governments and show them a better, friendlier, way. Friendlier governments have the potential to spread our friendship and honest, peaceful, intentions around the world, perhaps, for the first time in millennia, offering us the realistic hope of a thousand-year peace.

A THOUSAND YEARS OF PEACE

As we have begun to see, human beings are not some evil naturally warlike race. Deep down inside we all seek to be friends—we all seek peace. Why? It is how we:

- feel safe and secure;
- protect and care for our children, family, and communities;

- fulfill our humanity and feel most complete, as satisfied, fulfilled, human beings.

However, when it comes to creating lasting peace we have a problem. Certain desires nature gave us can make lasting peace next to impossible, as they have done for thousands of years. The good news is now we can recognize them, not just as individuals improving our lives, but as a greater people; as governments. Recognize and contain them, counter their damaging ways not just as individuals but as greater groups of people—as councils and governments—and we really could, for the first time in millennia, see the prospect of lasting peace not far on the horizon.

What malicious desires do governments need to counter, to cage and contain so they don't send us into endless cycles of wars and conflict? We can now recognize three, and as a government we have practical ways to counter each.

GOVERNMENTS COUNTERING WAR FROM WITHIN

The first and most threatening desires to lasting peace are our uncontrolled desires for wealth, power, and status. We have seen how catastrophic they are. But individuals aren't the only ones who can contain their inherent damage and destruction, governments can too.

For example, if every state ensured every other state all had enough food and shelter, for everyone, no exceptions, then the destructive desires of our inner beast would fade. (We have seen how our desires for wealth, power, and status rise if we feel insecure and under threat.) Similarly, if every state ensured other nation-states felt respected and heard, not abused, not forced to bend to another's will, not treated as inferior, and not looted by another's corporations or armies, then we would feel more secure and safe. If in times of disasters and famine we helped each other, we could all feel cared for, and secure and safe. If we protected each other from aggression, came together to protect the weak, we would all feel protected and safe. If we all let each other develop their own culture, even though it is different to ours, and not try to replace or change it, then we would all feel validated and approved—more secure and safe. If we all worked towards common goals of helping each other, such as towards making our citizens healthy, satisfied, human beings, we could bond using a common goal and feel a greater sense of sameness, of being similar, and not a threat. You have probably realized, this is simply applying the Ten Desires, our desires for friendship, on an international level.

Our Ten Desires can satisfy our human need for friendship and community on an international level just as well as they can personally.

The more of them we satisfy as governments interacting with each other—akin to individuals satisfying each other's same basic human desires—the more they suppress the desires of our inner beast that threaten lasting peace.

The second group of desires that threaten long-term peace that require controlling as a government are those for payback, or revenge.

We have seen payback ruin our relationships if we let it spark a tit for tat—you hurt me now I'll hurt you, and so on until we split—but it also readily leads to wars. As isolated tribes of Papua New Guinea remind us, wars can easily start just as acts of revenge. How do we solve this, so we don't go around killing our neighbors for taking another man's wife, or accidently killing their brother? In our societies, to counter our personal feelings for revenge and payback, we successfully—when applied impartially—use laws and policing, a judicial system that is fair and without favor. It works; it prevents us being at each other's throats. It is also a solution that can apply to us as nation states.

When we recognize nations and governments are driven by the same desires as individuals we can quickly see the benefits of using an international system of mutually agreed upon laws and policing. We already have international laws, courts, and judiciaries but not all countries abide by them. Until we come together to create—via consensus—rules and laws we can respect and enforce together (no exceptions)—we risk revenge and payback between countries, weakening our prospects of lasting peace. Of course, while our desires for wealth, power, and status, dominate the priorities of our countries there is little chance the most powerful players will ever seriously agree to or adhere to such laws. While everyone is out for themselves, the desires of our inner beast will drive us to break other countries to gain the advantage. By changing our government's priorities, making friendship the priority, we offer a way for all countries to finally abide by an international, enforceable, peace-making, law-based system. It gives us further incentives to ensuring we counter the desires of our inner beast as our primary goal, always.

And thirdly, all governments need be wary and learn to counter the threatening desires naturally raised in men.

As we noted earlier, men were made by nature to be stronger and faster than women and so were endowed with desires to primarily provide and protect, more so than their desires to care and nurture. The desires were designed to help keep our families and communities safe. But these desires can become less relevant in lasting peace, it can leave men struggling to find meaning and purpose. Such desires can lead men back to war and conflict just to give their lives meaning and purpose, to feel like they are real men, valuable to their families and community.

How can we counter this? Where might we find a solution?

In the past caring and nurturing kept desires to provide and protect in check. The women of our tribe would not want us to go to war, that would threaten the safety of our children. The only time to go to war was if we were starving, or to fend off those who threaten us. To know caring and nurturing was to know peace, in our life, and in our hearts. We saw a moment ago how the Iroquois found their solution. They gave ultimate power to the women, yet still kept and valued the men's ability to protect. They kept ambitions for conquest in check by only letting the women vote. Perhaps we could learn from them, and other tribes who found similar solutions, who revered women and their focus on creating peace and life and gave them great power and influence, so these qualities could improve life for us all.

We have a partial fix today, we call it sport. The men fight in controlled combat and represent our tribes (the teams we support). Better than staging open wars with death, brutality, and bloodshed!

When the fundamentals that lead to exploitation and disrespect are eliminated we can expect greater peace. When the foundations behind empires are neutralized, we can expect more peace. When we learn to be aware of and master our inner demons, we have the prospect of a peace that can last across generations. It is easy to blame our governments and representatives, but they are us. If we are truly serious about creating a peace that begins now and lasts for a millennium, then surely we need to be the example, to understand the threats to peace inside of each of us and work, personally, and as a society—governments included—on a fix.

Change us and we change our leaders, governments, and offer lasting peace to the world.

Yes, governments are broken, but they can be repaired. So too our communities. Wars can become an endangered species. The illness that has brought so much misery and destruction to our lives is easier to see; we have the self-insight to be able to recognize it. But are we prepared to try the potential cure, to take up and turn the key that unlocks a better future?

Are we prepared to put friendship first? Are we ready to try to satisfy in each other just Ten Desires?

KEY POINTS

- The Ten Desires can help us create governments that make our lives, communities, and the world a happier, and safer place.
- When governments meet our Ten Desires they will be much closer to working properly *for* us and we will be happier with them.
- **Six Principles of Friendship-Focused Government**
  - Flat hierarchies—long term—work best. Absolute rule will always be temporary; desires to be heard, valued, and respected will forever float to the surface demanding to be met.

- Consensus is the sticky grease that lubricates society, smooths over our individual needs and differences, and binds us together as a greater whole.
- Group meeting size matters: We cannot create consensus, help keep people informed, and let them all have their say, if the groups we meet in are too large; they need to be a manageable size.
- Individual liberties need respect: A group is made up of individuals all seeking to satisfy their individual expression of their humanity. If the group—community—doesn't respect this, then it will make life more miserable for everyone.
- Rules and laws are critical: If a government is to help us meet our Ten Desires, it must have laws and rules that help us respect each other's human desires and means of preventing payback getting out of control; such as rule of law and impartial policing.
- Individual and social responsibility: Society is guilty every time a crime is committed. Every crime is an indication of priorities and approaches that aren't meeting the people's needs; a failure in the approach and application of governance.

- **Best types of government for us:**
    - Democracy is always under threat while hierarchies exist, there is turmoil in the world, and our desires for wealth, power, and status remain strong.
    - The Iroquois of North America had perhaps the best democracy in history.
- **How we can improve our governments:**
    - Prioritize friendship: ask the friendship question.
    - Vote and be active.
    - Form local social groups.
    - Meet at community halls.
    - Help the marginalized and disadvantaged.
    - Create and support a village.
    - Be responsible.

- A thousand years of peace rests with us in our Ten Desires, which can satisfy our need for friendship and community on an international level, as well as they can personally.
- Change us and we change our leaders and governments.

CHAPTER 12

The Salvation in Us

> WE ARE MADE WISE NOT BY
> THE RECOLLECTION OF OUR PAST,
> BUT BY THE RESPONSIBILITY
> FOR OUR FUTURE.
>
> —*George Bernard Shaw*

When nature gave us crops to grow and animals to herd it is hard to imagine it had any idea of the devastation it would unleash upon itself. In an advanced primate species, it created one of its most adaptable creatures; they could roam the planet and survive on literally every continent in all manner of extreme conditions. But they were made specifically for roaming. When nature created just the right conditions to allow them to settle down and farm it was like strapping a bomb to a child and giving it the switch. New desires were unleashed that led them to become out of touch with the natural world. Worse still, it left them imbalanced in their heart (desires) and that imbalance led to overpopulation, exploiting the earth beyond its tolerance, poisoning it so it sustained less life, and now threatening to leave it a lifeless radioactive cinder thanks to the technology they developed out of constantly fighting among themselves. If the natural world's plan was to destroy itself, it was doing well. But perhaps nature wasn't as naïve as we might think. It seems it gave itself a failsafe, a way to restore the imbalance before it was too late. It gave these disturbed and tormented creatures that call themselves human beings an increasing ability of self-understanding.

It gave us not only the problem but access to understanding the nature of illness it inflicted upon us, and its cure.

Every one of us has evolved enough self-awareness to understand the basic human desires that drive us; that see us think, feel, and behave as we do. We have been given the ability to see what nature intended for us as a species and how it, unexpectedly, went off course. Each of us has the capacity to clearly see how our natural response to our environment—thanks to how nature made us—led to desires that would create ongoing wars, mass famines, division, hate, exploitation, inequity and imbalance, and to a vast destruction of the natural world. Nature gave us a gift of being able to bring forth into the light perhaps its greatest ever threat, an inner beast, uncontrolled, inside each of us, and an insight into simple things we can do to cage and restrain it. It gave itself, and us, realistic hope.

It has been at least 15,000–20,000 years since human kind first started farming, since the emergence of the desire for wealth. It has been over 5500 years since we developed civilizations and all the war and destruction they bring. Now the desires for wealth, power, and status dominate human beings in civilizations littered all over the world. We knew in our hearts this wasn't how we were supposed to feel, that despite the technical advances we were on a dangerous and destructive path, but we kept on it anyway. We have searched for saviors, we have lived with leaders telling us what to do for so long we thought our salvation could only be found with one of them. If only they could show us the way, if only they could help us fight off those who threaten us once and for all—our enemies—and finally make us forever safe. But as our focus was always diverted to the threats around us we failed to recognize, perhaps ignored, weren't ready, or didn't want to see, the demon we were trying to slay; the enemy that was always threatening our families was inside each and every one of us.

When we think of friendship we underestimate its power and influence. Like a special person in our life, it isn't until they are missing that we truly understand the fundamental, and heart-felt role, they played. To think of friendship till now has been to envisage it as not much more than a cure for a loneliness increasingly gripping our society, as a personal way to lessen a pain in our hearts. But friendship, seen in terms of the basic human desires that define it and make it work, has revealed a much more critical force. Friendship fell to the desires of our inner beast and havoc was the result, but friendship, with our conscious help, can cage it.

This is a unique time. Today we understand ourselves in ways we never have before; through science, and through peering deep inside. It is also a time of vast interconnection, of people being connected to each other all over the world so they can share their knowledge and wisdom to more people, quicker, than ever before. A time when no one country or people can completely dominate another with superior technology or take over the world; others can find similar technology and fight back. A time ripe for setting in place the seeds for positive change that restore balance, and with it, a lasting peace.

We can have a world where we no longer see wars killing our best and brightest, displacing millions, and the frightening acts of terror that often go with them. It is not an unrealistic dream to imagine restoring community spirit, of welcoming the marginalized or oppressed, being more tolerant, compassionate, and understanding. It is not some vague hope to have a stable and meaningful well-paid job, or that we will live in more equitable and caring societies, where the rich no longer get wealthier at our expense. Loneliness does not need to be on the rise; we can all enjoy more fulfilling relationships, caring, supportive, and stable loving families, and people around us who want us as friends. Nature has given us access to understanding one of its most mighty instruments for positive change: friendship. It has left the promise—the key—to a better future squarely at our feet.

Isn't it time we created a new and promising era of friendship?

Perhaps we should be asking ourselves more often: 'Am I putting friendship first?'

Are you?

FURTHER READING

Alexander, M (2011). *The New Jim Crow: Mass incarceration in the age of colorblindness.* New York: The New Press.

Alison, G (2017). *Destined for War: Can America and China escape Thucydides's trap?* London: Scribe Publications.

Beder, S (2002). *Global Spin: The corporate assault on environmentalism.* Vermont: Chelsea Green Publishing Company.

Cane, S (2013). *First Footprints: The epic story of the First Australians.* Sydney: Allen & Unwin.

Congress for the New Urbanism (2013). *Charter of the New Urbanism. 2nd Edition.* New York: McGraw-Hill Education.

Diamond, JM (1997). *Guns, Germs and Steel: A short history of everybody for the last 13,000 years.* London: Vintage.

Diamond, JM (2012). *The World Until Yesterday: What can we learn from traditional societies?* New York: Penguin.

Gammage, B (2011). *The Biggest Estate on Earth: How Aborigines made Australia.* Sydney: Allen & Unwin.

Gottman, J and Silver, N (1999). *The Seven Principles for Making a Marriage Work.* London: Orion.

Kiernan, B (2007). *Blood and Soil: A world history of genocide and extermination from Sparta to Darfur.* New Haven: Yale University Press.

Mann, CC (2011). *1491: New revelations of the Americas before Columbus.* New York: Vintage Books.

Perkins, F (1946). *The Roosevelt I Knew.* New York: Penguin.

Perkins, J (2005). *Confessions of an Economic Hitman: The shocking inside story of how America REALLY took over the world.* London: Ebury Publishing.

Robins, N (2012). *The Corporation that Changed the World: How the East India Company shaped the modern multinational.* New York: Pluto Press.

Sedhoff, W (2011). *A Balance of Self: A new approach to self understanding, lasting happiness, and self-truth.* Fremantle: Vivid Publishing.

Sedhoff, W (2016). *The Fall and Rise of Women: How women can change the world.* Melbourne: Ingram Press.

Snow, DR (1994). *The Peoples of America: The Iroquois.* Massachusetts: Blackwell Publishing.

Standing Bear, L (1933). *Land of the Spotted Eagle.* Lincoln: University of Nebraska Press.

NOTES

Introduction

1. The Step Family Foundation, 'Step family statistics', http://www.stepfamily.org/stepfamily-statistics.html (accessed 23 March 2018).
2. Statistics Brain, 'Infidelity statistics', 7 September 2016, http://www.statisticbrain.com/infidelity-statistics (accessed 23 March 2018).
3. PWC UK, 'UK economic outlook: Prospects for the economy, consumer spending and regional growth', March 2018, http://www.pwc.co.uk/services/economics-policy/insights/uk-economic-outlook.html (accessed 23 March 2018).
4. D Thomas, 'Why retail chains have suffered such a mauling', *Financial Times*, 17 March 2018, https://www.ft.com/content/83852f28-290f-11e8-b27e-cc62a39d57a0 (accessed 3 June 2018).
5. C Isidore, '31,000 Toys 'R' Us employees: No job and no severance', *CNN Money*, 16 March 2018, http://money.cnn.com/2018/03/16/news/companies/toys-r-us-employees/index.html (accessed 3 June 2018).
6. 'Private Equity: The barbarian establishment', *The Economist*, 22 October 2016, http://www.economist.com/news/briefing/21709007-private-equity-has-prospered-while-almost-every-other-approach-business-has-stumbled (accessed 3 June 2018).
7. Oxfam, 'An economy for the 1%', January 2016, https://www.oxfam.org/sites/www.oxfam.org/files/file_attachments/bp210-economy-one-percent-tax-havens-180116-en_0.pdf (accessed 3 June 2018).
8. Oxfam, 'Reward work, not wealth', January 2018, https://d1tn-3vj7xz9fdh.cloudfront.net/s3fs-public/file_attachments/bp-reward-work-not-wealth-220118-en.pdf (accessed 3 June 2018).
9. Statista, 'Total lobbying spending in the United States from 1998 to 2017', https://www.statista.com/statistics/257337/total-lobbying-spending-in-the-us/ (accessed 3 June 2018).
10. Wikipedia, 'List of ongoing armed conflicts', https://en.wikipedia.org/wiki/List_of_ongoing_armed_conflicts (accessed 24 April 2018).

11   M Chalabi, 'How many times does the average person move?', *FiveThirtyEight*, 29 January 2015, https://fivethirtyeight.com/features/how-many-times-the-average-person-moves/ (accessed 3 June 2018).

12   B Levin, 'Jews top target for hate crimes last year in New York City, again', *Huffpost*, January 2018, https://www.huffingtonpost.com/entry/jews-top-target-for-hate-crimes-last-year-in-new-york_us_5a553361e4b0baa6abf16224 (accessed 3 June 2018).

13   V Dodd, 'Police blame worst rise in recorded hate crime on EU referendum', *The Guardian*, 11 July 2016, https://www.theguardian.com/society/2016/jul/11/police-blame-worst-rise-in-recorded-hate-on-eu-referendum (accessed 3 June 2018).

14   The Sentencing Project, 'Trends in US Corrections', http://sentencingproject.org/wp-content/uploads/2016/01/Trends-in-US-Corrections.pdf (accessed 3 June 2018).

15   C Yeginsu, 'UK Appoints a Minister for Loneliness', *New York Times*, 17 January 2018, https://www.nytimes.com/2018/01/17/world/europe/uk-britain-loneliness.html (accessed 3 June 2018).

16   RD Semba, 'The discovery of vitamins', *International Journal for Vitamin and Nutrition Research*, October 2012, https://www.ncbi.nlm.nih.gov/pubmed/23798048 (accessed 3 June 2018).

17   JL Fisher-Blando, 'Workplace bullying: Aggressive behaviour and its effects on job satisfaction and productivity.' University of Phoenix, February 2008, http://www.workplaceviolence911.com/docs/20081215.pdf (accessed 3 June 2018).

18   G Marks, '21 percent of CEOs are psychopaths. Only 21 percent?', *Washington Post*, 16 September 2016, https://www.washingtonpost.com/news/on-small-business/wp/2016/09/16/gene-marks-21-percent-of-ceos-are-psychopaths-only-21-percent/?utm_term=.bcc191b3d13e (accessed 3 June 2018).

19   'Global estimates of modern slavery', International Labour Organization and Walk Free Foundation, Geneva 2017, http://www.ilo.org/wcmsp5/groups/public/---dgreports/---dcomm/documents/publication/wcms_575479.pdf (accessed 3 June 2018).

Part One:
The Friendship Crash and Rise of a Beast

20   J Carlin, 'Nelson Mandela: The freedom fighter who embraced his enemies', *The Guardian*, 7 December 2013, https://www.theguardian

.com/world/2013/dec/07/nelson-mandela-freedom-fighter-john-carlin (accessed 3 June 2018).
21 J Carlin, 'Mandela: A man of all the people', *Independent*, 18 July 2008, http://www.independent.co.uk/news/people/profiles/mandela-a-man-of-all-the-people-870727.html (accessed 3 June 2018).

Chapter 2: Rise of the Beast Within

22 'Strengths of Australian Aboriginal cultural practices in family life and child rearing', Australian Institute of Family Studies, CFCA Paper No 25, September 2014, https://aifs.gov.au/cfca/publications/strengths-australian-aboriginal-cultural-practices-fam/theme-2-children-need-freedom (accessed 3 June 2018).
23 B Gammage, *The Biggest Estate on Earth: How Aborigines made Australia*, Allen and Unwin, Sydney, 2011, p 298.
24 S Croucher, 'How rich is the Vatican? So wealthy it can stumble across millions of euros just "tucked away"', *International Business Times*, 5 December 2014, https://www.ibtimes.co.uk/how-rich-vatican-so-wealthy-it-can-stumble-across-millions-euros-just-tucked-away-1478219?hc_location=ufi (accessed 3 June 2018).
25 'Kim Kardashian West personality', *Forbes*, 2017, https://www.forbes.com/profile/kim-kardashian-west (accessed 3/6/18).
26 A Newbold, 'The highest-paid models of 2017', *Vogue*, 22 November 2017, http://www.vogue.co.uk/gallery/highest-paid-models-forbes-2017 (accessed 3 June 2018).
27 D Agren, 'Mexico drug cartel's grip on politicians and police revealed in Texas court files', *The Guardian*, 10 November 2017, https://www.theguardian.com/world/2017/nov/10/mexico-drug-cartels-grip-on-politicians-and-police-revealed-in-texas-court-files (accessed 6 May 2018).

Chapter 3: Slavery and Our Exploitation

28 'Sex trafficking, modern slave narratives, Shamere McKenzie', *End Slavery Now*, 3 January 2015, http://www.endslaverynow.org/blog/articles/shamere-mckenzie (accessed 3 June 2018).
29 'Our mission and values', *Shared Hope International*, https://sharedhope.org/about-us/our-mission-and-values/ (accessed 3 June 2018).
30 'Global estimates of modern slavery', International Labour Organization and Walk Free Foundation.

31 'Country study: United States', *The Global Slavery Index 2016*, https://www.globalslaveryindex.org/country/united-states/ (accessed 3 June 2018).
32 M Alexander, *The New Jim Crow*, The New Press, New York, 2012.
33 Wikipedia, 'Aztec slavery', https://en.wikipedia.org/wiki/Aztec_slavery (accessed 3 June 2018).
34 'United States average hourly wages 1964–2018', *Trading Economics*, https://tradingeconomics.com/united-states/wages (accessed 3 June 2018).
35 'Should the federal minimum wage be increased', *ProCon.org*, http://minimum-wage.procon.org (accessed 3 June 2018).
36 'Global findings', *The Global Slavery Index 2016*, https://www.globalslaveryindex.org/findings/ (accessed 24 July 2018).
37 'Country study: China', *The Global Slavery Index 2016*, https://www.globalslaveryindex.org/country/china (accessed 3 June 2018).
38 R Schimmer, 'Hispaniola. Case study: Colonial genocides', *Yale University Genocide Studies Program*, https://gsp.yale.edu/case-studies/colonial-genocides-project/hispaniola (accessed 3 June 2018).
39 'Massacre at the Great Temple of Tenochtitlan', *Wikipedia*, https://en.wikipedia.org/wiki/Massacre_in_the_Great_Temple_of_Tenochtitlan (accessed 3 June 2018).

Chapter 4: The Destruction We Support: Empires

40 '3 real stories from refugees', *World Economic Forum*, 17 December 2015, https://www.weforum.org/agenda/2015/12/3-real-stories-from-refugees (accessed 3 June 2018).
41 '3 real stories from refugees', *World Economic Forum*.
42 'The company that ruled the waves', *The Economist*, 17 December 2011, www.economist.com/node/21541753 (accessed 3 June 2018).
43 A Jadesimi, 'How China's $60 billion for Africa will drive global prosperity', 14 March 2017, https://www.forbes.com/sites/amyjadesimi/2017/03/14/how-chinas-60-billion-for-africa-will-drive-global-prosperity/#4c99b11038a3 (accessed 3 June 2018).
44 G Alison, *Destined for War: Can America and China escape Thucydides's Trap?*, Scribe, London, 2017.
45 B Kiernan, *Blood and Soil: A world history of genocide and extermination from Sparta to Darfur*, Yale University Press, New Haven, 2007.

46 'Obesity and overweight', World Health Organization, 18 October 2017, http://www.who.int/mediacentre/factsheets/fs311/en/ (accessed 3 June 2018).

47 'How close are we to #ZeroHunger?', *Food and Agriculture Organization of the United Nations*, http://www.fao.org/state-of-food-security-nutrition/en/ (accessed 3 June 2018).

48 'US and World Population Clock', United States Census Bureau, https://www.census.gov/popclock/ (accessed 7 May 2018).

49 'Debt relief under the Heavily Indebted Poor Country (HIPC) Initiative', International Monetary Fund, 8 March 2018, http://www.imf.org/en/About/Factsheets/Sheets/2016/08/01/16/11/Debt-Relief-Under-the-Heavily-Indebted-Poor-Countries-Initiative (accessed 3 June 2018).

50 S Fan, 'Where do the world's hungriest people live? Not where you think', *HuffPost*, 1 June 2015, https://www.huffingtonpost.com/shenggen-fan/where-do-the-worlds-hungr_b_6978434.html (accessed 3 June 2018); '2014–2015 Global Food Policy Report', International Food Policy Research Institute, Washington, DC, https://reliefweb.int/sites/reliefweb.int/files/resources/GFPR14-15_embargo_w.pdf (accessed 26 July 2018).

51 'Union Carbide's disaster', The Bhopal Medical Appeal, bhopal.org/what-happened/union-carbides-disaster/ (accessed 3 June 2018).

52 E Broughton, 'The Bhopal disaster and its aftermath: A review', *Environmental Health: A Global Access Science Source*, 10 May 2005, https://ehjournal.biomedcentral.com/track/pdf/10.1186/1476-069X-4-6 (accessed 3 June 2018).

53 'The United States of toxins', *Ode To Clean*, 24 October 2017, https://blog.odetoclean.com/the-united-states-of-toxins-1e219e5a701f (accessed 3 June 2018).

54 'Airbus A380 specifications', *Modern Airliners*, http://www.modernairliners.com/airbus-a380/airbus-a380-specs/ (accessed 3 June 2018).

55 'Fracking by the numbers', Environment America Research & Policy Center, 14 April 2016, https://environmentamerica.org/reports/ame/fracking-numbers-0 (accessed 3 June 2018).

56 'Fact sheet: Pollution—Facts that might surprise you', *Pure Earth*, 7 April 2014, http://www.pureearth.org/blog/pollution-15-facts-that-might-surprise-you (accessed 24 July 2018).

57 S Beder, *Global Spin: The corporate assault on environmentalism*, Chelsea Green Publishing Company, Vermont, 2002, p 25.

Part Two
The Friendship Key—Empowering Positive Change

58 F Perkins, *The Roosevelt I Knew*, Penguin Books, New York, 1946.

Chapter 5: Friendship: Prosperity, Peace, Respect

59 F Brown, 'Detroit's greener side/Detroit urban farming', visitdetroit.com, 20 March 2017, https://visitdetroit.com/urban-farming-detroit (accessed 3 June 2018).

60 R Grayson, 'Farmers of the urban footpath—design guidelines for street verge gardens', Australian City Farms & Community Gardens Network, April 2010, https://communitygarden.org.au/2010/04/09/verge-gardens (accessed 3 June 2018).

61 J Diamond, *Guns, Germs & Steel: A short history of everybody for the last 13,000 years*, Vintage, New York, 1997.

Chapter 8: Fixing our Relationship with Friendship

62 L Gottlieb, 'Does a more equal marriage mean less sex?', *New York Times*, 6 February 2014, https://www.nytimes.com/2014/02/09/magazine/does-a-more-equal-marriage-mean-less-sex.html (accessed 3 June 2018).

63 'Singles now outnumber married people in America—and that's a good thing', *PRI Lifestyle*, 14 September 2014, https://www.pri.org/stories/2014-09-14/singles-now-outnumber-married-people-america-and-thats-good-thing (accessed 3 June 2018).

64 L Standing Bear, *Land of the Spotted Eagle*, Lincoln, University of Nebraska Press, 1978.

65 L Standing Bear, *Land of the Spotted Eagle*, p 213.

66 A Lommel and I Campbell (translator), *The Unambal: A tribe in northwest Australia*, Takarakka Nowan Kas Publications, Carnarvon Gorge, 1997.

Chapter 9: Friendship, Better Pay, Jobs, Businesses, and Global Stability

67 'Our story', Bright Pink, https://www.brightpink.org/about-us/mission (accessed 20 May 2018).

68 C Reid and J Janisch, 'Wounded Warrior Project execs fired', *CBS News*, 10 March 2016, https://www.cbsnews.com/news/wounded-warrior-project-ceo-and-coo-fired (accessed 9 July 2018).

69 N Dolsak, S Christianna Parr and A Prakash, 'The Oxfam scandal shows that, yes, non-profits can behave badly. So why aren't they overseen like for-profits?', 19 February 2018, *The Washington Post*, https://www.washingtonpost.com/news/monkey-cage/wp/2018/02/19/the-oxfam-scandal-shows-that-yes-nonprofits-can-behave-badly-so-why-arent-they-overseen-like-for-profits/?utm_term=.65c2c01f6e9d (accessed 8 July 2018).
70 International Co-operative Alliance, *Cooperatives and the Future of Work*, 30 April 2018, https://www.ica.coop/sites/default/files/publication-files/ica-position-on-fowfinal07052018-510263159.pdf (accessed 30 July 2018).
71 B Venohr, J Fear and A Witt, 'Best of German Mittelstand—The world market leaders', 24 August 2015, https://dx.doi.org/10.2139/ssrn.2724609 (accessed 24 July 2018).
72 Venohr, Fear and Witt, 'Best of German Mittelstand'.
73 K Fastnacht, 'Robert Bosch: His life and work', *Journal of Bosch History*, Supplement 1, Robert Bosch, Stuttgart, 2010.

Chapter 10: Bringing Back Community

74 A Schmidt, F Zollo, M Del Vicario, A Bessi, A Scala, G Caldarelli, HE Stanley and W Quattrociocchi, 'Anatomy of news consumption on Facebook', PNAS, 21 March 2017, https://doi.org/10.1073/pnas.1617052114 (accessed 24 July 2018).
75 M Chalabi, 'How many times does the average person move?', *FiveThirtyEight*, 29 January 2015, https://fivethirtyeight.com/features/how-many-times-the-average-person-moves (accessed 3 June 2018).
76 B Ryan and G Stayner, 'African gangs in Melbourne are a problem, police admit, as Victorian Government defends strategy', *ABC News*, 9 January 2018, http://www.abc.net.au/news/2018-01-02/street-gangs-are-a-problem-in-melbourne-police-admit/9297984 (accessed 3 June 2018).
77 F Hunter and B Preiss, 'Victorians scared to go to restaurants at night because of street gang violence: Peter Dutton', *Sydney Morning Herald*, 3 January 2018, https://www.smh.com.au/politics/federal/victorians-scared-to-go-to-restaurants-at-night-because-of-street-gang-violence-peter-dutton-20180103-h0cvu4.html (accessed 30 July 2018).
78 N Bucci, 'Has the Apex Gang been mortally wounded?', *Sydney Morning Herald*, 20 February 2017, https://www.smh.com.au/national/victoria/has-the-apex-gang-been-mortally-wounded-20170220-gugziq.html (accessed 30 July 2018).

79 A Flagg, 'The myth of the criminal immigrant', *New York Times*, 30 March 2018, https://www.nytimes.com/interactive/2018/03/30/upshot/crime-immigration-myth.html?rref=world&module=ArrowsNav&contentCollection=The%20Upshot&action=keypress&region=FixedRight&pgtype=Multimedia (accessed 24 July 2018).
80 F Perry, 'My neighbour avoids me ... I was very unhappy: Your tales of urban loneliness', *The Guardian*, 24 March 2016, https://www.theguardian.com/cities/2016/mar/24/my-neighbour-avoids-me-i-was-very-unhappy-your-tales-of-urban-loneliness (accessed 24 July 2018).
81 RIM Dunbar, 'Coevolution of neocortical size, group size and language in humans', *Behavioural and Brain Sciences*, 1993, 16, pp 681–735.
82 M Konnikova, 'The limits of friendship', *The New Yorker*, 7 October 2014, https://www.newyorker.com/science/maria-konnikova/social-media-affect-math-dunbar-number-friendships (accessed 24 July 2018).
83 S Marche, 'Is Facebook making us lonely?', *The Atlantic*, May 2012, https://www.theatlantic.com/magazine/archive/2012/05/is-facebook-making-us-lonely/308930/ (accessed 3 June 2018).
84 Congress for the New Urbanism, *Charter of the New Urbanism*, 2nd Edition, McGraw-Hill, New York, 2013.
85 M Ghazali, 'Affordable and High-Rise Honeycomb Housing: How we create better homes for more people—a book in progress', http://www.tslr.net/2016/10/better-affordable-alternatives-to.html (accessed 3 June 2018).
86 Transition Bondi, http://transitionbondi.org (accessed 24 July 2018).

Chapter 11: Government by Us for Us

87 WikiQuote, 'Ronald Reagan', https://en.wikiquote.org/wiki/Ronald_Reagan (accessed 2 February 2018).
88 'Democracy Index 2017 Free speech under attack', *The Economist,* 2017, http://pages.eiu.com/rs/753-RIQ-438/images/Democracy_Index_2017.pdf (accessed 3 June 2018).
89 'Democracy Index 2017 Free speech under attack', *The Economist*.
90 Gettysburg Address, https://en.wikipedia.org/wiki/Gettysburg_Address (accessed 24 July 2018).

ABOUT THE AUTHOR

In his early 20s Dr Winfried Sedhoff faced a life-threatening personal crisis that sent him into self-imposed isolation. Over a 12-month internal quest he discovered not only answers to his crisis, but uncovered a sense of genuine self, a journey he documented in his first book, *A Balance of Self, A New Approach to Self Understanding, Lasting Happiness, and Self-Truth* (Vivid, 2011). For 25 years he has refined his approaches via his work as a family physician specialising in mental health, and has offered guidance and training to patients, colleagues, medical trainees, and the general public. His books convey his passion for history, tribal society, ethnography, psychology, and self-understanding.

Winfried lives in Brisbane, Australia.

ACKNOWLEDGEMENTS

To family, friends, colleagues, and the many patients I have had the privilege to know over my lifetime, every one of you has helped shape this book in some way and for that I am truly grateful.

To Jessica Perini, my editor, thank you for your guidance and invaluable recommendations. To Laura Duffy, a big thank you for a great cover design. And to Karen Minster, many thanks for applying your considerable creativity to the internals.

To those of you I have not yet had the privilege to meet may I also thank you. We all make the world. We all affect each other; you too have made this book possible.

To all who share the dream of a world filled with caring, respect, safety, and a sense of security for all no matter race, belief, gender, age, or sexual orientation, may we never lose our passion and energy to make this dream a reality.

Perhaps one day, we can truly claim we live among a world of friends.

INDEX

Aboriginal Australians, 17, 18, 19, 55, 125–26, 130, 168, 231
Abramovich, Roman, 39–40
absolute rule, 226
acknowledging people, 93, 195
active listening, 97–99, 134, 135, 188–89, 192, 196
actors, 24
adaptability, 127
affairs, xx–xxi, 120
Afghanistan, 54
Africa, loans to, 52, 58–59
African Americans, 32
'African gang crime', 205
African tribes, 211
Akhenaten, 22
Alexander the Great, 21
Al-Qaeda, 55
Alvarado, Pedro de, 42
ambitions, 17, 109, 139–40
Amish communities, 217
Ancient civilizations, 21–23, 25, 34, 37, 69–70, 208
anxiety, 3–4
Appreciated,
    for customers, 195
    day-to-day, 95–97
    for managers, 188
    in relationships, 147–48
    for workers, 192
Approved, *see* Validated/Approved
arguing, 98, 152–54
Armenian genocide, 54
armies, 25, 107, 208, 224
Asian Infrastructure Investment Bank, 52–53
attention, 91, 135
attitude, 89–90

attraction, 123, 125, 130, 134, 136
Aurangzeb, 49
Australian Aboriginal culture, 17, 18, 19, 55, 125–26, 130, 168, 231
Australian brush-turkey, 4–5
Austro-Hungarian Empire, 53
authoritarian rule, xxvi, 225, 235
Avner, Lindsay, 176–77
Aztecs, 34–36, 42, 74

Babylon, 37–38
Balance of Self Model, 6–9, 121–22
Bar Mitzvah, 103
barn raising, 217
basic human desires/needs, xxiv–xxv, 6–9, 56, 100, 228–29
'Bassem', 45–46
beast, *see* inner beast
Beder, Sharon, 61
beliefs, 22–23, 36–39, 56, 57, 71, 72, 77
Bhopal disaster, 60
Bible, the, 38
blaming, 154–55
boat people, 45–46
body language, 152
Bondi, 216
Bosch, Robert, 181
Brazil, 51, 59
bribery, 24–25, 26
Bright Pink, 176–77
Britain, xxii
British Empire, 48–50, 53, 59
brush-turkey, *see* Australian brush-turkey
bullying, xxvi, 18, 190–91, 194
Burke, Edmund, 49
Business Roundtable organizations, 61–62

business structure, xxxi–xxxii, 174, 175–83

Cacioppo, John, 209–10
Cared for, 12
    for customers, 197
    day-to-day, 107–9
    for managers, 190
    in relationships, 148–50
    for workers, 193
cars, 212, 213
caste system, 36, 38
casual friendship, xxiv, 87–89, 186, 208
Catholic Church, 23
CEOs, xxi, xxvi, 26
changing others, 147
Chas. T. Main, Inc, 51
chattel slaves, 38
'chemistry', 123
children, 17–18, 91, 112, 113, 126–27, 166
China, 25, 40–41, 50, 51, 52–53, 54, 75
choices, 81–83, 105–6, 147, 150, 186
Churchill, Winston, 65–66
cities, 89, 95
Civil War (1651), 49
'civilization', xxvii, 18, 72, 222, 250
close friendships,
    vs casual, xxiv, 87–89
    and equality, 146
    number of, 208
    with opposite sex, 161, 163, 164
    in relationships, 82–83, 119, 124–25, 131, 149, 162–66
    and sameness, 99–100
    at work, 186–87
Cold War, 52, 54
Columbus, Christopher, 41
common wealth, 69–70, 73
Communist Party in China, 40
communities, 203–221
    and business, 179, 185
    close, 167–69, 212, 233
community gardens, 70–71
community halls, 211, 214, 240
Community Self, 6, 8, 121–22, 156
community spirit, xxii, xxxii, 203–6, 215, 216, 219
compassion, 13

compatibility, 124–25, 168
competition, 17, 27, 40, 128
confidentiality, 98–99
consensus, 71–72, 227, 232, 244
contact, regular, 210–11
contempt, 153
control, need for, 147
Cooperative Home Care Associates, 172
co-operatives, 176, 177–80
corporate activism, 61–62
corporate empires, 47,
    see also hybrid empires
corporations, 175
corporatocracy, 235, 236
Corroborees, 168
corruption, 24–26
counseling, 110, 149, 155, 160–61
country people, 95
couples' therapy, 155, 160–61
crime, 232, 233, 241–42
criticism, 153
cultural differences, 93, 188
customer loyalty, 183–84, 197
customer service, 93–94
customers, 195–98
cynicism, 153

dances, 210–11
date nights, 132
'David', 205
deal breakers, 124, 166
debt, xxi, 34–35, 36, 58, 68–71, 172, 199–200
debt slaves, 35, 38
decision-making, 81–83, 105–6, 224
defensiveness, 153–54
democracies, 235–38
depression, xv–xvi, 3–4, 109
deprivation, 27, 39–40, 43
desires/needs, basic, xxiv–xxv, 6–9, 56, 100, 228–29
Desires of Friendship, Ten, xxv, 10–15
    for customers, 195–98
    day-to-day, 89–114
    on international level, 244
    for managers, 182, 187–91
    in relationships, 125–42, 145–49
    for workers, 182, 191–94
Detroit, 70

INDEX

Diamond, Jared, 88
dictators, 225, 234
difference, 11, 76, 124, 204
  see also Sameness
disagreeing, 98–99, 152–54, 193, 196, 227
disgust, 153
disrespect, 193, 197
diversity, 101, 240
'Doaa', 45–46
driving, 212, 213
drug running, 24–25, 48, 50
drug screening, 190, 193
'Dunbar Number', 208–9, 214

East India Company, 48–50, 59, 61, 174
Egypt, 22, 37–38, 45–46
elderly people, 217
elite, 22–23, 25, 27–28, 37, 49, 57, 59, 63, 146
Elizabeth I, Queen, 48
emotional involvement at work, 186–87
emotional pain, 225–26, 230
emotions, talking about, 134, 164, 165
empathy, 12–13, 97, 103
empires, xxviii, 45–64
  countering, 75–78
  definition, 47
employees, *see* workers
encouragement, 139–40
enemies, 76, 102
English language, 50
environment, 8–9
environmental destruction, 60–62, 77–78
environmentally responsible businesses, 185
equality, 71–72, 144, 146, 189
equity ratios, 181
escapism, 24
excess, 19–20
excluding others, 17–18
exclusivity, 163–65
expectations, 95, 96, 159–60
exploitation, xxvii, 33, 39, 43, 57
extremism, 55–58, 76
eye contact, 93

Facebook, xxiv, 204, 210
face-to-face contact, 209–10
family focused businesses, 184–85
Family Self, 6, 7, 121
farming, xxvii, 18–20, 249, 250
favoritism, 187
FDR (Roosevelt), 65–66
fear, 101–2, 127–8, 224–26
feelings, talking about, 134
femininity, 126, 134, 136, 137–38
festivals, 210–11
fights, 152–54
flat hierarchies, 183, 226
flooding, 152, 155
footpath gardens, 70–71
four horsemen, the, 152–54
fracking, 61
freedom, 228–29, *see also* slavery
friendship-friendly businesses, 175–87
friendship practice schedule, 114–15
friendship priority questionnaire, 80–81
friendship question, 79–84, 239
friendship with the opposite sex, 161, 163, 164–65
frustration, 159–60
fufillment, 127, 129

gender differences, 125–27, 137
gender roles, 126–30, 137–38
gender-sensitive friendship desires, 131–42
geo-economics, 53
Germany, 53, 54, 180–82, 225
Gettysburg Address, 242
Ghazali, Mazlin, 215
gifts, 91
give and take, 140
Global Financial Crisis (GFC), 172, 180, 181, 199–200
goals, shared, 184, 190, 194, 217
gods, 22–23, 37, 38, 43
gossip, 100, 135
Gottman, John and Julie, 152, 160–61
government, 222–48
government/corporate empires, *see* hybrid empires
government-owned businesses, 176
greeting people, 188, 192
group size, 207–9, 215–16, 227–28

habits, 84, 90
Haiti, 41, 67
hate crimes, xxii, 204–5
headphones, 211
Heard, 11, 91
    for customers, 196
    day-to-day, 97–99
    for managers, 188–89
    in relationships, 134–35
    for workers, 192
Heavily Indebted Poor Countries Initiative, 58
Hebrews, 37–38
helping others, 111, 193–94
hierarchies, 27, 59, 96, 105
    and belief systems, 37, 38, 39
    in business, 183, 187
    flat, 183, 226
    in government, 223–26
    military, 107, 224
    reducing, 71–72
Hindu beliefs, 38
Hispaniola, 41
Hitler, Adolf, 54, 225
holes, filling, 156–59
Holocaust, the, 54
Honeycomb suburbs, 214–15
Hong Kong, 50
hope, 22
housing, 213–15
hunger, 58–60, 243
hybrid empires, xxi, xxviii, 47–48, 50–53, 54, 57, 63

ignoring people, 93, 95, 132, 133, 195
illness, 148–49
immigration, 205
impartiality, 187
Incas, 69–70
inclusiveness, 17, 18
India, 36, 38, 48–50, 59, 60, 61, 174
individual responsibility, 232–33, 241
individuality, 7, 57, 71, 228–29
inequality,
    and belief systems, 36, 37, 38–39
    and farming, 20
    today, xxi, 36, 41, 57
infidelity, xx–xxi, 120
influence, 20–21, 24, 26

initiation ceremonies, 103
inner beast, 27–29, 63, 128
    countering, 73–74, 79–80, 156–57, 173–74
insecurity, 73, 128
instincts, 5–6, 230, 241
international law, 244–45
International Monetary Fund (IMF), 58, 60
intimacy, 132, 133
Iroquois people, 55, 237–38

Jefferson, Thomas, 67, 222
'Jenny and Tom', 118, 121
jobs, xxi, 17, 24, 33, 43–44
Judaism, 103
Judeans, 37–38
Julius Caesar, 25

Lakota Plains Indians, 10, 167–68
land, 6, 8–9
late, being, 91, 131, 132
laws, 230–32, 244–45
leaders, 21, 224–26, 250
liberal democracy, 235, 236
liberty, individual, 228–29, 237, 238, 242
life decisions, 82
Lincoln, Abraham, 17, 31, 102, 242
listening, *see* active listening; Heard
loans *see* Africa, loans to; debt
lobbying, political, xxi, 26, 49, 61–62, 63
local employment, 36, 180–81
loneliness, xxii, 203–4, 209–210
long-term approach, 181, 184
Los Zeta cartel, 25
love, 13, 148
loyalty, 183–84
lust, 168

maintenance, in relationships, 162
Malaysia, 215
malls, 212
managers, Ten Desires for, 182, 187–91
Mandela, Nelson, 1–2
manufacturing, 182
marginalized people, 102, 217, 240–41

masculinity, 126, 134, 136, 137–38
massacres, 42
McKenzie, Shamere, xxvii–xxviii, 31–32
meaningful tasks, 92
media, 62, 205
medicine, 18
meeting size, 227–28
meetings, 188
memories, 152
'men's business', 125–26
Mexico, 24–25, 59
Middle East, 52, 54, 57
military hierarchy, 107, 224
military power, 25
minimum wage, 35–36
mining, 61
minorities, 205, 229
Mittelstand businesses, 180–82
money, xxii, 35, 91
mothers, 126–29, 245
moving house, xxii, 204
music, 211

Nazi Germany, 54, 65, 225
needs, basic, xxiv–xxv, 6–9, 56, 100, 228–29
neighborhoods, 213
neighbors, xxii, 216
New Urbanism, 213–14
New York City, xxii, 205
New Zealand, 35
news, 204, see also media
Nicholas II, Tsar, 27
nomads, 19, 22, 34, 56, 71–72, 206, 231
Nong Chik, 215
non-profit corporations, 176–77
Noticed, 11
    for customers, 195
    day-to-day, 93–95
    for managers, 188
    in relationships, 132–33
    for workers, 192
nurturing role, 126–29, 245

obesity, 58
Old Testament, 38
Olmec people, 23

opinions, asking, 91
oppression, 57, 226
orders, giving, 105, 147
Orwell, George, 226
Ottoman Empire, 53–54

pain, emotional, 225–26, 230
Papua New Guinea tribes, 88, 230–31
parks, 213
parliament, British, 49
partnerships, 175
payback, 88, 230–31, 241–42, 244
peace, 74, 130, 225, 226, 242–43, 245–46
Perkins, Frances, 65–66
Perkins, John, 51–52
personal responsibility, 232–33, 241
Personal Self, 6, 7, 9, 121, 137, 156, 228
pharaohs, 22–23, 37
physical desires, 122, 123
Pinault, François, 39
plutocracy, 234, 236
police, 25, 231–32
politics, 239, 240
    see also lobbying, political
pollution, 60–61
Portuguese Empire, 59
poverty, 27, 39–40, 58–60, 77
power, 21, 24–26
PR, 62
practice schedule, 114–15
prestige, 24
primates, 208
private equity firms, xxi
problem solving, 135, 138–39
problems, recognizing, 151–54
profit vs people, 62, 174, 181
promises, 34
property development, 25–26
Protected, 12
    for customers, 198
    day-to-day, 112–14
    for managers, 190–91
    in relationships, 141–42
    for workers, 194
protecting assets, 20
providing/protecting role, 126–28, 245
public transport, 212

punishment,
  in business, 106
  in friendships, 90
  in relationships, 14, 132
  in society, 35, 227, 242

Qing dynasty, 75
quality time, 131–32

racism, 1, 32, 43
Ramos, Zaida, 172
Reagan, Ronald, 232
regular contact, 210–11
Reinders, John, 1–2
relationships, 118–71
  fixing with friendship, 151–61
  and the friendship question, 82–83
  Ten Desires in, 125–42, 145–49
religious beliefs, 22–23, 36–39, 56, 57, 71, 72, 77
Respected, 11, 14, 104
  for customers, 197
  day-to-day, 105–7
  for managers, 189–90
  in relationships, 145–47
  for workers, 193
responsibility, 92, 232–33, 241–42
restaurant workers, 35
revenge, *see* payback
revolution, 226
Roman Empire, 25, 208
Roosevelt, Franklin Delano (FDR), 65–66
royalty, 146, 234
rule of law, 230–32
Russia, 27–28, 51, 52, 53

safety, 28, 141, 207–8
Samaria, 23
Sameness, 11, 14–15, 90
  and community, 204, 217
  for customers, 196
  day-to-day, 99–102
  for managers, 189
  in relationships, 135–37
  for workers, 192–93
sarcasm, 153
Schultz, Howard, 39

secrets, 164, 165–66
security, 28
self-expression, 229
self-respect, 105, 121, 146
self-understanding, 103–4, 249–50
Sennheiser, 172, 180
sex, 7, 82, 123, 169
sex slavery, 31–32
shared facilities, 211–12, 214
shared goals/values, 184, 227
Shared Hope International, 32
sharing, 68–71, 73, 77
Shinto, 71
shopping centers, 212
shops, decentralized, 213, 215
showing off, 69
silent treatment, 154
single people, 166
skills, 10, 21–22
slavery, xxvii–xxviii, 31–44, 67, 68–74, 96–97
small talk, 100, 189, 196
Social Bees (SBs), 216–19, 240
social connection, 233
social gatherings, 167–68, 210–11, 239–40
social media, 99 *see also* Facebook
social responsibility, 232–33
social security, 70, 73
sociopaths, xxvi, 233
sole proprietorships, 175
Solomon Islands, 212
South Africa, 1–2
Soviet Union, 52, 54, 208
Spanish Empire, 41–42, 59, 74, 208
spirits vs gods, 22, 71
sport, 245
stability, 184
Stalin, Joseph, 65–66
starvation, 58–60, 77
status, 17, 21–24, 26, 136
stepping up, 154–55
'Steve', xix–xx
stonewalling, 154
Sundance ceremony, 167–68
superior beings, 39, 43
support groups, 217–18
Supported, 12
  for customers, 197–98

day-to-day, 109–112
for managers, 190
in relationships, 139–40
for workers, 194
survival, xxv, 7, 127
Syria, 45, 46

talking tree, 211
taxes, 23, 26, 180
technology, xxii, 74, 203–4, 251
teenagers, 92, 99, 102–3, 218
Tenochtitlan massacre, 42
terrorism, xxviii, 55–58, 76, 226
thanking people, 96, 148
therapy, 110, 149, 155, 160–61
threat, 101–2, 127–28, 224–26
time, 91, 131–32, 191
titles, using, 107
'Toby', 3–4, 13
'Tom and Jenny', 118, 121
totalitarian rule, 225, 226, 235
touch, 133
Toys R Us, xxi
Transition Bondi, 216
traumas, xviii, 112, 113, 142, 150
tribal societies, xxvii, 10, 55, 56, 71–72, 88, 103, 169, 208, 210–11, 227,
see also Australian Aboriginal culture; Iroquois people; nomads; Papua New Guinea tribes
Trump, Donald, 205
trust, 112, 165–66
Tsarist Russia, 27–28
Twin Towers collapse, 55

unemployment, 181
Union Carbide, 60
United States, 35, 51–52, 54,
see also New York City
Universal Declaration of Human Rights, 32
urban farming, 70–71

Validated/Approved, 11
for customers, 196
day-to-day, 102–4
for managers, 189
in relationships, 137–39
for workers, 193

Valued, 10
for customers, 195
day-to-day, 91–92
for managers, 187–88
in relationships, 131–32
for workers, 191
values, shared, 184
Vatican Bank, 23
victim, playing, 149, 153
Vietnamese refugees, 68–69
villages, 213–15, 241
virtual friends, 209–210
voting, 238, 239

wages, xxi, 35–36
walking, 212, 213
wars, xxi–xxii, 53–55, 74, 245
countering, 75
decision-making in, 224, 225
'war on terror', 76
see also World War 1; World War 2
weakness, 134, 153
wealth, xxi, xxvii, 19–21, 26, 34–36, 40–41, 68–71
weapons, 74
weekends away, 132
women, xvi, 237–38,
see also nurturing role
'women's business', 125–26
work, xxxi, 83
work environment, 186
workers,
exploitation of, 33
loyalty of, 183
Ten Desires for, 182, 191–94
World Bank, 51–52, 58, 60
World War 1, 53–54, 225
World War 2, 54, 65
Wounded Warrior Project, 177

Zeta cartel, 25

www.ingramcontent.com/pod-product-compliance
Lightning Source LLC
Chambersburg PA
CBHW070533010526
44118CB00012B/1118